Kinship, Islam, and the Politics of Marriage in Jordan

D1158742

PUBLIC CULTURES OF THE MIDDLE EAST AND NORTH AFRICA
Paul A. Silverstein, Susan Slyomovics, and Ted Swedenburg, editors

Kinship, Islam, and the Politics of Marriage in Jordan

AFFECTION AND MERCY

Geoffrey F. Hughes

INDIANA UNIVERSITY PRESS

This book is a publication of

INDIANA UNIVERSITY PRESS
Office of Scholarly Publishing
Herman B Wells Library 350
1320 East 10th Street
Bloomington, Indiana 47405 USA

iupress.org

Manufactured in the United
States of America

First printing 2021

Library of Congress Cataloging-
in-Publication Data

Names: Hughes, Geoffrey F., author.
Title: Kinship, Islam, and the politics
 of marriage in Jordan : affection
 and mercy / Geoffrey F. Hughes.
Other titles: Public cultures of the
 Middle East and North Africa.
Description: Bloomington : Indiana
 University Press, 2021. | Series: Public
 cultures of the Middle East and North
 Africa | Includes bibliographical
 references and index.,
Identifiers: LCCN 2020043820 (print) |
 LCCN 2020043821 (ebook) | ISBN
 9780253056436 (hardback) | ISBN
 9780253056443 (paperback) | ISBN
 9780253056450 (ebook)
Subjects: LCSH: Marriage—Jordan. |
 Marriage customs and rites—Jordan. |
 Man-woman relationships—Jordan. |
 Sex role—Jordan. | Kinship—Jordan. |
 Marriage—Religious aspects—Islam.|
 Jordan—Social conditions—21st
 century.
Classification: LCC HQ664.3 .H84 2021
 (print) | LCC HQ664.3 (ebook) |
 DDC 305.3095695—dc23
LC record available at https://
 lccn.loc.gov/2020043820
LC ebook record available at https://
 lccn.loc.gov/2020043821

TO BLAIRE

Contents

Acknowledgments

LIKE ALL INTELLECTUAL ENDEAVORS, THIS ETHNOGRAPHY IS the result of a collective project involving hundreds of different minds. In my case, this book was made possible by an incredible amount of generosity—spanning multiple languages across multiple continents, encompassing those responsible for my education and upbringing in the United States and those Jordanians who graciously accepted me into their lives and taught me about their lifeways. I also cannot forget my colleagues here in the United Kingdom who have supported me since I finished the PhD dissertation that became the basis for this book. A full accounting of all of the debts I have incurred in the process of writing this ethnography would be impossible, but I hope these acknowledgments will somewhat suffice.

My greatest debts are to my mother and father, the two people who gave me life. They were my first teachers, my first travel companions, and my most reliable, tireless, and consistent mentors. I am also deeply indebted to my adoptive Jordanian family, which includes countless individuals who have treated me as a brother, a cousin, an uncle, or a son over the years. Leading in generosity, I would like to thank Abu Yazin and Abu Abdullah and the rest of their families. The warmth and hospitality that they showed was superlative—even for a country in which warmth and hospitality are foremost national pastimes. I was also honored by the generosity of the houses of Abu Bassam, Abu Muhammad, Ishhada, and Abu Suleiman. I would further like to express how grateful I am to friends and teachers like Nader, Abu Riyad, Ghassan, Wael, Mu'tasim, Muhammad (Abu Abdullah), and Abu 'Ala'.

The various institutions I studied were also incredibly hospitable toward me. I was repeatedly struck by the professionalism and incisive wit of the employees I encountered at the Housing and Urban Development Corporation, the Sharia courts, and the Chastity Society. Employees were also always exceedingly honest and self-critical, making me wary of thanking them by name lest their candor be used against them. Instead, I would like to thank the institutions themselves—trusting that the key figures who enabled my research know who they are and know how much I appreciate the risks they took to make this project happen. However, I am happy to acknowledge Ms. 'Afnan and Abu Hassan from Jordan University's archives for being some of the most helpful, knowledgeable, and generous archivists imaginable. Most historians I have talked to would give anything to work under the conditions that they helped to foster.

The difficulties involved in thanking the myriad colleagues and professors who helped with the book are hardly any less daunting than the task of thanking the countless Jordanians who facilitated my research. Andrew Shryock was everything I could have asked for in a mentor: involved, supportive, and generous with his time. Gillian Feeley-Harnik read countless drafts and provided fine-grained critiques that helped me fully realize the theoretical stakes of my argument. Much of the initial impetus for the project emerged from a series of classes I took with Matthew Hull. Frances Hasso helped me think more deeply about how to balance the anthropological stakes of the book with its potential contributions to the literature on gender and the state in Jordan, Palestine, and the broader Middle East. I would also like to thank Conrad Kottak, Henry Wright, Sally Thomason, Judith Irvine, Webb Keane, Damani Partridge, John Mitani, Krisztina Fehervary, Stephen Jackson, Yousef Al-Yousef, Stuart Kirsch, and Alaina Lemon for giving me the intellectual tools I needed to take on this project. Since coming to the UK, I have benefited immensely from the collegial and supportive environment at the London School of Economics and the University of Exeter. Matthew Engelke and Harry West have been excellent mentors. David Hein-Griggs provided crucial last-minute assistance with the rainfall map, for which I am grateful. I would also like to honor the memory of

David Graeber, a long-time inspiration who was always generous with his time up to his untimely death in 2020.

I was also privileged to receive support from a number of grants and fellowships that gave me the time and money needed to conduct this research and write up my findings as a book. I would especially like to thank the National Science Foundation (award number 1154785) and the University of Michigan's Horace Rackham School of Graduate Studies. Further support has subsequently been provided by the National Endowment for the Humanities, the American Center of Oriental Research, the London School of Economics and Political Science, and the University of Exeter.

We always learn at least as much from friends and peers as we do from professors. I owe a lot to my friend and mentor Warren Emerson, whose consistent correspondence while I was in the field was a constant source of insight, humor, and emotional support. I also owe a lot to all of my roommates and colleagues over the years: James Meador, Stuart Strange, Katharina Erbe, Denise Dooley, Ujin Kim, Gregory Storms, Lamia Moghnie, Bryce Adams, and Alison Joersz. They fed me, listened patiently to my anxieties, and, in many cases, read draft after draft of what became this book. Hoda Bandeh-Ahmadi, Sandhya Narayanan, Chris Sargent, Nama Khalil, Kimberly Powers, Ismail Alatas, Bridget Guarasci, Lindsey Conklin, Maxim Bolt, and Dan Birchok have also proven to be important interlocutors. Ashley Lemke, Bethany Hansen, Kristen Munnelly, and Andrew Gurstelle were always willing to provide moral support and prevent my intellectual growth from being stunted by my anthropological subdisciplinary specialization. Saving the best for last, I would like to thank Blaire Andres, who has helped me throughout the book project, reading drafts and believing in the project when even I had started to doubt it. Any errors are mine alone.

Note on Transliteration

TRANSLITERATION PRESENTS REAL PROBLEMS FOR ETHNOG-raphers working in a country like Jordan where pronunciation can vary greatly from place to place and dialect to dialect (especially between town and country). To make matters more complex, Jordan is now home to Palestinians, Syrians, Egyptians, Iraqis, Yemenis, and many others who bring their own sensibilities about pronunciation with them. Given that the pronunciation of a given word or phrase can vary greatly from person to person (even within the same household), I have tried to render all Arabic transliterations according to the simplified transliteration system of the *International Journal of Middle East Studies*, sticking as close to Modern Standard Arabic spelling as possible. My hope is that this will render key terms recognizable to the expert and novice Arabic learner alike without asserting a level of precision that is not actually there (and sparing the non-Arabic speaker a lot of potentially distracting and potentially alienating diacritics). In general, those hoping to pick up Jordanian Arabic should be warned that the letter *qaf* can be pronounced as a *g*, a voiced uvular stop (especially among Bedouins), or a glottal stop (especially among city folk). The letter *tha* is sometimes pronounced as a *t*, and the letter *dhal* is sometimes pronounced as a *z* (especially, again, among city folk). Meanwhile, the letter *kaf* is sometimes pronounced as a *ch*, especially among older Jordanians and others living in rural areas. There are plenty of other variations in pronunciation, but, at least at the time of writing, these were the most marked shibboleths of dialect variation within Jordan.

Kinship, Islam, and the Politics of Marriage in Jordan

Introduction

A Crisis of Marriage, A Crisis of Legitimacy?

THE WORD *CRISIS* IS OFTEN ASSOCIATED WITH THE MIDDLE East—both within the region and globally. It certainly was for me when I first arrived in Jordan as a Peace Corps volunteer teaching English in a rural primary school in 2006. Since then, I have seen first-hand how the effects of wars and occupations in Iraq, Palestine, Lebanon, and Syria have overflowed preexisting territorial divisions, profoundly affecting everyday life. This is to say nothing of the widely felt impacts of the excitement turned to disappointment of the so-called Arab Spring and the very real fears of people in the region of Al-Qaeda and, more recently, the so-called Islamic State or *da'esh*. Today, Jordan is a resource-poor country that plays host to refugees from all of these crises. Significantly more than half of the population can now say that their ancestors lived elsewhere when the country was founded in 1947.

Another crisis coexists with these violent geopolitical struggles. It is what people across the region have come to call "the crisis of marriage" (*azmat az-zawaj*). According to the historian Hanan Kholoussy (2010), this crisis helped to constitute the modern Arabic-language public sphere more than a hundred years ago. For those who have been conditioned to view the region through a foreign policy lens that emphasizes war, civil strife, and urgent humanitarian appeals, the focus on marriage might seem odd—even frivolous and misplaced—amid this violence and displacement. Of all the threats to the longevity and legitimacy of Middle Eastern social orders and states, the difficulties that young people have marrying might seem to rank quite low. Indeed, I would be lying if I said I came to the subject matter of this book through any great original insight on my own part. To the contrary, it was the constant talk of matchmaking, weddings, and house construction—much of which initially bored me to tears—that eventually brought me, kicking and screaming, to the topic. I am deeply grateful too, for year after year, the crisis of marriage remains an enriching source of social insight, whereas so many other crises are quickly eclipsed by the seemingly ever-escalating horrors of their successors.

One of my early attempts to approach this marriage crisis as a potential object of study brought me to the office of a distinguished professor—a demographer, sociologist, Christian, and self-described liberal—at a leading Jordanian university. After listening politely to my enthusiastic project pitch, he shared a study that he was working on arguing that there was actually no marriage crisis at all. Based on the then-current demographic data, he had constructed a longitudinal data set that, he argued, contradicted the widely held belief that "spinsterhood" was a growing problem in the kingdom.[1] This study involved questioning whether, in fact, a growing number of Jordanian women were never marrying, presumably for economic reasons. In the study, he went on to speculate that the so-called marriage crisis was actually a displacement of anxieties about technology, changing gender roles, economic restructuring, and other broader social changes. My gracious host added in conversation that, first and foremost, the whole thing was a transparent attempt by the Muslim Brotherhood to make the government look bad and challenge its legitimacy.

Without discounting any of this perspective, I argue that explaining this marriage crisis discourse in terms of "bad faith" (Sartre 1965) or "misrecognition" (Bourdieu 1984) would be missing the point insofar as it fails to explain why marriage in particular serves as such an appealing subject for this discourse of crisis. It will become clear that the Muslim Brotherhood and the broader Islamic movement are very actively promoting the idea of a marriage crisis (discussed in detail in part 2, "The Proposal"); however, that marriage crisis also produces the Islamic movement in powerful ways. Disproving or even just challenging particular claims about the crisis in this manner can be revealing, but it can also fail to defend the stakes of its own intervention in an oddly self-defeating manner: if the marriage crisis is really about these other things, then why would people be convinced that it doesn't exist by debunking these highly delimited claims about spinsterhood? As it turned out, the data on falling marriage rates among women in subsequent years eventually led the professor to back away from these arguments and accept that rates of spinsterhood were on the rise. But to return to an earlier question, with all of the other problems facing Jordan, why would people across the kingdom's political spectrum see the marriage crisis as such a potent threat to the government's legitimacy?

The answer would seem to be that the idea of a crisis of marriage is, as the anthropologist Claude Levi-Strauss might say, "good to think" (1963, 89). As a notion, it opens up space for thinking about alternative family structures and life trajectories. It nurtures what C. Wright Mills (1959) has termed a "sociological imagination" that allows people to abstract from their own individual experiences to situate their lives within broader contexts of collective struggle and collaboration. It also exemplifies what Robert McKinley (2001) has called "the philosophy of kinship" by posing questions about how humans can coexist with one another within trusting relationships. But the marriage crisis is not all imagination and philosophy: it catalyzes political movements, crystallizes institutional arrangements, and remakes the physical infrastructures of people's home lives. What makes the "marriage crisis" so appealing is its ability call forth a range of contradictory social engineering projects by connecting numerous scales, ideals, institutions, technologies, and forms of sociality simultaneously.

Against a vision of the Middle East as a zone of violence and instability, a crisis of marriage is quotidian and everyday in the extreme. It decenters war, violence, and the machinations of primarily male political and economic elites who are often distant from their people. In its place, it substitutes a vision of a region that, although constantly picking up the pieces, carries on with the basic work of social reproduction day in and day out. This work often goes unacknowledged, tends to be carried out primarily by women and the poor, and rarely provides occasion for spectacle—although I hasten to point out that it was precisely by engaging with my male Jordanian interlocutors that I overcame my own culturally inculcated tendency to reduce marriage and gender to "women's issues."[2] The goal in this view is not to downplay the real, spectacular violence that has marked the region and the everyday violence to which vulnerable people around the world are often subjected. Rather, the goal is to devote the appropriate amount of attention to the rebuilding and care that constitutes the counterpoint to such violence and the stress that it places on broader systems of large-scale population management. This is where I focus my ethnographic gaze. This introduction begins by exploring why marriage makes such an attractive target for various social engineering projects. I provide a brief overview of Jordan's unique historical trajectory before outlining the study's research design and its scale and scope. I end with a brief overview of the structure of the book's chapters.

KINSHIP AND THE SOCIAL ENGINEERING
OF "AFFECTION AND MERCY"

In 1995, reflecting widespread contemporary popularity, this verse was added (with little fanfare) to the preprinted Islamic marriage contract form that the Jordanian government's Sharia courts use to register the marriages of its Muslim citizens, who make up over 97 percent of the population: "And of His signs is that He created for you from yourselves mates that you may find tranquility in them; and He placed between you affection and mercy. Indeed in that are signs for a people who give thought" (Qur'an Surat Ar-Rum 30:21). As anodyne as the sentiment may seem (that marriage is a sign of the benevolence and justice of God's plan for humanity), other Islamic precedents could be relevant here. One could imagine emphasizing individual rights[3] and self-actualization.[4] One could also imagine emphasizing community and social reproduction,[5] with the need to attend unromantically to property and labor relations.[6] In fact, Islamic marriage contracts still seem to be practically focused on both of those issues rather than attributing an almost foundational role in Islamic cosmology to the marital bond.

Nevertheless, these different configurations of kinship and personhood remain potent possibilities for contemporary Jordanians, with wide-ranging implications for people's day-to-day lives and the ambitions of larger institutions. Such institutions may seek to extricate individuals from their familial ties, or they may seek to absorb and instrumentalize kin groups. The success of the Islamic movement in mobilizing marriage as a political issue seems to stoke widespread anxieties and to politicize marriage in a self-reinforcing manner. Following the above Quranic verse, I use the terms "affection and mercy" to describe the emerging compromise among different kinship obligations. This ideal places the husband-wife dyad at the center of familial, social, and political life while holding that dyad in productive tension with both the extended kin group and a fully individuated form of personhood. Regardless of which political tendency is winning out at any given moment, marriage remains a key site for contesting how personhood will be autonomous of—or beholden to—kin-based familial roles.

The topic of kinship has a long and storied history within the social sciences. What began with the earliest attempts by anthropologists to understand other peoples' conceptions of relatedness and belonging has been taken up as a powerful tool of social engineering by states and private institutions. The study of kinship carries this baggage with it but also anticipates and prefigures aspects of contemporary gender and queer theory. Over the course of its development, the concept has undergone a series of radical transformations. When Europeans and Americans began to develop the concept, they took for granted that there were certain "biological facts" that might or might not be acknowledged by the kinship systems of other peoples but that were universally operative. Conveniently, these "facts" were the central categories of Euro-American kinship, like *mother*, *father*, and *blood*. Consequently, the concept of kinship has come up for critique. People became aware that the seemingly incontrovertible materiality of things like blood might actually be more metaphorical than early anthropologists were wont to accept. Early anthropologists also made a lot of assumptions about what makes family "family."

In turn, the critique of kinship fed into a more voluntarist perspective that all but rejects any sort of biological or "natural" underpinning to kinship. The anthropologist Signe Howell (2006), for instance, has drawn on her studies of transnational adoption to argue persuasively for more attention to the ongoing social processes of "kinning" and "dekinning," through which various others are either brought into the familial fold or excluded from it. Today, the tendency is to assert the importance of what anthropologist Kath Weston (1991) aptly termed the "families we choose" in her study of lesbian and gay surrogate families. Even more recently, the revolution in assisted reproductive technologies has occasioned a whole raft of fascinating research showing how a better understanding of the biological "facts" of kinship does not settle controversies about the true nature of kinship. Ironically, it simply provides more points of intervention, multiplying possible permutations of kinship and creating new tools for contesting their validity, as surrogates, donors, and other novel social actors vie to define their relatedness to one another (Edwards et al. 1999; Inhorn 2012; Strathern 1992).

As the anthropologist Morgan Clarke (2009) has shown in his study of new assisted reproductive technologies in Lebanon, Middle Eastern kinship ideologies (including Islam) challenge this voluntarist take on kinship. They insist that neither biological nor social components of kinship are sufficient on their own. On the one hand, the idea that procreation involves the combining of male and female substances is a clear and unambiguous truism within the Islamic tradition—one in keeping with the region's broader Abrahamic tradition. In fact, it is arguable that much of what Europeans and Americans consider to be biological about kinship owes far more to this Judeo-Christian tradition than to more recent scientific discoveries that have been grafted onto it (Delaney 2001). Like Jews and Christians, Muslims readily adopt modern biomedical terms like *DNA* and *genes*. Nevertheless, the degree to which the use of such terms remains beholden to much older beliefs is often palpable: these beliefs are taken to be common sense. Therefore, the people I met in Jordan were no more or less incredulous than Europeans or Americans when I told them about human societies like the Trobriand Islanders, who believe that women are impregnated when spirits of their matrilineal ancestors tire of living on a neighboring island and make their way across the sea and into the body of one of their female descendants (Delaney 1986; Leach 1967; Malinowski 1929). There was a deep commitment among the Jordanians I met to the idea that paternity was a real, intrinsically material phenomenon linked with sexual intercourse.

On the other hand, although my Jordanian friends (much like Clarke's Lebanese interlocutors) considered the exchange of substance through intercourse a necessary condition for the creation of kinship, it was almost never considered sufficient in itself. The issue was legitimacy, specifically, the legitimacy of paternity. I often encountered people who were deeply disturbed by the European and American films they saw, with their frequent recourse to plotlines involving beautiful people who jump in and out of bed with each other at the drop of a hat. There was a widespread sense that Americans and Europeans were all bastards because they could never "know" who their "real" fathers were. Through frequent questioning on the matter, I became adept at explaining that, in fact, people in my American society were deeply fixated on such questions—to the point where the biomedical paternity test was not simply a fixture of family law but also its own genre of reality television. However, I cannot recall a single instance in which anyone seemed even slightly convinced that such tests were a compelling solution to the problem of legitimate filiation (i.e., the kinning of children).

Clarke (2009) seems to have had plenty of analogous experiences in the course of his own fieldwork. He explains that the Arabic concept of *nasab* (similar to English-language concepts of filiation and "consanguinity") is "dependent on being conceived and born within wedlock, not mere 'biogenetic' relatedness" (189). "Sexual propriety" and the nuptial rituals that constitute social recognition of the idealized legitimate sexual relationship are "a material condition with regard to kinship relation." In other words, for people who accept this explicitly "biosocial" model of kinship, in which "legitimacy is a material component of filiation" (198), there is no doctor, no medical test, and no court order that can provide a compelling substitute for the ritual act of marriage.

Without discounting the fact that these beliefs are often deeply held, it is important to emphasize that kinship systems like those found in Jordan cannot be divorced from the more objective social and legal structures in which they exist, specifically regarding citizenship and inheritance. A person born in a country like Jordan does not necessarily gain basic citizenship rights by virtue of existing. Citizenship in Jordan and neighboring countries is generally conferred on the basis of the father's citizenship alone—and men are under little official obligation to recognize their illegitimate children. Without citizenship, people are confined to the shadows—unable to work, to run a legally recognized business, or to own property. This is no small matter in a nation of refugees where the fear of statelessness is all too real. Social and legal norms emphasizing the importance of aggressively legitimating sexual relations are mutually reinforcing.

This unapologetically patriarchal and exclusionary approach to the legal recognition of kinship in the Middle East is fully conscious and much discussed both in activist circles and among the relatively apolitical. It has also led sociologists, historians, and political scientists to take up the study of marriage in the Middle East with a good deal of alacrity. Although the topic of marriage was once a mainstay of anthropology (cf. Bourdieu 1977; Evans-Pritchard 1966/1990; Levi-Strauss 1949/1969; Morgan 1871; Needham 1973), it seems to have been ceded to neighboring academic disciplines as anthropologists sought out greener pastures. The biologizing, heteronormative, and androcentric tendencies of some of this older marriage literature has been rightfully critiqued (cf. Carsten 2004; Gough 1971; Holy 1996; Schneider 1972; Strathern 1992). However, this need not diminish the urgency of studying marriage from an anthropological perspective. The contemporary efflorescence of critical kinship studies provides exciting opportunities to "make the familiar strange" regarding one of the most staid and venerable modes of producing new kin relations—through legitimate, community-endorsed, heteronormative sexual intercourse within the confines of wedlock.

Marriage can no longer be considered an intrinsically important topic of study. Nevertheless, the continued insistence of so many powerful institutions on the importance of marriage begs investigation. As the sociologist Frances Hasso writes, marriage has become a site for a variety of "postcolonial legal and pedagogical projects absorbed with managing, developing, and protecting the national family" (2011, 3). Like Hasso, in her comparative study of marriage and family law in Egypt and the United Arab Emirates, I quickly found that powerful forces in Jordanian society—the Islamic movement, the Jordanian government, and major banks—were committed to the transformation of marriage. Hasso calls the prevailing logic of such projects "corporatist," implying a sort of "vision" that "posits families, states, or communities as naturally hierarchical systems in which members harmoniously play their assigned roles" (2011, 14).

The simultaneous action of different corporatist social engineering projects targeting marriage need not produce a wholly coherent outcome, corporatist or otherwise. "Family" is not a neutral concept here. To take one particularly useful contrast that Hasso (2011) develops, the Arabic terms *usra* and *'a'ila* represent two notably distinct ways of thinking about "family." The word *usra* connotes "a modern spatial understanding of confinement" and the so-called "nuclear" family (husband, wife, kids), whereas *'a'ila* represents a more relational mode of family associated with patrilineal extended kin groupings or *tribes* (Hasso 2011, 26). I will argue in the next section that every shift in the balance between the prerogatives of the family-as-*usra* and the family-as-*'a'ila* has historically represented a complex shift in the fortunes of different political tendencies, genders, age groupings, classes, and ethnic identities. The result is that the manner in which banks, the Islamic movement, and the Jordanian government set out to order these nested hierarchical systems can quickly put them at odds—with each other and with the families they seek to reorder. In the resulting struggles, terms like *tradition* and *modernity* (to say nothing of *Islam* and *law*) become difficult to deploy in analytically precise ways because social actors are eager to use them strategically—only to discard them later when convenient.

In this context, what Islamic law can mean (and has meant) for people's family lives is a major topic of debate. As the sociologist Mounira Charrad puts it in an apt turn of phrase, family law serves as "a mirror of the polity" (2001, 109). Charrad's work focuses on the comparative study of family law reform initiatives in North Africa in the twentieth century. She correlates reform initiatives with the strength of the modernizing states and their ability to defeat "traditionalist" coalitions of tribal power brokers and religious groups. This leads her to emphasize the ways in which "the thrust of Islamic law in general is to permit the control of women by their male relatives and to preserve the cohesiveness of patrilineages." She also argues that Islamic law generally "tolerates a fragile marital bond" and "identifies ties among agnates ... as the critical bonds for individuals even after marriage" (31). Charrad's research highlights the precarity women could face as the result of weak marital bonds and their resulting dependence on male kin.

The historian Amira Sonbol (2008) has conducted extensive archival work on marriage contracts in the Nile delta going back to the fourteenth century BCE. She shows how Islamic and pre-Islamic legal structures provided women with ways to contest the prerogatives of tribes and their male relatives. She portrays women representing themselves in court and often having their prerogatives upheld by the courts against recalcitrant husbands. Women could include elaborate stipulations in their marriage contracts (as they continue to do in Jordan to this day), which provided grounds for divorce and (often substantial) payments known as *mahr*.[7] Such payments might be given to the woman at the time of marriage (i.e., the "prompt" *mahr* payment) or in the event of divorce or the husband's death (i.e., the "deferred" *mahr* payment). Sonbol highlights how the weak marital bond could work to women's advantage by allowing them to escape from bad marital arrangements or at least use the threat of leaving to leverage their options.

Sonbol (2008) argues that the introduction of French legal theories to Egypt, through direct colonial rule under Napoleon and later indirectly through the *Tanzimat* ("reorganization") reforms of the late Ottoman Empire, weakened the status of women in the region. She argues that given increasing European influence, nineteenth-century family law evolved with increasing emphasis on "keeping the family together" (in this case, the "nuclear" family) as "the central discourse in allowing the father to reign over his children and his wife" (112). In the nineteenth and twentieth centuries, courts curtailed the ability of Egyptian women (and women throughout the broader region) to stipulate conditions for their marriages, and wifely "obedience" became legally enforceable (see Cuno 2009).[8] This shift between *'a'ila* and *usra* happened within a broader Islamic framework and had complex and ambivalent effects for individuals and their families. Although some see women's interests as better served by the stronger marital bonds of the *usra*, others see promise in the weaker marital bonds of the *'a'ila*. It is probably best to see potential in all arrangements for creative subversion while being sensitive to the ways in which strong and weak marital bonds can represent different ways of "bargaining with patriarchy" (Kandiyoti 1988).

Despite the ambivalent effects of changing marital relations, marriage remains an attractive target for those interested in changing how people relate to one another. As Hasso argues, the reordering of marital life in the Middle East in the postcolonial era has generally been less a function of "more democratic and antipatriarchal orientations" than of "governance agendas ... [that] compete with the still relevant values and norms associated with shari'a and tribal authority systems, themselves often in tension and responsive to sociohistorical conditions" (2011, 25). As the currency of affection and mercy demonstrates, older precedents (e.g., Sharia and tribal authority systems) often provide the raw materials for innovations in these governance agendas in Jordan. In general, the tendency among both social scientists and proponents of affection and mercy has been to posit the more confined *usra* as the replacement for the more expansive *'a'ila*, in line with much of modernization theory. However, this approach is more complicated in countries like Jordan where sovereignty has been seized by the most powerful *'a'ilas*, who present themselves as royalty and often build ruling coalitions on the basis of kinship (see Baram 1997; Bonte et al. 2001; Dresch 1994; Khoury and Kostiner 1990). They may normalize and naturalize the *'a'ila* as a privileged mode of kinship—or they may selectively encourage and cultivate particular *'a'ilas* at the expense of others. Jordan's history can be read as an ongoing struggle between the family-as-*usra* and the family-as-*'a'ila*, enlivened by intense and ongoing inter- and intrafamilial conflict and a small but growing fear that kinship itself might be facing obsolescence. Although the discourse of modernization may be widespread among Jordanians (whether they love it or hate it), there are good reasons to question its teleological and deterministic tendencies.

HISTORICAL CONTEXT: KINSHIP IN CONFLICT

At this point, it is necessary to take stock of what "Jordan" actually is in this context. As a nation-state and an increasingly viable social world for its inhabitants, Jordan is a relatively recent invention. The country was carved out of the Ottoman Empire by the British and the French in the aftermath of World War I, combining a diversity of peoples and ecological zones. The Hashemites, a leading Meccan family with a strong claim to being descendants of the Prophet Muhammad and good relations with the British Foreign Office, quickly ascended to the thrones of Jordan, Iraq, and Hejaz (in present-day Saudi Arabia). Whereas the other Hashemite kingdoms would fall, Jordan's Hashemite dynasty lives on, with its King Abdullah II serving as the fifth Hashemite king. On its path to independence, Jordan was forced to cede much of its most fertile, populated territories to the west to the state of Israel, leaving the kingdom with the East Bank of the Jordan River as the country's western border. At the same time, Jordan has taken in millions of refugees and economic migrants over the years from Palestine, Iraq, Syria, and Egypt. Of these, only those from the West Bank usually have Jordanian citizenship. No official figures are maintained given the contentious nature of Jordan's demography; however, it is widely accepted that well over half of Jordan's citizenry hails from elsewhere. Given how historically porous and malleable Jordan has been, kinship ensures Jordan's coherence as a viable social world in some key ways. Most important, family ties confer citizenship and sovereign authority on some and not others. The area that is now Jordan was quite marginal to the Ottoman Empire but has come to feature increasingly exacting modes of governing the family. These developed under the Ottoman Empire's Tanzimat, or reorganization, and then later under the British Mandate and then under Jordan's postindependence authorities.

Ottoman rule was often markedly indirect, especially in places like present-day Jordan that lacked natural resources and received little rainfall (thus producing little agricultural surplus). In those regions where governance was remunerative, the primary mode of Ottoman intervention in the interpersonal relations of its subjects was through the patronage of a range of religious specialists, with each faith community allowed a degree of self-governance. This arrangement, known as the *millet* system, lasted for hundreds of years. Arguably, this basic paradigm of family law remains in countries like Jordan today, with separate laws for Muslims and different Christian sects under the broader regulatory umbrella of the Jordanian state. The Ottoman Empire promoted its own brand of Sunni Islam and gave precedence to the Hanafi legal guild in matters of Islamic law. For most of Ottoman history, effective administrative control south of Damascus was limited to the coast in the *sanjaqs* (districts) of Lajun, Nablus, Jerusalem, Jaffa, Gaza, and Ramla. These districts were prosperous enough to pay taxes to the empire (all dutifully preserved in notebooks) and support towns with rudimentary manufacturing industries and courts (Cohen 1973, 144–172). Across the Jordan River, moving from the West Bank (Palestine) to the East Bank (present-day Jordan), Ottoman control quickly dissipated. Without much to tax, there was little reason to provide security or courts. The chief concern of the Ottomans was to pay off the local tribesmen to "protect" the annual hajj pilgrimage to Mecca, lest they decide to raid it instead (Rafeq 1966, 70–72).

Many initiatives described in this book can be traced back in one form or another to either Islamic legal precedents or the Tanzimat, a belated attempt by the Ottoman Empire to reorganize itself along the lines of a modern European nation-state in the twilight of its rule. As the historian Eugene Rogan (1999) argues, after suffering a string of military defeats at the hands of the Russians and the Hapsburgs while fighting off internal insurrections, the Ottoman regime found its sovereignty challenged in the nineteenth century. It was also running out of money and seeing its territory and the base of workers necessary to exploit it shrink. This was the Ottoman version of what Michel Foucault has called "the emergence of the problem of population" (1991, 99). As in much of Europe (Donzelot 1977/1997), the increasing cost and complexity of warfare and other forms of political competition began to drive widespread anxieties that the empire's vital energies were not being channeled properly. With the ruler acting as a father to his people, the patriarchal family would not longer merely "model" all other relations of authority, as it had for so long. Rather, the family would become "an element internal to population . . . a fundamental instrument in its government" (Foucault 1991, 99). This Tanzimat meant bypassing tribal and faith leaders to manipulate the finer points of people's familial relations more directly in the hope that the empire might extract more from its territory and population than it had in the past.

On the southern frontier, the reforms meant major initiatives to pacify raiding groups on the periphery, to reorganize taxation, to convert communal property regimes into an individual freehold property regime, and to individuate its subjects to hold them personally responsible for their actions. Following a number of unsuccessful attempts to pacify the region, the Ottomans slowly began to extend communications infrastructure (roads, bridges, a ferry, railroads, telegraphs) and a security presence east of the river. They encouraged refugees from places like Chechnya and Circassia to settle and farm the area and only recognized the land claims of those who held a title and paid taxes. The apparent stability helped attract merchants (Rogan 1999, 1–20). In 1867, Mehmed Rashid Pasha finally succeeded in appointing administrators and judges in Salt (Rogan 1999, 69). Of course, there was resistance. Karak revolted in 1910, burning all property records (Fischbach 2000, 31–32). The "Great Arab Revolt" of 1916–1917 cemented the alliance between Jordan's future Hashemite rulers and the British war effort against the Ottomans.

With the dissolution of the Ottoman Empire, old identities of profession (e.g., peasant, Bedouin) and confession (e.g., Sunni Muslim, Christian) gave way to new identities that were increasingly tied to the emergent nation-states the European powers were carving out of the old empire. The most infamous impetus for this was the Sykes-Picot Agreement between Britain and France to divide the Ottoman Empire between them. Britain took Iraq, Transjordan, and Palestine (which would be promised as a Jewish homeland). France took over the northern swath of the empire, which would become Syria and a new, French-backed Christian homeland in the region: Lebanon. Jordan would become the buffer between the emerging Jewish homeland and Iraq and Saudi Arabia (Barr 2011; Hourani 1991, 318–322; Wilson 1987). In time, Jordan would become a major destination for refugees fleeing conflicts in most of these neighboring countries. However, even before Jordan's indigenous population was joined by refugees from its more urbanized and heavily governed neighbors, the British were zealously pursuing their own state-building project. As Rogan (1999, 3–13) argues, much of this activity (e.g., land reform, individuation of subjects) was a continuation of the Tanzimat and what he calls (following Michael Mann) Ottoman "infrastructural power": bureaucratic technologies allowing for the greater "penetration" of "society" to increase tax collection and support ever-larger military apparatuses. The British would later continue these efforts with an aggressive land-registration campaign in the west of the country (Fischbach 2000) and successive changes to Jordanian family law and the "personal status law," which placed ever-greater emphasis on the individuation of citizens (Moors 1995; Welchman 1988).

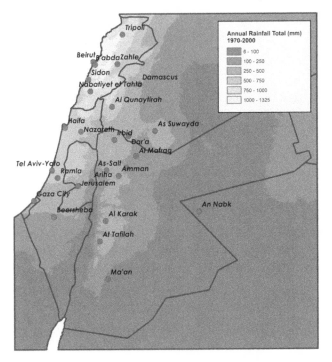

Figure I_01. Jordan's arid climate historically rendered it marginal to the states and empires that dominated the more agriculturally viable regions to the west and north.

From the 1920s onward, Jordan and its leadership could not help but be drawn into the midst of the controversy in neighboring Palestine between the indigenous Arab population and Jewish settlers. Conflicts over land sales and future infrastructure projects only escalated as the relationship between the two groups increasingly soured. Meanwhile, the British sought to buy the quiescence of the Hashemite Emir Abdullah however they could (Wilson 1987, 103–127). Nevertheless, buying the emir's quiescence would be far from sufficient to allow for the orderly management of Britain's post-World War II withdrawal. Having failed to broker an agreement between the competing sides, Britain simply left. Fighting broke out, and the settlers quickly gained the upper hand against the indigenous population. In response, neighboring Arab governments occupied the primarily Arab portions of Palestine. Egypt was left with the Gaza strip and Jordan annexed the West Bank. In the process, two-thirds of the Arab population of Palestine became refugees, settling primarily in Arab controlled parts of Palestine, Jordan, Egypt, Lebanon, and Syria. Under the direction of the United Nations, the various sides reached an armistice agreement in 1949 (Hourani 1991, 358–363). However, the conflict continues to define Jordanian politics.

Although the British Mandate in Jordan ended in 1946, it was replaced by a monarchy heavily dependent on foreign aid, military aid, and remittances with close ties to Britain and the United States. Relatively easy access to funds without the need to tax its population allowed the Hashemite state to build up an elaborate security apparatus while distributing its largesse to a coalition of supporters—primarily those from the East Bank but also important capitalists from the West Bank (Baylouny 2008; Brynen 1992; Peters and Moore 2009). Increasingly denied its agricultural base to the west and obliged to accept more and more refugees from those areas, Jordan has developed what Pete Moore (2004) called a "Political Economy of Acronyms." The United Nations was involved from the beginning, accommodating refugees and acting on their behalf. The various agencies of the United Nations have been joined subsequently by the World Bank, the International Monetary Fund, USAID, innumerable trade deals, and "special economic zones." Throughout, the Hashemites have worked to maintain "a highly disparate regime coalition that consists of a Syrian/pre-1967 Palestinian merchant elite and Transjordanian tribes" (Peters and Moore 2009, 257). Even the mechanisms (public employment for those from the East Bank and business advantages for the West Bank "merchant-industrialists") have remained remarkably constant (Peters and Moore 2009, 265; Massad 2001, 10–17).

There has also been a good deal of antagonism between East and West Bank communities. Palestinian nationalists assassinated King Abdullah I at al-Aqsa mosque in Jerusalem in 1951. The killing sparked rioting by the king's guard in the Old City and sporadic attacks on Palestinians east of Palestine in Salt and Amman (Wilson 1987, 208–209). When Jordan lost the West Bank in 1967, tensions increased greatly. Palestinian *fida'iyyun* (guerrillas) continued to operate out of Jordan, calling the legitimacy of King Hussein into question. Beginning in 1970,

King Hussein traveled to tribal meetings, rallying support for his cause and transferring funds from the military budget to the tribes so they could buy weapons. Following an attack on the king's motorcade, Bedouin units began shelling two refugee camps in Amman. Meanwhile, King Hussein demanded that the tribes of the south evict the *fida'iyyun*. Ultimately, foreign journalists put the death toll for the civil war, known as "Black September," between seven thousand and twenty thousand. Following the war, officials commenced with a wave of newspaper closings, mass arrests, and a purge of Palestinians from the bureaucracy. By the 1980s, the Palestinian portion of the armed services had fallen from more than half to less than a quarter (Massad 2001, 204–245).

The war and the subsequent purges of Palestinians from the government bureaucracy led to resentments. These included nativist "Jordan for Jordanians" sentiments but also the sense that the East Bank population had abandoned its Muslim and Christian coreligionists and fellow Arabs (Massad 2001; Shryock 1997b). To some degree, this feeling was mitigated by an explosion of employment opportunities in the Gulf Region. Many Palestinians leveraged their educational credentials and Arabic language skills to move into lucrative positions in the oil industry and subsidiary development projects, funneling billions back to their families in Jordan in the form of remittances. The international relations scholar Laurie Brand groups the Palestinian community shaped by this history of dispossession and migration into four categories: relatively poor and unintegrated Palestinians who live in the camps and form the basis of the urban underclass, better off small business owners and low-level bureaucrats who demonstrate some allegiance to Jordan, the most successful Palestinians and thus most enthusiastic about the Jordanian project, and then those Palestinians based abroad for whom a Jordanian passport is mostly a passport of convenience (Brand 1995, 49).

If the Palestinian population has been sustained largely through aid, remittances, and government support for well-connected merchant-industrialists (Reiter 2004), the native Transjordanian population has been sustained by the military—and selling their lands to Palestinians. Members of the armed services in Jordan enjoy access to steady pay, free education, subsidized housing, health-care services, special stores stocked with low-cost goods, and retirement benefits. The pay may not be good, but it has always been sufficient—at least for those who own their own homes. The dual nature of the economy for Palestinian Jordanians and native Jordanians adds an important economic dimension to these identities, as Jordanian and Palestinian identities have increasingly been mapped onto the division between public- and private-sector employment.[9]

Despite direct governmental support, the East Bank population has also been the most restive in recent years—especially when inflation (often brought on by the influx of new refugees and their money) threatens to erode the social position of public-sector employees (Baylouny 2008, 288–291). Furthermore, because they predominate in the public sector, native Jordanians are hit especially hard by Jordan's frequent economic liberalization pushes—and tend to experience them as a morally inflected sleight. As in most places, Jordanian public-sector employees consider the stability afforded by their steady (if modest) prerogatives to be their just compensation compared with groups that are allowed to strike it rich in high-risk, high-reward economic pursuits centered on investment and remittances. It would be a mistake to explain East Bank-West Bank tensions solely in economic terms when both sides have invested a good deal of their identities in particular moral, political, and historical accounts.

As the ethnographer Andrew Shryock (1997a) has shown, whatever the current events of the day may be in Jordan, they tend to be zealously interpreted through a lens that dramatizes them as part of a centuries-old conflict between farmer communities to the west and the nomadic desert tribes to the east. Prominent politicians construct coalitions through genealogical claims, publishing their own histories and family trees to endow ancient rivalries with contemporary relevance. The Hashemite monarchy has zealously promoted this rivalry and inflected it with its own mode of patriarchal rule, which allows the monarchy to play the various factions off against each other—alternately offering succor and treating them like unruly children. Shryock terms the resultant political form, "dynastic modernism," in recognition of the manner in which "modern institutions and technologies are resources leaders (and their subjects) can use to organize, resist, revitalize and dominate 'traditional' identities" (2000, 67–72). Within the schema provided, Palestinians are to be interpellated through a self-narrative of loss and betrayal by Arab regimes, whereas native Jordanians are urged to see themselves as gracious but overwhelmed hosts (Brand 1995, 52). With the death of King Hussein, this paradigm became embodied by kinship relations as the torch passed to King Abdullah II. His marriage to a Palestinian woman (Queen Rania) is emblematic of the ongoing effort to work through Jordan's ethnic tensions through the idiom of marriage.

Armed with a large security apparatus and substantial government revenues from abroad, the Hashemite monarchy has little need or incentive to extend democracy or civil rights to the population. Parliament becomes little more than a calculative device for determining which coalitions are well organized enough to warrant the distribution of largesse (Brynen 1992; Peters and Moore 2009; Shryock 2000). The situation is analogous to Egypt, where the political scientist Diane Singerman notes in her study of the lower classes (known as the *sha'b*), "The government has reduced the realm of politics to distribution.... From their end of the bargain, the *sha'b* participate in formal politics [by consuming]" (1995, 39). So while elites may criticize the materialism of the common people, as they find themselves subject to demands from foreign patrons for fiscal discipline, the crisis is of their own making. Because access to a decent standard of living is the price that the *sha'b* extracts from elites in return for quiescence, they are highly sensitive to even small fluctuations to the cost of living. This leaves the regime's international backers to determine the price they are willing to pay for quiet in Jordan.

These shifting ethnic and kinship affiliations have attracted the attention of powerful institutions that see great geopolitical import in their development. Leaked US embassy cables indicate that US officials are engaging local kin networks in their efforts to aid the intensely pro-US Jordanian government in thwarting the opposition Muslim Brotherhood's political party, the Islamic Action Front (IAF). Both the embassy and regime loyalists were clearly concerned that the IAF would expand from its perceived base in the Palestinian refugee camps in places like Zarqa (deemed by the embassy a "hotbed of Islamist Activity" and the IAF's "natural constituency") to more "tribal" areas like Madaba. These rural areas have traditionally helped fill parliament with independent, progovernment candidates who see their function as fighting for their constituency's share of largesse. Usually, such candidates run primarily on their last names to signal their tribal affiliations to potential constituents (Antoun 2006; Shryock 1997b). Of particular concern to the embassy in the 2007 mayoral elections in Madaba was a member of the Shawabkeh family who was intent on running with the IAF. In a cable, embassy officials claimed, "Observers count 8000 votes as his base— 4000 from his family and home turf, 3000 Palestinian votes from IAF sympathizers in the camp, and 1000 scattered IAF votes among other demographics."

The problem for the embassy and regime loyalists was that the two "independent tribal candidates" had threatened to throw their support behind the Islamist candidate "if regional power brokers support the other." Although some of these power brokers go unnamed, the cable goes on to report:

> Local Christian power brokers told poloffs [political officers] that they had the support of key figures close to the central government, including former Prime Minister Faisal al Fayez, and claimed some Muslim candidates are prepared to ally with them in order to stop the IAF. However, they will not launch their campaign without a green light from the government—which is to say, the General Intelligence Directorate (GID). Such a go-ahead does not appear to be forthcoming. A well-placed observer and supporter of Shawabkeh told poloff a Christian candidate could not win because moderate Muslims would align against said candidate, even if that meant supporting the IAF. "Christians can be king-makers in Madaba," he said, "but not the king." (Amman Embassy 2007)

The cable is merely an artifact of what residents have long assumed. Jordanians repeatedly shared suspicions with me that the US embassy is closely monitoring (if not outright manipulating) the ethnic and tribal dimensions of local Jordanian politics. They believed that the maintenance of the status quo relied on the ability of the General Intelligence Directorate and the rest of the state apparatus to strategically punish and reward different families to build sustainable governing coalitions along kin lines.

However, the long-term viability of this divide-and-rule strategy and the ethnic and kin-based categories it has helped to reify depend on the ways in which millions of everyday people in Jordan come to construct their own social worlds. The cable tempers the somewhat common assumption in Jordan of the embassy's omnipotence. "Power brokers" treat the embassy's political officers as fellow power brokers. But they also talk back. Take the IAF backer, for instance, who taunts the embassy official by saying, "Christians can be king-makers in Madaba, but not the king." Understanding these various competing efforts to remake Jordanian politics requires careful attention to the making and breaking of kin bonds through research grounded in everyday life, emplaced communities, and face-to-face interactions.

SCALE AND SCOPE: MANAGING JORDAN'S DIVERSITY

How can one hope to represent the social world that has given rise to this crisis of marriage? Who speaks? How much do they speak? What do they get to speak about? Questions of ethnographic research and exposition are inextricably linked with questions about the power of social display and self-representation. I designed my research to encompass the major cleavages that Jordanians spoke about. This took me to both urban and rural areas in and around Jordan's capital, where most of the kingdom's population is located. Over time, I came to know people from across the socioeconomic spectrum, hailing from the many nations that have sent refugees to Jordan in recent decades, especially Palestinians. I was always keen to capture women's voices and perspectives but also tended to be directed toward other men given my positionality as a male ethnographer.

Consequently, the resulting mode of representation is inherently situated and partial. On the one hand, I have no interest in flattening the diversity associated with Jordan's marriage crisis by seeking out some sort of lowest-common-denominator "native's point of view" (cf. Malinowski 1922/2014). There could never be a single authentic Jordanian, Arab, or Muslim perspective. On the other hand, I have little desire (or ability) to achieve a meticulous, almost statistical form of representation, with space in the account precisely allocated to different identity categories on the basis of their prevalence within the larger population. In a way, this book is an account of the inability of institutions to fully represent populations and their marriages in such a precise manner. Against a simplistic view of ignorance that takes it to be the mere absence of knowledge, I follow the historians of science Robert Proctor and Londa

Scheibinger (2008) in tracking how ignorance is actively produced as a generative social reality that constrains and precipitates a variety of individual and collective projects. In this spirit, I sought to engage in what Proctor calls "agnotology" (the study of ignorance) to draw attention to how the perspectives of different categories of people can be distorted and effaced in the normal course of events in Jordan. Silence (and processes of silencing) can reveal a lot—a point I will repeatedly emphasize throughout the book.

The "Bechdel test," named after the feminist critic Alison Bechdel (1985), famously asks whether a work of fiction contains at least one scene in which two or more women talk about something other than a man. It is used as an index of an artist's willingness to develop strong female characters and give them agency within their imaginative worlds. To the degree that this book fails to live up to this relatively low bar of gender representation, I can only blame its nonfiction characters, the relatively gender-segregated context of its production, and my positionality as a male ethnographer. I believe that trotting out an ethnographic vignette to fit that metric would give the wrong impression about how Jordanian women generally chose to engage with me, often preferring to refuse my ethnographic gaze and force me to account for myself in the face of an inquisitive, united front. I want to emphasize that knowledge in this kind of social context moved across gendered barriers with some difficulty— by design. At points, I will need to impart to readers some sense of the frustration of coping with the inherent partiality of social knowledge and how the realities of gender segregation can intensify those frustrations. On this count, my male Jordanian interlocutors—constantly, throughout the book, imagining women's evaluations and talk—might be more progressive than the book itself. I hope to capture some of this gendered fragmentation of Jordanian lifeworlds through my exposition, but I also want to suggest that there are other ways of thinking about the relationship between public acknowledgement and power. In certain contexts, power may be more about one's ability to act without having to provide any verbal account of oneself. As such, women may figure in the narrative more in terms of their ability to enact forms of power at a distance, to the degree that this seemed to be their preferred mode of social engagement. The same holds for other identity categories within Jordan's diverse social field.

It may be true that, as Giyatri Spivak famously argued, "the subaltern cannot speak" (1988), but those in dominant positions may well choose not to speak. As Shryock's research on oral history among Jordan's Balga Bedouin has repeatedly shown, for example, the most powerful lineages often demonstrate their agency not by talking; rather, they act in ways that compel others to narrate their exploits for them (Shryock 1995, 1996; Shryock and Howell 2001). This approach is part of a larger, historically specific set of sensibilities in the region that we also see reflected in Lebanese ethnography (cf. Gilsenan 1986, 1996). These sensibilities perhaps reached their furthest elaboration (bordering on *reductio ad absurdum*) in the court etiquette of Jordan's former Ottoman rulers. Ottoman sultans communicated by sign language because "ordinary speech was considered undignified. . . . The sultan had become a showpiece and sat silently on his throne in a three-foot turban, like an icon, immobile" (Baer 2008, 141). Voice and visibility have complex relationships to power. People's experiences are often molded in no small part by how their own gaze is directed and fixed on particular positive and negative exemplars, like a sultan or (perhaps) a family that enacts a particularly sumptuous or abject wedding.

I am particularly concerned with how and why more marginalized community members like women, youth, and the poor efface their own practices and involvement in community matters—and in what we lose when we fail to attend to these sorts of active, self-conscious forms of erasure. For instance, how do we judge the social salience of rarer, larger weddings and engagement parties that everyone sees—and everyone sees everyone seeing, and talks about seeing everyone seeing—versus more mundane weddings and engagement parties that might be much more common and, therefore, unremarkable? How do we judge the social salience of deeply entrenched traditions of marriage versus novel but controversial compromises? How salient are youths who follow the rules versus youths who flout convention and cause huge conflicts that people recount in hushed tones for years to come? How salient are the marriage practices of wealthy elites (perhaps despised or idolized) versus those of the impoverished masses (perhaps also despised or idolized)? We might even question the intense social focus on the wedding itself: after all, the hard work of marriage is only just beginning when the wedding is over, and a successful wedding in no way implies a successful marriage. Even if the wedding is a focal point for (often patriarchal) anxieties about intergenerational male kinship ties, the sorts of social reproduction that marriage is supposed to precipitate will take decades to realize. The investment of time, money, and emotions into weddings could seem misplaced retrospectively.

Be that as it may, extraordinary events and individuals often seem to play far larger roles in people's imaginations than their own mundane day-to-day experiences, especially when appreciating the nature of marriage in its mass-mediated "crisis" form. Marriage may be for life, but particular places, institutions, ideologies, and public figures are associated with marriage more closely than others. An important dimension of this dynamic was the conscious spatialization of the past in rural areas. Urban and rural folk alike considered such areas to constitute the privileged repository of "tradition," particularly regarding marriage and kinship. Consequently, I made a conscious effort to incorporate rural perspectives and practices, even though that decision flies in the face of the region's rapidly urbanizing demography (cf. Abu-Lughod 1989). Amid concerns that anthropologists have overcorrected and abandoned the countryside (Deeb and Winegar 2012), I wanted to be mindful of how rural areas can exert an influence that is disproportionate to their share of the overall population—in politics, culture, and other domains. My basic research strategy was to take up residence in a rural family compound in Madaba, at the edge of the capital, and then commute into urban Amman, where I could work with the institutions most directly concerned with remaking marriage in their own image. These included the Sharia courts, the Chastity Society, and the Housing Corporation. Each of these institutions offered a unique vantage point on marriage that was markedly distinct from the view from the village.

Some Jordanians were skeptical of my desire to study rural marriage patterns and wisely cautioned me against overlooking the dynamism and diversity of Jordanian marriage practices. Nevertheless, most people seemed to attribute my decision to an admirable (if quixotic) commitment to authenticity. I found hosts in rural Jordan through the kin networks I had been introduced to while working as an English teacher in a rural school some years before. I based myself in Madaba governorate, taking advantage of its diverse mix of nomadic and sedentary folk; Jordanians and Palestinians; Christians and Muslims; rich and poor; and urbanites, suburbanites, and long-standing farming communities. As time went on, I had to "pick sides" in ways that are reflected in my findings. While the effect of these cleavages on my findings may be seen as gaps, they are also indicative of the reality (and importance) of these cleavages themselves. Notably, the idea of me living in a working class rural village alongside Palestinian and Jordanian Muslims seemed to make a lot of more educated, urban, and wealthy Jordanians visibly uncomfortable—all the more when I insisted on the hospitality and generosity of my hosts. Christians in particular seemed concerned that my experiences implicitly denigrated their own claims of persecution at the hands of Jordan's Muslim majority. Despite my best efforts to remain humble and open to all (and my relative success in maintaining cordial relations all around), I will always wonder if I could have done more to include such voices in my study.

For their part, my hosts in the village were the best hosts I could have asked for, and they never made me regret the decisions to design my research so that I would be well placed to capture their perspectives. My hosts were always eager to show me what their "traditions" were about while apologetically acknowledging the fallen times in which we lived (a subversive inversion of the normal modernization discourse so often wielded against them). They took me to massive proposal delegations where hundreds of men assembled to ask a woman's family for her hand in marriage on behalf of their "son." They brought me to well over fifty weddings and engagement parties over the years. I also became involved in house construction—the most expensive and time-consuming aspect of marriage for most rural Jordanians. As I was frequently told, with a complex mix of braggadocio and humility, things had been bigger, more communal, and more lavish in the past. People in the village told me plainly that, these days, they were increasingly focused on acquiring the certification to get stable employment (often in the public sector). Unable to afford rent, they relied on the fact that they owned their own land and homes to offset their relatively meager salaries. Without space of their own or money to rent, young people were expected to postpone marriage at the risk of never owning their own home and becoming downwardly socially mobile.

In this context, putting together the money for marriage (including a *mahr* payment, wedding, and house) was a constant source of familial tensions, but people looked to the institutions offering to help with a mixture of hope and cynicism. In their own ways, the courts, the Chastity Society, and the Housing Corporation were all suspected of threatening the family's independence and self-reliance. At the same time, they could be highly appealing. The courts promised to protect the prerogatives of individuals without recourse to their families. The Chastity Society offered the community of the Islamic movement and a learned form of political critique of the status quo—family authority figures included. The Housing Corporation offered new financing mechanisms that could help young couples buy houses on the basis of their future earnings instead of waiting for help from their families. Moving between these ideologically polarizing sites helped sensitize me to Jordan's internal diversity.

As the main arbiter of legal marriage in Jordan, the Sharia courts were an obvious first place to look for data on marriage; however, the courts' own struggle to represent and regulate the marital practices of its population is akin to my own in many ways. For hundreds of years, going all the way back to the sixteenth century, learned men in places like Jerusalem have been recording certain quantitative and qualitative dimensions of people's marriages, a topic I explore in part 2 of the book. They have long faced widespread disinterest and noncompliance. Thus, the view provided by court registers is not as synoptic as their dutiful keepers might hope, century after century. So-called "customary marriages" that are never recorded by a court may emerge as a religiously defensible option in cases where courts are simply too distant and unable to enforce their own writ. However, customary marriage may also occur because of distrust of the local courthouse, its procedures, its personnel, or even its broader political entanglements. Many Palestinian refugees, for instance, deliberately avoided registering their marriages with the Sharia courts into the 1980s because they feared that such documents could serve as grounds for being denied their "right of return" to Palestine should the conflict ever be resolved. Orthogonal to this specific concern, plenty of other people from various backgrounds (especially among the more nomadic) told me proudly that their ancestors would never have given any human institution a say over their marriage practices.

I conducted extensive fieldwork at the Sharia courts in winter 2011, primarily in Madaba. I observed more than one hundred contract signings, but I also collected and coded a representative sample of marriage contracts.[10] This sample included 377 marriage contracts taken from the Amman Courthouse covering the years 1926–1953, the period during which the court had jurisdiction over all of central Jordan, including Madaba. I also took a representative sample of 433 contracts from the more recent Madaba Courthouse, covering the years from its opening in 1954 to 2011. Despite their inherently partial depiction of the social field in which they were produced, these marriage contracts reflect the history of the region in its broad outline: signs of urbanization, monetization, and increased literacy abound. Whereas the category of "peasant" was the most common occupation in the period before Jordan's independence and the subsequent administrative overhaul of the courts and their contracts (33% of men), the many categories of military and civilian government functionary came to predominate in even rural areas like Madaba after 1953 (41% of men). Although 70 percent of women in the Madaba contracts were listed as housewives, court records revealed their growing participation in the workforce over time. The shift from thumbprints to signatures indexed the rapid strides that Jordan made in terms of education and literacy in recent decades. The waves of refugees from Palestine in 1948 and 1967 showed up in the places of birth that court applicants listed. One can even catch glimpses of people's wealth and their marriage traditions by looking at the forms that people's *mahr* payments took (e.g., cash, gold, livestock), although the accuracy of these claims was often questioned by court officials and the public alike.

Finally, it was possible to track the growing role of the courthouse itself in marriage—especially over the course of the past century, as the courts became more central to the documentary process through which the Jordanian state comes to know its population. The Islamic marriage contract-signing ceremony, once merely grafted onto a familial ritual involving a delegation at the home of the bride, is increasingly divorced from its familial context through recourse to the courthouse's facilities. In extreme cases, the courthouse may replace the customary festivities at the bride's home. Although the majority of contract-signing ceremonies still happen in homes, the courthouse has been rapidly gaining in popularity as a site of contract signings since the 1980s and may surpass the home as the primary site of contract signings in the coming decades. In part 2, I emphasize the marked differences in how marriage contracts were officiated in people's homes and the courthouse. Equally important, however, was that the circumstances of these marriages tended to be rather different. Contracts signed in people's homes tended to reflect the traditionalism of the families involved, whereas more urban, deracinated families preferred the courthouse. The courthouse also served as the site where officials dealt with the sorts of marriages they felt were the most prone to being exploitative or abusive. My fieldwork in the courthouse exposed me to marriages involving second wives, divorcees, minors, and refugees far out of proportion to their overall presence in the records of the courts. As one might expect, courthouses tend to attract contention.

The Chastity Society also courted contention, often by drawing attention to precisely the types of people who court officials perceived to be the most vulnerable: spinsters, divorcees, youths, and women in general. Its activists were committed to both studying and ameliorating the marriage crisis. They published prolifically, hosted conferences and training courses, and organized mass weddings to help cut down on the cost of marriage. In partnership with the Jordan Islamic Bank (Jordan's largest Islamic bank), they distributed more than $10 million in interest-free loans to young people hoping to marry. At one point, they arranged a matchmaking service (staffed only by women, for modesty's sake), but that was no longer active at the time of research. I was privileged to be provided an extensive selection of their published research, generous amounts of interview time, and invitations to a range of events, including fundraisers, mass weddings, and training courses for newlyweds. The activists were part of a broader Islamic movement that has been active in Jordan in recent decades. Their leader, Dr. Abdul-Latif 'Arabiyyat, had previously been the most successful leader of Jordan's Muslim Brotherhood-aligned IAF party, even serving as a speaker in the kingdom's parliament for a time. Happening on one of Jordan's most famous Islamist opposition figures in his retirement as he worked to organize weddings for young people was one of the more serendipitous discoveries of my research.

I also conducted extensive research at the Housing Corporation, attempting to understand the relationship between Jordan's marriage crisis and its housing crisis. This connection is made frequently in everyday conversation but is much less commonly addressed in marriage crisis discourse. Housing is incredibly scarce in Jordan because of the constant influxes of refugees and the country's rapidly growing population. With a median age of 22 amid rising life expectancy, Jordan will need to build hundreds of thousands of housing units in the coming years simply to accommodate organic population growth (to say nothing of the refugees). Having spent years watching how families in rural areas that were lucky enough to inherit land worked tirelessly to build their own houses, I wanted to understand how the Jordanian government was planning to accommodate the vast majority of Jordanians who lacked such means (especially in cities and refugee camps). I had initially hoped to study a royal initiative to build one hundred thousand housing units in five years, called Decent Housing for Decent Living. By the time I returned, the Housing and Urban Development Corporation had placed the project on hold amid recriminations over corruption. This situation encouraged me to focus on archival work. Through the archives, I came to understand how the construction projects of my neighbors (sometimes even involving myself) were shaped by the corporation's subtler project of engineering the creation of a housing market in an attempt to alleviate shortages.

I also met powerful leaders of a number of different communities and political movements, with various ties to the Islamic movement, the security services, and some of the most powerful kin groupings. I tried to chart a middle course among the vying power bases by focusing my attention on the struggles of middle- and working-class people whose primary concerns were their own families. I tended to see the embassy officials, senators, parliamentarians, and sheikhs I met as seeking to marshal forces that were hopelessly beyond their control. Despite their (often cynical) machinations, I have gone out of my way to present my research in a way that carries the least risk of revealing the identities of anyone who is not a published interlocutor and intellectual. I hope that readers avoid trying to "out" participants as the region's instability and ever-shifting alliances could potentially put people at risk when their main intention in talking to me was friendliness, hospitality, and curiosity about the world around them.

OUTLINE OF THE BOOK

The book itself is structured around the three major ritual prestations associated with marriage: the house, the proposal, and the wedding. Marriage is typically a housed relationship. For the couple to take up residence in a house after the marriage, the groom's family is expected to secure housing for him and his bride. When the man is ready to marry and a suitable match has been arranged, the bride and her family—and there was a lot of slippage here—would historically be promised a certain sum of gold, furnishings, and other goods (known as *mahr*) in a proposal delegation. This would be followed by a wedding hosted by the groom's family, at the bride and her family would be presented with the "prompt" portion of her *mahr* payment (with the "deferred" portion to be paid as a sort of alimony in case of divorce or on the husband's death).[11] Today, the basic succession of ritual prestations remains unchanged, although that proposal is likely to be accompanied by a trip to the government-run Sharia courts, where the *mahr* payment will be duly recorded in court records and become a legally enforceable entitlement for the bride. This will be followed—often after an arduous wait because of the difficulty of securing the funds—by a wedding and the couple's move to their new house, still all at least notionally provided by the groom and his family. Although the process of getting married remains relatively stable in its broad outlines, the changes in how young people secure the basic prerequisites of marriage feed into the ongoing struggle between the *'a'ila* and the *usra*. They also offer new opportunities for various individuals and groups to assert themselves. Each part of the book explores the recent history of this struggle in depth by following families and institutions as they struggle to retain or remake older marriage practices.

In part 1 of the book, I take up the home to show how contemporary gender roles are both reified in the here-and-now and projected onto an imagined past. Emphasizing the malleability of notions of gendered space and "public" and "private," I trace a series of rapid shifts in property relations and gender roles over the course of the past century that can be easily occluded by the apparent continuity of the public-private distinction. In chapter 1, I look at how domestic space was constructed (materially and symbolically) both historically and more recently, using a combination of oral historical accounts of past practices and participant observation. Juxtaposing the goat hair tents of the eldest generation with the new generation's cinderblock houses purchased with wage labor, I emphasize how intergenerational male kinship bonds continue to be crucial to these projects, from securing the land on which the house is built to marshaling the money and labor necessary to build it. I also underscore how the home has increasingly become the most insurmountable barrier to marriage for all classes (whether they seek to own, rent, or mortgage), exacerbating contemporary anxieties around the increasing need for women to work outside of the home to support it.[12]

In chapter 2, I look at how the Jordanian government has long sought to respond to the bottleneck in housing production through financialization and how initiatives designed to empower the "individual owner-builder" have challenged the grip of the extended family but also valorized its prerogatives in unexpected ways. I suggest that the price of housing is a major factor driving women into the workplace. Women's employment has the potential to decrease the dependence of women and young people on men and their extended kin groups in the future. However, this will happen only so long as land maintains and deepens its current commodified form and the gendering of space continues to facilitate women's movement in "public" space. If the male individual owner-builder of an earlier era of housing policy remains tied to ancestral lands and the good graces of his father and uncles, there is reason to suspect that attempts at even further individuation may likewise produce unintended and even contradictory results.

In part 2 of the book, I consider the ritual pageantry surrounding the initial proposal—the official start of the process of getting married—to understand how people and other sorts of moral agents are constructed through marriage in the context of the broader economic challenges outlined in part 1. In particular, I explore the implications of the intro-duction of government Sharia courts for marital and familial dynamics in Jordan. Chapter 3 is centered on a comparison of the delegation and courthouse rituals to explore what sorts of people and families they seek to reproduce, emphasizing the deindividuating tendencies of delegations and the individuating tendencies of courthouse rituals. I show how the Jordanian state has increasingly come to be held accountable for the plight of those deemed most vulnerable through the information infra-structures of its own increasingly elaborate system of Sharia courts.

Chapter 4 builds on this comparison by showing how courthouse procedures create new forms of individual and collective voice that open up new spaces for critiquing existing kinship configurations. I focus on the ways in which courthouse rituals highlight the voices and needs of women in particular. This becomes even more apparent as activists from the Chastity Society increasingly appropriate the courts' data and statistical categories to level their own critiques of state and society on behalf of vulnerable groups like "spinsters" and women "divorced before consummation." This latter category is particularly interesting because it emerges from the courts' own knowledge practices and the disjunc-ture between the rituals of the proposal delegation and the courthouse contract signing. As the state becomes more involved in legitimating people's marriages, it opens itself up to attacks on its own legitimacy and enables people to imagine—and demand—new ways of marrying and relating to each other.

In part 3 of the book, I consider the wedding itself and the sorts of alliances and identities that emerge through the enactment of dif-ferent sorts of wedding rituals. I focus on three types of weddings in particular: the "traditional" multiday wedding extravaganza, the newer and distinctly urban abbreviated wedding celebration hosted in a hotel or wedding hall, and the mass weddings of the Chastity Society. In chapter 5, I focus on how Jordanians use different types of weddings to promote competing forms of legitimacy. Jordanian weddings bring people together and support relationship building through proximity, gift exchange, shared commensality, and the collective effervescence of singing and dancing. It is through attention to these sorts of details that people make more or less subtle statements about who they hope to include through such rituals—and who they hope to exclude. Adherence to wedding "traditions" becomes a means to valorize and extend the 'a'ila, whereas novel forms of wedding (usually briefer and cheaper) may protect the usra's resources. Increasingly, weddings become sites where class warfare, ethnic conflict, and the urban-rural divide are enacted. In this sense, weddings are often rightly seen as a means of not only making relations but also cutting them off.

In chapter 6, I build on this local understanding of what weddings communicate and instantiate by focusing on why weddings have become a privileged site for contesting alternative notions of legitimacy. I draw primarily on the mass weddings and training courses of the Chastity Society. Although they represent a minority opinion, the comprehensiveness and didacticism of their critique and its ritual elaboration help to emphasize how Jordanian weddings have historically bolstered the 'a'ila—and how newer models could emerge that favor the usra. The society's agenda builds on—and only makes sense in the context of—a widely held sensibility that the husband-wife bond valorized by marriage and enacted through the wedding are the foundations of civilization and human life itself. If the state currently offers one vision of affection and mercy, the Chastity Society's version attempts to prefigure a more expansive future welfare state that would take a more intensive role in nurturing the usra and protecting the vulnerable through education, legal protections, and material support. In all likelihood, though, the realities of most people's actual relationships will continue to be shaped by a variety of competing ideals without ever fully conforming to any of them.

Although marriage crisis discourse is transnational and long-running, marriage can still mean radically different things to different people. The history of marriage in Jordan showcases this, with its vacillation between state-backed ideologies of Islamism, monarchism, and tribalism. Despite its particularities, broad patterns can be discerned, like the struggle between extended and more closely delimited kin groupings that I have highlighted throughout. Moreover, key aspects of the postcolonial order in Jordan, like the Muslim Brotherhood and particular, politically powerful extended kin groups, grew (of necessity) from precisely those social domains that British colonial institutions defined themselves in opposition to—namely, religion and the family. This arrangement will be familiar to students of other postcolonial contexts (cf. Chatterjee 1993). An emphasis on legitimate filiation is quite widespread and has important implications for property and labor relations. It remains to be seen what conditions will actually emerge on the ground as people organize themselves to make various demands in the name of marriage and its crises.

Jordanian families struggling to meet the material preconditions of their own reproduction do not necessarily reproduce the increasingly familiar American and European model of the autonomous, self-actualizing individual or, at its most collectivist, the isolated, so-called nuclear family. Such a model (the *usra*) is instantly recognizable, even among the most provincial Jordanians; however, a more expansive model (the *'a'ila*) remains dominant within the central halls of power and along the margins. Where generations of social scientists have confidently predicted the decline of the extended kin group and the rise of ever more individuated, self-actualizing consumers, this study sounds a note of caution. Jordanian modes of making and breaking kin bonds—kinning and dekinning—remain creative, complex, and difficult to reduce to a simple narrative of progress toward the putatively modern nuclear family, or *usra*, and the autonomous individual and away from the broader and more relational *'a'ila*.

NOTES

1. The sociologist Rania Salem (2014, 2016) has also shown that, compared with available statistics, public perceptions of the Middle East's supposed marriage crisis are often overblown in both Jordan and Egypt, where people tend to vastly overestimate the inflation in wedding expenses, rising marriage ages, and rates of spinsterhood.

2. Through a fascinating analysis of the development of European legal norms around a whole variety of contracts (e.g., marriage contracts, work contracts, prostitution contracts, slave contracts), the political theorist Carole Pateman (1988) has argued that there is a "sexual contract" that precedes the "social contract" at the heart of liberal political theorizing, excluding women from the latter in the process. I fear I would never have fully appreciated the wisdom of her analysis were it not for my time in Jordan and the prodding of my interlocutors.

3. Verse 4:24, for instance, focuses on a man's right to marry multiple women and a woman's right to her *mahr*: "And [also prohibited to you are all] married women except

those your right hands possess. [This is] the decree of Allah upon you. And lawful to you are [all others] beyond these, [provided] that you seek them [in marriage] with [gifts from] your property, desiring chastity, not unlawful sexual intercourse. So for whatever you enjoy [of marriage] from them, give them their due compensation as an obligation. And there is no blame upon you for what you mutually agree to beyond the obligation. Indeed, Allah is ever Knowing and Wise."

4. Verse 24:33, for instance, urges men to exercise self-control until God blesses them with the means to marry: "But let them who find not [the means for] marriage abstain [from sexual relations] until Allah enriches them from His bounty."

5. Verse 4:1, for instance, emphasizes the centrality of marriage to human reproduction: "O mankind, fear your Lord, who created you from one soul and created from it its mate and dispersed from both of them many men and women. And fear Allah, through whom you ask one another, and the wombs. Indeed Allah is ever, over you, an Observer."

6. Verse 2:187, for instance, takes a pragmatic view of marriage: "They are clothing for you and you are clothing for them." In other words, spouses are meant to "cover up" for each others' flaws.

7. As I will show in chaps. 3 and 4, women often struggle to protect their *mahr* from the depredations of both their husbands and their kin, and this struggle has long been integral to the workings of formal Sharia courts in the region and how they attempt to insert themselves into family life.

8. Gerber (1980) makes a similar argument for the relatively high status of women in Bursa in present-day Turkey under Ottoman Rule.

9. See also Joseph Massad's (2001) account in chap. 4 of *Colonial Effects* ("Nationalizing the Military") for a fuller discussion of how Palestinians came to be consciously excluded from the military. Nevertheless, I personally know a number of Jordanians of Palestinian descent in the military and plenty of East Bank Jordanians in the private sector.

10. Because it was the least likely to be damaged, I took the middle contract from every book of 50 contracts: contracts xxxx25 and xxxx75. The sample is representative because the contracts are always meticulously filled in, in order in every book, and every book is filled in completely, so no couple is more or less likely to have the twenty-fifth or seventy-fifth contract in a book than anybody else. However, thanks to population growth (much like contracts truly chosen at random), contracts chosen by my methodology are more likely to be more recent.

11. The first half of vol. 2 of Granqvist's *Marriage Conditions in a Palestinian Village* (1935) is devoted to a detailed ethnographic description of this progression as she found it at the time. Her accounts of people's sensibilities and the variations among peasants, Bedouin, and townsfolk are strikingly consistent with the recollections of my Jordanian and Palestinian interlocutors who were alive in the 1930s and 1940s.

12. For a discussion of analogous issues with the decreasing importance of *mahr* payments in relationship to the increasing cost of housing in Palestine in the 1980s, see Annelies Moors's (1995, 119–121) *Women, Property, and Islam*.

Part 1

The House: Changing Conceptions of Property and Domestic Space

1

The House

MY FRIEND OMAR'S FAMILY COMPOUND HAD SEEN A FLURRY of activity over the week, with a new concrete and steel rebar structure springing from what had been a vacant lot. I saw him on the street, greeted him, and teasingly asked when he was going to get married. As a man in his midtwenties with a prestigious job in the military[1] and as the eldest son in the family, he immediately grasped the subtext. "I want to wait until I finish the house," he said and smiled back. Continuing with a line he had probably been using all week, he winked a bit and said, "I want to bring a girl the size of the house." The local common sense was that the more prestigious the house, the more prestigious ("bigger," so to speak) a bride he would be able to marry. A year later, as the house was nearing completion, he finally got engaged. Omar eagerly described his bride to me in terms of her job (an engineer), her salary, and the combined household income he was looking forward to when her salary was added to his sizeable military salary and benefits package. His good news was accompanied by a palpable sense of exhilaration and relief at the prospect of being able to support a large and prosperous household that would meet the high expectations that his family and neighbors had for him.

I begin with this bit of banter because it exemplifies how men seek to reconcile exacting standards of masculine competence and feminine modesty with the dynamic economic realities they often face. As I will show, the most striking thing about Omar's account of his house and impending marriage is the erasure of the driving impetus provided by his father and the broad support of his extended family—to say nothing of the affective bond between him and his prospective wife. This kind of status competition and conspicuous consumption are banal and ubiquitous in Jordan. However, it is important to attend to the novelty of its shifting manifestations over time—especially because people may attempt to naturalize gender roles and erase any evidence of their historical dynamism. In this chapter, I argue that the attempts of Jordanian men to stake their status on their ability to house women in accordance with an exacting code of modesty can lead to an incredible diversity of accommodations. This diversity can occur even within a small community over a short period of time, like the three generations represented by Omar, his father, and his grandfather.

This quest of the middle and upper classes for bigger, more elaborate, and more permanent houses is transforming gender and kin relations across the country. Increasingly robust economic activities are required to actualize such houses that draw women out of the home and into the labor market to support them. In comparison, when Omar's grandfather married half a century ago, he initially lived in a goat hair tent made by his mother and sisters, on patrimonial lands that he and his brother claimed on the basis of having worked it themselves and their collective willingness to defend it with force if necessary. Family relations have grown to conform to the model of men like Omar and his father (creatures of an external "public" world) who perform wage labor, acquire capital, and use it to house women (in this case, associated with a cloistered, private, or domestic realm). The contemporary Jordanian home reifies this conceptual gendering of space, labor, and property relations and continues to materialize it in the built environment despite radical change.

Nevertheless, money and commodity circulation increasingly suffuse village sociality to the extent that even this model of "public" men (Carver 1996) housing women is growing outdated. There is something quite novel about a man who describes his prospective fiancée in terms of her occupation and salary—although it is increasingly the norm in Jordan.[2] In contrast, a number of Omar's uncles and grandparents remarked to me at various points that "I never touched money until I served in the army." The statement was intended to emphasize that their access to money—even as military-aged men—had been viewed as a challenge to the preexisting gerontocratic order. Thirty to fifty years ago, senior men claimed (not always convincingly) the right to dispose of the family's capital as their sole prerogative. The older generation's complaints about changing expectations for the role of money and other commodities in mediating relations between older and younger men tended to fall on deaf ears. What people could not ignore was the issue of women's participation in wage labor and the money economy. At the time of research, both men and women in Omar's village were speaking with trepidation of the imminent tipping point at which career prospects would shift from being a detriment to a woman's marriage prospects to being an asset.[3]

Despite this widespread conviction that "tradition" was now on the verge of collapse, earlier ethnographies show how adaptable beliefs about the importance of men housing women can be in the face of rapid social change. A recent example is provided by Linda Layne (1994, 73), who noted that a particular (and highly gendered) bodily "posture" was an important source of continuity in the process of sedentarization as Bedouin families shifted from tents to houses in the 1980s. The way that women moved within—and almost exclusively within—the home was important in maintaining the coherence of gender ideologies at a moment of rapid social transformation. In contrast, I found that the physical space of the home has become a newfound source of continuity as women's labor is redefined. When Jordan's median age is twenty-two years old, even comparatively novel architectural arrangements are all that most have ever known. However, the materiality of the home and its ties to broader spatial, labor, and property relations makes it even more difficult to ignore. As a growing literature in English and Arabic shows, fewer and fewer men are able to provide a house and financial support for a wife (if women even want that). These financial barriers to marriage raise the possibility of rising marriage ages and growing populations that never marry unless women contribute financially to household income (Badraneh 2009; Badran and Sarhan 1999; Hasso 2011; Schwedler 2010). In this context, the house itself has become a new way to enlist and transform people's lived realities into props that support standards of female modesty that are nearly unattainable: if women must leave the home to marry and be properly housed, then that is what they must do. The idea persists that women should be housed and, consequently, ideologically erased from public space—even if women have to go to work to realize some semblance of those modesty standards.

The contradictoriness of these attitudes toward women's circulation in public space is nothing new—a reality that seems to have been effectively occluded for most younger Jordanians, who tend to assume such contradictions are recent. Drawing on his fieldwork among Jordanian peasants in the 1960s, the anthropologist Richard Antoun (1968) argued that such ideals of modesty remained a cherished model of village sociality, despite the practical impossibility of peasants living up to them. He writes of the complex work of "accommodation" that was necessary to reconcile the realities of agricultural labor with the gender relations valorized by "townsmen," "Bedouin," and others who "do not need their wives and daughters to perform agricultural duties and . . . can afford to keep them in a secluded and unproductive state" (Antoun 1968, 677). From the time when Antoun wrote this analysis until Layne wrote hers in the 1980s, the trend was toward the increasing confinement of a growing percentage of women to the physical house. Meanwhile, men were drawn out of village household economies to sustain the household through their participation in an increasingly formalized labor market. There is growing acceptance that the rising costs and expectations associated with the home and the market relations that undergird that home's construction will eventually pull women into the workforce—reworking notions of personhood, gendered space, labor, and property in the process. What is striking is the degree to which this change can be justified—indeed, often is justified—through appeals to the "traditions" of modesty and propriety themselves.

The first part of this book is located at a point of doubled liminality: the threshold of the home itself and its construction, arguably an obligatory passage point for social reproduction in any community. When the succeeding generation constructs its homes differently, it also constructs its families differently. To track this transformation in the relationship among gender, labor, property, and space, I attempt to trace two phenomena in this part: in chapter 1, I consider the construction of a house, whereas in chapter 2, I consider the construction of a housing market. Chapter 1 is focused on house construction through ethnographic research in rural Jordan. It is built on growing literature on "house societies" (Bahloul 1999; Carsten and Hugh-Jones 1995; Levi-Strauss 1987) and a number of previous studies that foreground the construction of those houses (Dalakoglou 2010; Melly 2010; van der Geest 1998). Chapter 2 is focused on the construction of a housing market through ethnographic and archival research at the Housing and Urban Development Corporation (HUDC). It is built on growing literature that shows how economic markets are literally constructed—much like houses (Callon 1998; Mackenzie 2006, 2009; Zaloom 2006).

Chapter 1 uses the juxtaposition of the tent (which was a common form of housing in Jordan as late as the 1960s) and the various implements of public policy to emphasize the peculiarity of contemporary houses and housing markets and their role in radically shifting the gendering of labor, property, and space in Jordan in a relatively short time. When tracking the experiences of Omar and those of his grandparents' generation, ideas of public and private serve as an important conceptual pivot point guiding recent shifts in the gendered political economy of the Jordanian household. In addition, its ramifications are important for broader national and international political economies. These shifts in logics of gender, labor, property, and space are transforming the modes through which so-called public and private "spheres" or "domains" (cf. Cannell and McKinnon 2013; Chatterjee 1993; Collier and Yanagisako 1987; Franklin and McKinnon 2001; Strathern 1988) are co-constituted.

"OIKONOMY" OF HAIR, MUD, AND STONE

The emergent liberal notion of private and public as a contradictory mixture of oppositions (between individual and collective, interiority and exteriority, market and state) is fully present in Jordan. Use of the terms 'amm ("public" or, more literally, "general") and khass ("private" or, more literally, "particular" or "special") has increased. Jordanians now speak of privatization (khiskhisa) and the public sector (al-qita' al-'amm), just like everyone else who encounters the logics of neoliberal globalization and its avatars. In fact, the HUDC is one of the numerous bi-bi-bis (PPPs; public-private partnerships) proliferating across the Arab world and elsewhere. Such conceptions of public and private remain in tension

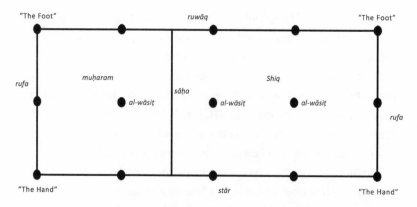

Figure 01_1. A diagram of a hypothetical tent. It uses some of the most common terms and emphasizes the bodily metaphors and deixis used to discuss the house and its constituent parts. However, there is a lot of variation in terminology, especially when it comes to the names of the poles. For instance, the *saha* is often called the *mu'and*. The pole on each side in the middle is usually referred to as the *kasir*, but some people use the term *'amr*—despite the fact that this term is more commonly used to refer to poles in the rear. *Zafir* is another term for these rear poles. Moreover, even the terms that evoke parallels with the body are not universally used. For instance, "the hand" (*al-iyd*) is sometimes called the *muqaddim*, whereas "the foot" (*ar-rijl*) is often called the *fahiq*.

with older local conceptions still embedded in the physical structure of the household and its peculiar gender, labor, and property relations. This means that certain aspects of these older conceptions continue to exert significant effects, even among young people like Omar. First, I will attempt to provide a brief sketch of the tent's structure and its animating logic. Second, in contrast to the highly abstracted notion of public and private that these organizations promote, I will discuss the home's relationship to literal "bread and butter" issues: the production of wheat, barley, milk, and meat. From these, I will turn to the home's relationship to a tangible set of concerns around interiority and exteriority, visibility and invisibility. In the second half of the chapter, I will contrast this pastoral mode of dwelling with those of the latter half of the twentieth century. These newer modes of dwelling have emerged with the advent of government jobs, concrete houses, and a veritable army of consultants and experts eager to bring their own Anglo-American notions of labor relations, domesticity, and property to the region.

The goat hair tent is a vexed but central image in a diverse array of ideological depictions of Arab heritage and culture. It simultaneously serves as a focal point for certain strains of nationalism and chauvinism (see the widespread popularity of Bedouin soap operas in the Middle East) and as a trope in orientalist imaginaries of the region. The Bedouin tent has arguably served the same functions in orientalist discourse that the tepee has in certain racist depictions of Native Americans by rendering its inhabitants primitive, close to nature, and, above all, easily separated from their land and any resources it might hold. Such discourses obscure the subtle but widespread transformation of the landscape by both Native Americans (Berkes 1999 Cronon 1996; Peacock and Turner 2000) and Bedouins long before the arrival of White settlers and resource extractors. My goal in highlighting the tent is to draw attention to the broader ecology in which it is implicated. I acknowledge the problematic uses to which the image of the tent has been put in the past. However, the tent can also put into sharp relief the peculiarities of the gendered political economy of public and private promulgated by various facets of contemporary global governance such as the World Bank, the US State Department, and the United Nations.

The basic architectural principles of the Bedouin goat hair tent are relatively simple. The tent forms a vaguely rectangular shape that is achieved by stretching a piece of fabric over a more or less rectangular grid of poles. These poles are held perpendicular to the ground by the tension of the ropes and the fabric pushing downward on the them. The poles are arrayed so that a longer center pole[4] (al-wasit) is flanked by two shorter poles stretching the length of the tent. I have spent a fair amount of time visiting with friends in Jordan who put up such tents while tending crops on land rented far from their permanent homes. Today these tents are likely to be made of burlap sacks or repurposed United Nations Refugee Works Administration tent fabric rather than painstakingly woven goat hair; however, the effect is the same. People passing the growing season in a tent emphasize that it can be a good way to save on gas and take advantage of the cooling summer breezes.

I used to make a point of asking elderly Bedouin men in Jordan about the names for the constituent parts of the Bedouin goat hair tent—not

the least because everyone seemed to enjoy teaching the foreign anthropologist the obscure minutiae of a bygone era. A number of elderly men
were even kind enough to draw diagrams for me. At first, I thought it
would be useful as a conversation starter that might lead comfortably
into stories, jokes, and ad hoc social theorizing. Indeed it did. It soon
became clear that there was also great diversity of experiences and termi-
nologies that people would express through their narrations of the tent.
Some aspects were ubiquitous: The tent was always conceived as divided
into two parts—the masculine *shiq* and the feminine *muharam*. But
was the *shiq* on the right or the left? A man once told me it varied by
tribe: his tribe put the *shiq* on the left. Seeming to contradict his thesis,
he then added, "but the path here is on the right so I put the *shiq* on the
right so [male] guests wouldn't walk by the *muharam*."

Nevertheless, there was a certain spatiotemporal ordering of this
gendered polarity that seemed to transcend the countless individual
experiences of the tent. For my part, I was taught and later experienced
the tent as a man.[5] The long sides of the tent would usually be raised up
to some degree. The front flap (usually known as the *star*) would be parallel to the ground, whereas the back flap (usually known as the *ruwaq*)
would be raised only enough to allow the wind to enter. I was told in no
uncertain terms that only dogs and children enter through the *ruwaq*.
Men must enter through the front. Ideally, a man should approach from
the back of the tent, which allows the family to be shielded from his
gaze by the lowered *ruwaq*. When he is within earshot, he should call
out, "Peace be upon you" (*salam 'alaykum*), "O protector, O family of the
house!" (*ya satir, ya ahl-al-bayt!*), or some other greeting. With permission granted, the visitor should approach one of the rear corner poles
known as the "foot" (*shadih ar-rijl*) or *al-fahiq* while making sure to
give the various ropes, which are staked in the ground around the sides,
a wide berth. Passing the stake jutting out from the front pole (known as
the "hand," *shadih al-iyd*), the male guest could expect to find his hosts
waiting to greet him.

Similar accounts of gendered space could be provided for other types
of homes in Jordan and in other times and places. When I have gone for
strolls among the ruins of the stone houses of the peasantry from the
early twentieth century, my Jordanian friends have always described

them in terms of the same gendering of space. The examples could be multiplied across the Mediterranean[6] and across the Arab world.[7] Domestic space is treated as though it were polarized into male and female aspects (*shiq* and *muharam*), whereas the home forms a feminine pole (*am-mharam*) in relationship to the masculine exterior. Admittedly, this is contradictory.

To use the language of Susan Gal's (2002) essay, "Language Ideologies Compared: Metaphors of Public/Private," this kind of "fractal recursion and erasure" is associated with most extant discourses on public and private. In fact, members of both genders move throughout the house and throughout the community over the course of the days, weeks, months, and years (Layne 1994, 70–73). Yet so firm is the ideological commitment to the maintenance of these polarities that people can speak of the masculine and feminine portions of the home and then, in the next breath, declare the home to be wholly feminine vis-à-vis the masculine market, *suq*, *bazaar*, or *agora*. I will return to the gendering of space within the "oikonomy"[8] of hair, mud, and stone, but I would like to begin by describing the activities of a family that, at the time of my research, continued to herd goats and engage in household food production. I hope the account will highlight some of the most striking recent changes in the gendering of property and labor relations and their ability to reify new ideas of public and private.

Subsistence, Property, and the Gender of Work

One of the more enjoyable ways to collect ethnographic data and oral history in rural Jordan is to go tend goats with retirees. This activity lends itself exceedingly well to storytelling, and the work need not be grueling—especially in the spring and fall when the weather is nice. These operations can range from hardscrabble subsistence work to major business ventures with migrant employees. Many efforts also seem hobbyist in orientation. For all the scorn often heaped upon those who continue to work in the agricultural economy, participants tend to turn it around. They tout the wisdom of biding one's time until the urban service economy inevitably implodes, maintaining one's body, sensibilities, and skills in order to adapt. In this section, I focus on one of my earliest such trips.

I arose as usual around six in the morning, but instead of going off to work, I set off with my neighbor Abu Fulan for a day of goat herding. Tall, cheerful, and retired from his job as an administrator, he enjoyed passing his days tending his flock. With a good pension and without the responsibilities of multiple wives or many sons, he could prioritize his own modest family's consumption—and their performance of a very particular sort of propriety with deep resonance. At seven, I went downstairs to meet him. He was holding the goats while his wife (Umm Fulan) milked them, and he told me to sit with a glass of tea and wait for him to finish.

Such marked but simultaneously partial division of labor has been widespread historically. Even their names denote their respective statuses: father (*abu*) of so-and-so and mother (*umm*) of so-and-so. Their respective roles were also highly overdetermined by local modesty standards. As I was repeatedly told, it is shameful (*'ayb*) for a man to milk an animal—and here Abu Fulan was, very studiously taking over the most masculine-coded aspect of the task.[9] Martha Mundy, writing about Yemen in the 1970s, argues, "Here as in most highlands, the division of labor stresses the defensive role of men and, correspondingly, the reproductive and domestic roles of women" (1979, 163). In particular, Mundy points out that women in highland Yemen were intimately involved in production but "[did] not direct plowing, irrigation, or building of irrigation channels and of walls separating fields" (163). Antoun (1968) recorded a more detailed but largely similar set of complementary gender roles covering most of the peasant agricultural economy in Jordan in the 1960s. At one level (as the villagers surely explained to Antoun), "men carry out all of the tasks requiring appearance in public places . . . only men handle the oxen and plow the fields, construct houses and roof them, and work with the sickle during the harvest period." Yet he observes, "women help in specified tasks even when the job is mainly men's," "digging up areas missed by the plow," "picking up the missed stray blades," and "drop[ping] the seeds . . . in the furrow" (Antoun 1968, 682). Again we see this pattern of fractal recursion and erasure, this time in the gendered division of labor.

In many ways, Umm Fulan was not so different from a *rabbit bayt* or housewife.[10] She relied on her husband for access to money and, by extension, the market while remaining at home in a space that was gendered female. Nonetheless, the urban ideal of the housewife would be spared this level of intimate involvement in the earliest stages of food production. The more notable economic transformation, however, has been in the male gendered aspects of labor and property relations: Abu Fulan's ability to use his independently obtained salary and pension to provide food and shelter and render Umm Fulan's intensive involvement in food production less and less integral to the household's survival. What is unprecedented is the way in which this inconspicuous consumption—this ability to shelter family members, especially female family members, from such labor[11] and cloister them—was expanded globally to encompass a much larger section of the male population in the post–World War II era.[12]

The weather was pleasant as we set off with about ten head of goats. We descended the steep path leading away from the densely packed settlement and toward Abu Fulan's grazing areas. We moved through his nephew's olive trees quickly, lest the goats take the opportunity to eat from the trees. Once we reached the valley, we followed the dry riverbed toward Sid al-mishmish. The grass was lush and green and littered with patches of yellow, purple, red, and blue flowers. Various herbs gave off a pleasing smell. Sid al-mishmish was a place where the riverbed gave way to a steep limestone cliff followed by a gorge filled with limestone boulders. We slowed to allow the goats to begin grazing. Abu Fulan pointed to a patch of wheat about two to three meters wide and about ten meters long and cautioned me to make sure the goats did not eat from it, as it belonged to our neighbor Sweilem. A goat would edge toward the wheat. Abu Fulan or I would pick up a rock and toss it at the patch of wheat the goat was eying, and the goat would back up a little.

I had always thought the shepherd was supposed to protect the livestock. I was surprised to discover that we were primarily concerned with protecting the plants from overgrazing. I have to admit that, on this point, I had paid too much heed to the ways that urbanites have portrayed Bedouins for over a thousand years. As a scholar from an aristocratic Jerusalem family once gleefully exclaimed to me—quoting the thirteenth-century historian ibn Khaldun—*yajid al-'arab yajid al-kharab* ("where the tribes are found, destruction is found"). There is a common view of pastoralists and other nomads being, if not exactly savages, anti-thetical to civilization, cultivation, and building. The image is of hordes that take what they need and move on, leaving the landscape exhausted. Instead, I learned about a complex set of overlapping property rights that rendered the land neither communal nor private; the protection of certain portions was a collective responsibility—but only really because of one person's insistence.[13]

Once the goats had moved beyond our neighbor's wheat, we sat on a boulder. I asked Abu Fulan about the land tenure arrangements in the area and the economics of his goat herding. Facing away from the gorge, he gestured at the steep slopes on either side. He explained that this land was *musha'* (often glossed as "communal") that was technically state owned (*lil-dawla*) but available for grazing and collecting firewood. He grazed his goats on it for free eight months out of the year. On top of the ridge to our right sat a new farm owned by "the Pasha," a wealthy capitalist from Amman who was starting to build a mansion. The land had been purchased from Sweilem and presaged the increasing subur-banization of the area as locals abandoned barely profitable agricultural ventures and cashed out to the tune of millions of dollars. The valley running perpendicular to us was owned by Abu Fulan's mother's broth-ers, who rented about five hundred square meters to Abu Fulan for sixty Jordanian dinars (JD 60)[14] a year. There he was able to plant enough barley to last his goats two months. During the dead of winter, he relied on feed (*'alaf*) that he purchased for about JD 60. Every year he was able to sustain ten to thirty goats for the cost of JD 120 (about $170). Given that goats typically reproduce once per year and that a goat could easily fetch JD 200–250 at market at the time, this welcome supplement to his pension kept him active and occupied.

It is important to emphasize that I have only spoken of Abu Fulan's attitudes about land rights—not about the underlying legal system per se of either the present or the past. In fact, property relations have been greatly in flux for the past few hundred years. Tribesmen, Ottoman administrators, British colonial officials, Jordanian bureaucrats, and World Bank consultants have questioned not only the private or com-munal nature of various plots of land but also the natures of the catego-ries themselves. In *State, Society, and Land in Jordan,* a thorough study of documentary evidence,[15] Michael R. Fischbach (2000) describes an Ottoman land regime in which very little land outside of urban areas was private, freehold land (*mulk*). The vast majority of land was the property of the state (*miri*); it was there to be improved and used by subjects in return for taxes. By working the land, Ottoman subjects gained rights to the fruits of the land (*tasarruf*, or usufruct[16]), but the "neck" (*ar-raqaba*, or ultimate ownership) continued to reside with the state and served as the basis for taxation.

This situation was beginning to change in the late nineteenth century because of the *Tanzimat* reforms of the late Ottoman Empire. Fischbach (2000) argues, however, that it was only with the onset of British rule that property relations in Jordan's agricultural regions really started to shift. He claims that for the British, there were "two fundamental assumptions. The first was that all land was owned by someone. The second was that land should be managed efficiently in order to maximize its productive potential" (79). The cadastral surveys the British conducted in the wake of their conquest of the Ottoman Empire sought to institutionalize private property with a precision that had never been attempted before.[17] All cultivated land was to be assigned by the state to individuals—even if the ownership of uncultivated land remained ambiguous. To be fair, early results were quite partial. The oral historical accounts of *mahr* in the post-Ottoman era that I recorded are full of examples of land transfers that were not recorded in either government-issued marriage contracts or government-issued land deeds (*sanads*). To this day, the privatization and commodification of land in Jordan remains a partial—if increasingly successful—project that the World Bank, the United Nations, and the HUDC continue to promote with mixed results.

Abu Fulan's use of the word *musha'* (so-called communal land) and its conflation with state-ownership (*miri* land) is telling. It reflects the conflicts that have marked the shift from tents, grains, and goats to concrete houses and government jobs in rural Jordan. Tribes have repeatedly fought to maintain what they call their communal (*musha'*) lands. The Jordanian State has argued that these lands, which lack recognizable cultivation (at least from the perspective of sedentary urbanites and farmers), can be appropriated by the state and privatized as necessary.[18]

People like Abu Fulan occupy land in a different way: they range over a wider area, extracting less from each zone they pass through. They seize, they grift, they submit, and, if necessary, they pay. Such people do not really concern themselves with the finer points of property law. They confront land as both individual and collective, public and private. As the day wore on, we moved toward the valley running perpendicular to Sid Al-mishmish. I noticed Abu Fulan keeping the goats away from particular shrubs that had been overgrazed or "tired" (ta'ban), in his words.

Around eleven o'clock, we headed back to the house to water the goats and eat breakfast. Abu Fulan brought out tea, fresh goat cheese, olives, hummus, and eggs. In contrast to Abu Fulan's labor, I could be only indirectly aware of his wife's contributions based on the unmistakable qualia of a fresh, home-cooked breakfast. Her labor was, if not quite invisible, not particularly visible to me, no matter how much her family appreciated it. In the next section, I turn from discussion of the gendering of property and labor to the relationship among gender, space, visibility, and interiority. In particular, I turn to one of the rare times during fieldwork when a woman made an effort to put herself at the center of my research, using her performance and its implicit critique of local modesty standards to illustrate how the home can help work out (or inflame) contradictions between economy and standards of modesty.

The Seed (Al-Bizr)

After weeks of hearing some friends of mine talking about their neighbor, 'Authba, an elderly woman with a reputation for being a character, they insisted on taking me to visit her. We hailed the men from the road as we walked by their land, and they demanded we come and drink tea. Inside the tent, the dirt floor was covered with a brightly colored plastic mat and a number of upholstered foam mattresses. I explained that I was doing research on customs and traditions around marriage and made small talk. Soon enough, 'Authba burst into the room with her scarf over her face and declared, "I hear there's a foreigner here!" I made a slow gesture to stand up while putting my hand over my heart to greet her. She let forth a volley of effusive praise, and we all laughed at the mock sycophancy. I repeated my introduction and explained my research focus on marriage.

'Authba immediately launched into a story: "In the old days, the man and the woman never saw each other until their wedding night." She paused for dramatic effect. "So on my wedding night, I was alone in the tent and this man walks up and I covered my whole face except for one eye." As she did this, she revealed one of her eyes. She continued, raising her pitch by a few octaves, "I said, 'Who are you?'" She dramatically lowered her voice as she let her scarf down, "I am your husband, girl!" Everyone burst out laughing again. She asked me what I wanted to know and repeatedly proclaimed her "expertise" while gesturing with her scarf. In this manner, she held court as she bantered with my friends and her sons. She seemed to take great pleasure in her ability to simultaneously challenge local norms around female modesty (even for an older woman[19]) and my ethnographic gaze and presumably cosmopolitan gender norms, embracing (and mocking) a perception of herself as a helpless victim of rural backwardness.

Eventually, I asked her about the names of the various parts of the tent. To this day, I am not sure what she said when she responded by asking whether I had heard of one particular part of the tent, but everyone burst out laughing. The men were too bashful to repeat the precise word she had used, but they explained to me that it was a word for the gap between the *saha* (the piece of fabric separating the putatively masculine *shiq* from the *muharam*) and the *ruwaq* (the back of the tent). It was clear that she had likened the gap to the human pudendum—a clever play on the anthropomorphization of the tent and an extension of what one would expect to find behind the tent's "hands" and between its "legs." My friends would later refer to it as simply *al-bizr* (the seed). As I pondered its possible significance, a teenage girl's voice rang out from the other side of the divide: "Mom! Your TV show is on!" 'Authba yelled back, "What do I want with my TV when I have a foreigner right here!" That was the first time I realized the laughter was coming from both sides of the tent.

This story highlights the inherent difficulties and hazards of rendering the interior exterior and the invisible visible. 'Authba, a gifted performer, handled it expertly. She could turn it into a joke. However, as we will see, this is not always the case. Such renderings can be fraught with misunderstandings, arguments, and violence. And as I have intimated, this problem is not merely a Jordanian one. In "Forms of Time and Chronotope in the Novel," Mikhail Bakhtin (1981) goes so far as to argue the drive to exteriorize and render visible the interior and the invisible is central to the development of literature in general and the novel in particular. I suggest that ethnography itself is ancillary to this preoccupation. Bakhtin argues that "the public and rhetorical unity of the human image is to be found in the contradiction between it and its purely private content. . . . Although personal life had already become private and persons individualized, although this sense of the private had begun to infiltrate literature in ancient times, still, it was only able to develop forms adequate to itself in the small everyday genres, the comedy and novella of common life" (110). In the essay, Bakhtin attempts to illustrate the "historico-literary process" through which various forms of time-space have developed in literature and the arts from the Greek Romance to the Rabelasian novel.[20] It is important to note, however, that we have not yet arrived at the liberal notion of public and private. This shift markedly divides market from state and associates the former with the private and the latter with the public. Here, the dialectics of interiority and exteriority, visibility and invisibility, still predominate.

CONCRETE RELATIONS: BUILDING
THE CINDERBLOCK HOUSE

As an ethnographer, and even more so as a male ethnographer, I was always acutely aware of this literary conundrum hit upon by Bakhtin. When the action was masculine, visible, exterior, and collective, I was well equipped to narrate it, but such action failed to exhaust the ethnographically relevant data. Much like generations of World Bank consultants, colonial administrators, and Jordanian bureaucrats, I found myself compelled to consider (if not necessarily understand) that which was feminine, invisible, interior, and individual—what Bakhtin would call "private." As he observes, "By its very nature this private life does not create a place for the contemplative man, for that 'third person' who might be in a position to meditate on this life, to judge and evaluate it.

This life takes place between four walls and for only two pairs of eyes."
Instead, in the following section, I focus on the construction of that
space "between four walls" of interiority and invisibility: the home.
Although my primary focus will be on the logistics of actually building
a house from cement, steel, water, and gravel, I hope to use the concrete
house's juxtaposition with the pastoralist oikonomy of goats and tents to
highlight the peculiarities of recent shifts in property, labor, and spatial
relations—specifically regarding gender and the creation of the conditions of possibility for male individuality and autonomy within a market
context.

Previously, Bedouin homes were a form of women's wealth bound
up in a subsistence economy where money played a relatively small role
in mediating day-to-day social relations.[21] With the adoption of concrete
houses, the home became men's wealth as men abandoned pastoralism,
joined the army and bureaucracy (or went abroad to work in industries
such as construction), and increasingly used their personal salaries to
pay for the materials and labor necessary to build houses.[22] As British
and American military advisers and development consultants poured
into Jordan in the mid-twentieth century and set about "modernizing"
the country, women became increasingly interiorized, invisible, and distant from economic power. As we will see in the next chapter, part of
this shift involved development consultants becoming convinced that
there were "individual owner-builders" who needed to be empowered
through the creation of a "private" housing market. The elusiveness of
actual individual owner-builders has not served as any obstacle here.
House construction remains a collective endeavor concerned with fashioning the physical house as a corporate body for the married couple and
their progeny. Nevertheless, Jordan's political economy has increasingly
been designed to serve "him"[23]—the individual owner-builder.

"For a Relative"

In order to have housing while doing research without displacing anyone
else, I made an agreement with a friend who I will call Harun to build
a two-room house instead of using my research grant money to try to
find a place to rent.[24] This arrangement would have the added benefits

of allowing me to learn about house construction first-hand and giving his teenage son a head start on getting married once he had finished his studies and found a job. I had yet to begin work at the HUDC archives, where I would learn about the decades-long project to empower "individual owner-builders" to build their own homes—and I would probably have scoffed at the premise of someone building their own house alone, even if I had not attempted it. Yet over the course of constructing the house, I would learn just how collective house construction remains in rural Jordan to this day.

The process began normally enough by soliciting bids from various subcontractors (*mu'allims*). Harun and I settled on the lowest bidder: an Egyptian by the name of Ahmad who agreed to organize all of the labor of constructing the pillars, roof, and walls for JD 700.[25] We began by going to meet with him in a downtrodden section of Madaba city. He flagged us down on the street and took us into an alley with a strong, rotten stench. We headed up the stairs to the second floor, where we found about thirty pairs of flip-flops and shoes strewn about. Ahmad led us into a dilapidated room with a TV, some worn mattresses, and a few mass-produced plaques with verses of the Quran. A number of young (and not-so-young) men sat around. Two sat listening to music on their mobile phones through headphones while an older man fiddled with his prayer beads and a young man flipped through satellite TV channels. A bottle of orange soda quickly appeared, and the men began to discuss the materials that would be needed. Harun presented a piece of paper that another foreman had written for him. Ahmad spoke at a rapid pace, swerving between his Mansouri dialect (they were all from the Egyptian city of Mansour) and an approximation of Jordanian Arabic. They went through the various quantities of materials one by one as Ahmad fired off multiplication problems. He agreed with the various figures and launched into a brief discussion of steel and cement procurement. After no more than ten minutes, everyone had finished soda, concluded business, and taken their leave.

Harun explained on the way back that he did not trust the foreman at all. Sure, Ahmad was building a house for a cousin's nephew, but the foreman was totally transient. On the bright side, Harun reckoned himself too poor to be swindled. He claimed that the biggest problem was that workmen would steal materials. This was why the family would have to be careful to buy only as much as he needed and make sure it was delivered and supervised such that thievery was kept to a minimum. The first step would be to get the steel. He would buy it by the ton in the form of a kit that included everything from rebar to nails and wire. The next day, once the steel frames were set up, the merchant would have the sand, gravel, and cement delivered. Harun was able to provide some evidence of a need to be wary: a Qatari man had built himself a home in the area without ever visiting, and the neighbors reported seeing trucks coming every night to take away load after load of materials.

The next day, we went to the largest cement dealer in town to price materials—a constant topic of male conversation in the village. Price swings had become normal since the state monopoly had been sold to the then-French multinational Lafarge and, when buying by the ton on a limited income, could threaten to put marriage out of reach. However, three new cement factories had opened in 2010–2011. Harun was taken aback to discover that the "Cement of the South," which he and his family had relied on for decades and considered better than the cement made at the northern plant, no longer existed as such. The trader tried to mollify him by talking up the new government-backed quality rating system, but we were not in a good position to buy from him anyway. He quoted the going price for cement paid in cash, and such a distributor would be unlikely to offer good terms for a loan. We wanted more flexibility in the terms of payment. So with the materials priced, Harun went to buy the materials from his friend, neighbor, and distant uncle Abu Hashim. He generously quoted the same prices as the Madaba distributors and agreed to deliver the materials bit by bit on an installment plan.[26]

Abu Hashim's store was emblazoned with a large green sign advertising Lafarge cement and the words "building supplies" (*muwad al-buna'*), written in Arabic. To the left of his store were hundreds of bags of carefully stacked cement, and down the road was a cinderblock factory run by a single Egyptian man supplying Abu Hashim's customers with blocks, which could be purchased from Abu Hashim on credit. The interior of the store had three sections: a storage area for white cement, a tiny office for receiving customers, and the shop itself, which overflowed with tools and basic supplies for plumbing, painting, and wiring.

Out front, there was a wall of paint cans about one meter high and two meters long. On top of the paint cans sat a water cooler and a thermos of Arabic coffee. Abu Hashim could almost always be found out front. He was a light-skinned man with a light brown mustache, kind eyes, and a headscarf. He always wore trousers and a long-sleeved dress shirt, which would be rolled up to reveal his muscular arms. Next to him sat his assistant, an Egyptian youth who served coffee, carried supplies, and drove the truck for deliveries.

There were two reasons to buy from Abu Hashim: proximity and his willingness to accept interest-free debts in a Muslim community where *riba* (roughly "usury") is frowned upon. While the debate about *riba* and its relationship to interest and usury is complex and beyond the scope of this chapter, a few points are key. Specialists on the topic like anthropologist Bill Maurer (2002, 9; 2005) are absolutely correct that Christian connotations render these words less than ideal as potential translations. At the same time, these words are ubiquitous whenever the subject of *riba* arises in the literature on Islamic finance, and they are often judged to be more similar than different—despite the objections of certain politically connected religious authorities. Usually, there is some agreement that *riba* includes the exchange of a smaller amount of money at one point in time for a larger amount of money later. Whatever *riba* actually is, the sayings of the Prophet Muhammad are clear on its permissibility. It is related that, "The Messenger of Allah cursed the one who consumes riba and the one who pays it, the one who writes it down and the two who witness it" (see Muslim 2007, 319).

When I asked about his customers, Abu Hashim readily mentioned the importance of proximity but neglected to mention the role of money lending. As we sat one day, he told me what I suspected: with Ramadan approaching in the middle of the building season, an initial burst of activity had given away to rather slow going. There was no *haraka* (movement). He explained, "Summer is a busy season because people come back from the Gulf and they want to build. Kids are out of school so they can help." He predicted a flurry of activity once Ramadan was over. It would be difficult to make money in the building supply trade if everyone offered such soft terms for loans as Abu Hashim had. In a different side of the business, a customer arrived and asked the owner for a plastic shutoff valve for water tanks. The Egyptian assistant ran inside to find the parts and put it together. The owner asked for five dinar and the man pleaded, "for your relative." The owner muttered about it being difficult and the man accepted the device and left—presumably with the intention of paying later. After he had left I asked, "Where is he from?" The owner pointed across the street: "the house with the green windows." He then added, "he's military so he gets paid at the end of the month." Most people's need for credit was less urgent than that of the man with a broken water tank, but a steady stream of people had enough of a need to build that they found their way to such provincial suppliers.

Customers of such establishments would be in a better bargaining position if they could pay in cash and would likely go to the nearest town to buy their supplies from the main suppliers. Customers who could not pay cash had to pay a premium to such local proprietors—who inevitably knew exactly how every customer fit into the local kinship structure, what their job was, whether they would pay back their debts, and when they would be able to pay them back. In this sense, the building supply store was primarily a money-lending operation—albeit one that was fully in accordance with Islamic law, as it was based on an exchange of material goods for money and not money for money. The figure of Abu Hashim forces us to reconsider the idea of an individual owner-builder. At the time of my research, such building supply stores were ubiquitous. They tended to rely on the same business model centered on monetizing one's kinship bonds and meticulously precise local knowledge by lending money in the manner with which Jordanian Muslims were most comfortable.

"Work Isn't Shameful"

Money and building materials alone cannot build a house. Kinship remains integral to the construction of houses because of its ability to mobilize labor. Despite most Jordanian men having some ability to use cash to hire transient migrant labor to do the most dangerous work, the local construction industry in Jordan depends on the labor of the entire family to provide proper food, supervision, and coordination. My hosts constantly had to weigh the cost of hiring others against the physical toll

Figure 01_02. A rural cinderblock factory. Given their weight, cinderblocks tend to be produced locally, often by migrants working for local Jordanian building supply store owners.

on their own bodies from doing it themselves. They made this most clear at those times when my attempts to "help" were summarily rejected with clinical descriptions of the deleterious effects I would suffer. Although my friends in the village were often fond of saying that "work isn't shameful," the necessity of constantly repeating the phrase—either to rationalize one's own labor or that of someone else—is telling. In some ways, the phrase actually trivializes the issue: much of this work is not just degrading but also entails serious risks of scarring, loss of limb, or blindness. The aim is to limit the exposure of oneself and those one cares about to such hazards. Consequently, as construction shifts from the coarseness of gravel and steel to the softer and smoother surfaces of stucco, tile, and paint, the labor becomes less anonymous and disposable and becomes increasingly based on the intimate ties of kinship. Nevertheless, even in the earliest phases when dealing with migrant workers, there were attempts by all involved to take some of the anomic edge off of the relations—most notably through shared commensality.

The workers (referred to in the othering local idiom of "the Egyptians") showed up at 7:45 a.m., about forty-five minutes late. Because it was summer and Harun, his sons, and the rest of the family had to take care of the morning's harvest no matter what, I had been charged with being at the site to receive the workers with tea and provide anything else they might need. Immediately, the requests started flowing. They seemed to have shown up with no tools whatsoever with the exception of two devices for cutting and bending steel rods. They asked for a sledgehammer. Next they wanted to know where the "owner of the house" was, and all I could say was that he was on his way. While I was looking for a sledgehammer and trying to make tea, they announced their displeasure with the nails. I went over and served them tea. One man was on the roof demolishing the cinderblocks that sat over the steel rebar of the columns from the first floor. Because they were building on the roof of a preexisting structure, there was no need for blueprints or consultations. The workers were simply extending the existing columns.[27] The other two were cutting the lengths of steel to form the columns. After drinking the tea and granting that I could (if nothing else) make a good cup of tea, they moved to the roof, where they rigged up a table to bend the short lengths of steel into rectangles. They would use six long bars and twelve rectangles to make a column. After spacing the rectangles along the length of the six rods, they would use steel wire to attach four of the rods at the corners and the remaining two in the middle of the long sides. While the foreman worked on this task, his two assistants hammered boards together to make the molds for the concrete they would pour the next day.

At this point, it was about thirty minutes into the process of building the house. I found that the workmen would need at least this much attention for the remainder of the process. When they requested a broom, I ran next door to Harun's brother, Mahmud. As I was on my way, a man began honking loudly because a truck was parked in the road. I said I did not know who owned the truck, so he kept honking until the owner emerged from Mahmud's house. I went over to ask about the broom. I was ordered to sit down and drink tea while they sent a son to deliver the broom. They asked, "How are the Egyptians with you?" I whined that they seemed to think I was a building supply store and recounted the whole list of things they had requested. Just then, Harun called to ask how many "Egyptians" there were so he could bring the right amount of breakfast. I said three and then told him about the problem with the nails. I explained that, from what I could tell, they had nails that were short and thin along with nails that were long and wide but that they wanted nails that were long and thin. Mahmud told me what such nails were called and added "just like Harun's," at which point they started laughing hysterically at the idea of treating nails as a phallic symbol.

Harun showed up with a breakfast of bread, two kinds of beans ("Egyptians love beans," he said), and tomatoes. He told me to make sure I did not feed them until 10:30 a.m., lest they want another meal. He presented me with the nails and left to take care of his other business. At 10:30 a.m., I presented the food and began to make tea. It was clear to Harun that everyone was annoyed. The workers wanted a ten-year-old who would snap to and run errands for them and bring a steady supply of tea. The problem was that we were both trapped within the gendered expectations of young manhood. In the words of Antoun, we were aware that the other "should not undertake chores which marked his formerly adolescent status" and that our counterpart "regards himself . . . as no man's servant and only undertakes chores out of the generosity of his own heart" (1967, 295). Harun could immediately see that this was not going to work and promised to send his ten-year-old son the next day to ease things along.

All of these requests for food, tea, and tools were integral to the logic of immigration. The workers would stock up on caffeine and calories at the employer's expense and then go back home in the evening to sleep—saving almost all of the money for their Jordanian work visas and their own marriages back home. After all, they had come to Jordan for the opportunity to make JD 15 as laborers or perhaps JD 20 or JD 25 as a skilled ironworker (*haddad*), carpenter (*najjar*), block layer (*tubanji*), or stucco worker (*kasir*). I often sat and listened to them talk about how their own migration was tied up with dreams of saving up enough to build their own houses back in Egypt and get married. Mahmud and Harun understood this but did not necessarily like it. Mahmud could both complain about the constant requests and hard-nosed negotiating stance and then say, "What can they do? They need a thousand dinar a

year for the visa to work here so Harun here can draw a pension from
the government and sit here laughing and smoking his water pipe."
However, they were less sanguine about the sudden insistence of the
workmen a few hours later that they would need more cement. Harun
exclaimed, "Just because I wear a headscarf, they think I'm stupid." He
was convinced that they were inflating the amount of cement needed in
an attempt to get work for one of their friends loading and unloading the
extra materials. Nonetheless, in one day, they had erected eight columns
and laid the mold for the staircase. They would begin pouring the cement
the next afternoon.

Ahmad showed up the next day with more workmen and a cement
mixer, which they used to speed the process of pouring the pillars. Two
weeks later, they were back building a mold to pour the roof, placing
cement blocks into it, and fashioning the steel rebar or *'asab* (nerves).
With that, the roof or "back" (*zahr*) of the house was complete. After the
roof, we had cinderblocks delivered and the block layer and his assistant
set to work laying them. In three weeks, Ahmad and his workers had
fashioned the steel rebar, poured the pillars and the roof, and built the
walls—what my neighbors referred to as the "bone" (*'azm*). Rather than
continue with a step-by-step account of house building, I want to focus
on the ways in which, as the project wore on and we began to work on the
skin or finishings (*jilda*),[28] the workers became more intimately related
to the community. Increasingly, Harun did not solicit bids from strangers so much as he turned to people with whom he had preexisting ties.

Exteriority

I could go on for pages about the extensive supervision, support, and
assistance that the various workers expected as they built the house.
There is no way they could have worked so diligently and so continuously
without the constant supply of water, caffeine, food, and tools—not to
mention the frequent need for Harun's sons, nephews, and me to move
multiple cubic meters of building materials (cement, tiles, sand, and
cinderblocks) into place in preparation for the next phase of building.
In between the various stages of the process, there was a need to water
(*asqi*) the fresh green (*akhdar*) cement to help cure it. There was nothing

out of the ordinary about this. If anything, it was strange that someone like myself, without kin bonds, was caught up in such a project. Virtually everyone in the neighborhood helped at one point or other. Much as I have carried cinderblocks, made tea, supervised workers, and watered cement for my Jordanian friends and neighbors, they proved even more generous when I attempted my own building project. Although it is possible to insulate oneself from this kind of work with enough money, only the very wealthiest where I lived could afford to do so.

With the steel and concrete in place, the men of the village became more and more actively engaged in the construction of the house. Harun's and Mahmud's sons set to work doing the electrical and plumbing work. They worked with hammers and chisels, carving out a path through the concrete cinderblocks for the wires and pipes. They had already run plastic tubing for the wires through the roof before pouring the cement, so they just had to link up the holes they had carved out for the electrical outlets with the ceiling while linking up the holes they had made for the plumbing fixtures with the floor. They would take a healthy swing at the cinderblock, causing the lining of one of the holes in the cinderblock to crumble as it gave way. Then they would take the chisel and work their way through the solid concrete, separating the holes that ran to the floor.

The mere fact that one was male was not necessarily sufficient to embody this particular sort of masculinity. When I tried to help, I managed to scrape about half of my knuckles to the point of bleeding as the chisel gave way with unexpected force, sending my left hand careening into the rough concrete. I managed to do the same to my right hand by misjudging the angle as I swung at the chisel. I also developed some nasty blisters on my palm and the inside of my thumb from the motion of the hammer, no doubt exacerbated by the fact that the handle was made out of steel. Attempting to keep up, I wrapped my hand in medical tape such that each blister was covered. Needless to say, my body was not accustomed to such work. As one of the Egyptian workers exclaimed with wonder one day as they took turns feeling my hands, "they're soft and fair like a woman's." Eventually, Mahmud's son Muhammad (age eighteen) arrived. He was faster and better at it than the younger youths. He was also less shy about breaking through to the other side. He told me it was the *kasir*'s (stucco worker's) job to "clean up." Once the wiring and plumbing was in place, they mixed up some cement on the floor and smeared it over the channels they had chiseled out, making sure everything was at least somewhat flush.

As construction neared completion, the labor involved became less anomic and more driven by bonds of kinship and modes of affiliation based on long-term exchange relations. As Mahmud and his sons helped with the wiring and plumbing, Harun made arrangements with the *kasir*: the person charged with adding the final layer of concrete or stucco to the exterior and interior of the house. Here, Harun had specific ideas about who he planned to hire. His village had been hiring people from a particular family in Syria to do their stucco for more than a decade—largely because they were willing to do the work and then take payment in monthly installments. This would probably be one of the first jobs in the village for which they were paid in cash. Next, Harun's friend 'Abed did the tile work (Harun's brother Mahmud was very skilled with tile, but Harun had already asked a lot of him and his sons). Harun was able to get the windows from a business associate who ran a *jama'iyya* (a kind of charitable society or nongovernmental organization) that owned a window factory, a carpentry shop, and a blacksmith's shop.

The Syrian stucco workers in particular related to the village in a manner that only a specific kind of long-term indebtedness can engender. Unlike the Egyptian team, which involved a shifting cast of characters who tended to be standoffish and quiet, the Syrian stucco workers more or less insisted that the family watch them work as they told us about their own marital and house-building projects back in Syria. When they finally arrived (a day late), they said they would be working only two hours that day but would be looking forward to lunch, naturally. It was hard to argue so long as Harun's brother and a number of his cousins still owed them for work they had long since completed. The assistant mixed the "mud" or *tin* (which consisted of water, finely ground limestone, and cement) and occasionally helped his uncle apply it to the walls. They watered the cement and set to work, covering a palate with the mud and flinging it at the wall with a trowel. Once they had covered the walls with patches of this mixture, they applied thicker swathes in bars on each wall so that, once it had dried, they could get an even coating. When

Figure 01_03. Shared commensality. Food, water, and tea were crucial to the process of construction. I once calculated that building a house in Jordan required one hundred grams of sugar and 2.25 tea bags per square meter.

the mud had been applied, they used thick wooden beams to level it. Through multiple coats and the use of increasingly fine sponges, the texture became smoother and smoother.

The addition of stucco represented the completion of the exterior of the exterior and the exterior of the interior. Harun opted for the most utilitarian finish for his son's future home, even though some of his neighbors suggested I opt for paint (inside and/or outside) or a limestone "face" (*wajh*) for the house. The choice of finish presented a clear status competition in which people vied for superiority in different ways simultaneously. A house could be judged on the basis of the stone's quality.[29] At the same time, there were people who put stone on only the front of their house or on all of the sides except the back. Some people put stone only around their windows and on the corners. Inside, Harun once again opted for the simple, durable and inexpensive materials favored by the rural Jordanian working class: concrete floor tiles, wooden internal doors, a steel exterior door, and aluminum windows. As Harun was fond of saying, "everyone cuts *halawa* [a sugary sesame paste] according to the size of his tooth" (others preferred to describe the calculus of investing in houses by saying "everyone extends their legs according to the size of their mattress"). The point was that, to some degree, houses seemed to provide almost endless opportunities for embellishment so long as the money was there. While Harun's preferred proverb subtly critiqued the overindulgence of some of his neighbors, others framed things in a language of compromise and making do with less. Among the wealthy, houses are increasingly embellished with elaborate plaster (*jibsin*) designs, wallpaper, curtains, carpets, and overstuffed couches—especially in guest rooms.

These forms of surfacing, smoothing, and softening constitute the "interior" exteriors, spaces that form the backdrop to so much of the stagecraft of hospitality in Jordan. Such stagecraft is clearly discernible in migrant flophouses, construction sites, and building supply stores but finds its fullest expression in the houses that inhabitants of these other sites seek to actualize. As Andrew Shryock and Sally Howell have argued, contemporary hospitality and "house politics" are "a mode of domination in which families . . . serve as instruments and objects of power" (2001, 248). This is a distinctly masculine form of power that relies on the invisible but essential work of females and subordinate males to properly execute the performance. It involves the creation of "tactical facades" for "projecting, in a very private place, a very public reputation" (Shryock and Howell 2001, 255). However, this notion of public and private has far more in common with that of Bakhtin (1981) than with the interpretation in the next chapter. In chapter 2, attention will turn away from the activities of households and toward those of technocrats working for a variety of development organizations including the United Nations, the World Bank, and the HUDC.

In the latter half of the chapter, the focus has been almost exclusively on exterior male workspaces, which have grown more important as market relations have become more central to mediating gender relations through the emergent opposition between public and private. In the meantime, property relations have fallen into the background but have not been forgotten. Their erasure is a reflection of the ethnographic context I have described: in rural Jordan, residents generally had strong claims to property, which were couched in a language of indigeneity. Such claims were legitimated by a nationalistic discourse that often portrayed those who hailed from Palestine as less deserving of the rights of citizenship (property, access to government jobs, and the ability to organize politically without the fear of persecution) than their compatriots from the East Bank.[30]

It took Harun months after finishing construction to get a building permit,[31] but no one ever had to seriously consider the possibility that they might be dispossessed—not all people were, or are, so lucky. For many Jordanians (especially those of Palestinian descent), property relations continue to be a constant source of sorrow (due to the memory of past dispossession) and anxiety (due to the fear of future dispossession). More important, housing for those who do not build on inherited land is fundamentally different from what I have described. It is challenging for most Jordanians to assemble the money to build a house, and those who lack land are even more dependent on the help of outside institutions—banks, the HUDC and, increasingly, large rental companies—for housing.

NOTES

1. To get a sense of how normal this involvement with the military is, more than a quarter of men in the Madaba sample of marriage contracts were employed by the security services.

2. These new standards of desirability are not necessarily monetary either—or at least directly so. In one case, a young woman from a working-class Palestinian background became the subject of local gossip as a hot marriage candidate after the *tawjihi* (national college entrance examination results) were released and she became known as "the girl who got a 95."

3. The increasing participation of Middle Eastern women in the workforce is a topic of intense focus among development practitioners and academics alike. Homa Hoodfar's (1997) work in urban Cairo depicts working-class women engaged in a variety of paid and unpaid work inside and outside the home as they struggle to make ends meet. Fida Adely's (2004, 2012) ethnographic work in a more rural, conservative, and somewhat better-off community in Jordan traces the relationship between education and women's life aspirations and shows how young women balance competing objectives (work, family, faith) and the compromises they must make to realize their dreams. The issue of women working outside of the home is one of the key places where one can discern what Lila Abu-Lughod (1998, 243) has called Islamists' "selective

repudiation" of Western feminism. This leads Islamic activists and authorities to defend certain rights associated with nineteenth-century women's rights activism (e.g., work, education, ideals of bourgeois marriage) while opposing others that are associated with later feminist activism (e.g., sexual independence and public freedoms) due to association with the corrupt and morally decadent West. Kenneth Cuno (2015) and Ziba Mir-Hosseini (1999) have identified a similar dynamic in debates about women's roles in society in Egypt and Iran, respectively. As I will show, Islamic activists and authorities are not the only people in Jordan engaged in such practices, which are ubiquitous.

4. A classic index of sheikhly status was the number of these center poles in one's tent. More center poles meant more room to accommodate guests, which meant the need for more surplus to meet the obligations of hospitality (see Layne 1994, 59–60).

5. Linda Layne (1994) offers a complementary account of domestic space from a woman's perspective in chap. 3 ("Arab Architectonics") of *Home and Homeland: The Dialogics of Tribal and National Identities in Jordan*. As one might expect, she emphasizes the importance of maintaining one's modesty while moving through space—the counterpart of my focus on lowering the gaze and moving with care, announcing my presence with every step.

6. Cohen (1989) offers a relatively nuanced account of women's movement through various gendered spaces in ancient Greece, drawing on a combination of archaeological and textual evidence. Herzfeld's (1985) ethnography of a town in Crete finds gendering of the town square itself. The most famous example of the Mediterranean house literature is Bourdieu's (1977) research on Kabyle homes in North Africa.

7. The gendering of domestic space both internally and in relationship to the exterior is a recurrent theme in ethnographies and histories of the Arab world (cf. Ghannam 2002; Khater 2001; vom Bruck 1997).

8. As Timothy Mitchell (2002) has argued, the notion of the economy is a mid-twentieth-century European invention. It presupposes a nation-state as its locus and demands technocratic management. It is "a distinct social sphere." Before the twentieth century, *economy* was used primarily as a term for practices of maximizing efficiency (Mitchell 2002, 81). It is derived from the ancient Greek *oikos* (house)—the original locus of the term. My use of *oikonomy* is meant to re-center *economy* away from the nation-state and toward the home—at least for the first half of this chapter. This is in keeping with the broader Mediterranean sensibilities I am trying to foreground and should not be taken as any sort of invocation of the "Western canon." Nevertheless, the conflation of the two through the term *economy* recalls Foucault's (1991) later work on "biopolitics" and "Governmentality."

9. A common context in which I heard about the shamefulness of a man milking was when my friends sought out shepherds to tend to animals that they did not have time to watch. Syrian men were preferred for such work precisely because they were willing to milk the animals as well as tend to them.

10. The term *rabbit bayt* is completely absent from my sample of marriage contracts until the 1950s, when it suddenly became the default designation for women's employment. In my sample of contracts from the Amman courthouse stretching from 1926 to 1953, the term does not make a single appearance. The majority of women (71%) do not have any occupation recorded. This primarily indicates a lack of interest in their economic activities and, relatedly, the assumption that women's economic activities would likely mirror those of their husbands. The prevalence of the latter assumption is

consistent with the fact that most of the remaining women are classed on their marriage contracts (using quotation marks) as "peasant" or "farmer"—just like their husbands and fathers. Three of the 377 brides were seamstresses. No doubt those three represent a fraction of women who performed such work, but their contracts show some very limited interest on the part of court officials in women's economic activities during this period. In contrast, nearly 70% of Madaba brides (spanning the years 1953–2011) have their occupation listed as "housewife." The shift to "housewife" in court documents represents a notable shift not necessarily in women's labor but at least in its social recognition.

11.   The cloistering of elite women is a widespread phenomenon that has been written about in different times and places. Kenneth Cuno argues that in late-nineteenth- and early twentieth-century Cairo, "Upper- and ruling class households practiced the strictest seclusion of women, ostensibly to guard their modesty, but also making ostentatious displays of wealth and respectability" (2015, 47). Intriguingly, however, a wealth of historical studies have shown how variable the nature of this cloistering can be and how it can be connected to everything from subsistence strategies to statecraft. Cuno (2003), for instance, shows how Egypt's Khedival rulers took up monogamy in the span of a few generations in the late nineteenth century. They abandoned a system of concubinage and polygyny that entailed households that "contained anywhere from several hundred to over a thousand female slaves . . . all but a few of these women . . . celibate, and subject to a strict rule of discipline under the master's mother and wives" (Cuno 2003, 251). He argues, "The ruler's household, including its harem, was an instrument through which a dependent elite was created and reproduced" (255). However, the system was abandoned in the nineteenth century. Cuno asserts that this was due to endogenous strategies of dynastic succession and conformity to exogenous European mores around companionate marriage. In *Modernizing Marriage*, Cuno (2015) extends this subtle analysis of changing conceptions of gender and marriage in nineteenth-century Egypt more broadly by turning to another group that supported companionate marriage for different reasons: modernizing social reformers like Muhammad Abduh and Qasim Amin. However, even as these reformers promoted a vision of marriage that entailed women leaving the home for work, education, and other social activities, they took for granted that this would be in the service of an exchange of women's obedience (*ta'a*) for men's maintenance (*nafaqa*) (Cuno 2015, 77–122).

12.   The expansion of a highly gendered conception of wage labor that brought with it a freedom from the constraints of kin bonds is central to the political potency of transnational feminist projects like the "wages for housework" campaign described by Sylvia Federici (2012).

13.   Andrew Shryock (1997a) has studied the roots of this confusion in some detail and presents a convincing explanation. He observes that among the Balga Bedouin, property is generally believed to be obtained by seizing it from another group, by being granted it in return for political support, or by "marital exchanges or as terms of reconciliation between groups in conflict" (42). The mistake is that despite the open acknowledgment that the land was obtained collectively and is constantly defended collectively, various subgroupings and members can assert much more specific rights— at times by simply working a particular bit of land more intensively.

14.   At the time of research, most people in rural areas made about JD 300 per month—although most owned their own homes. Urbanites tended to make slightly

more but not enough to make up for the high rents they had to pay. The official exchange rate was $1.40 for JD 1. However, goods tended to be cheaper in Jordan, so, for instance, a small can of soda would cost JD 0.25, meaning that JD 100 could buy 400 cans of soda assuming no bulk discount. Needless to say, local meat is not one of those cheap goods. One kilo of local meat cost JD 8–13 at the time of research.

15. Lars Wahlin (1988, 1994) and Shryock (1997a) have questioned the degree to which Ottoman records can be trusted—where they still exist (Fischbach [2000, 31] points out that the land records for southern Jordan were burned during an uprising in Karak in 1910). The case for the veracity of the later records is stronger, but there is probably a degree to which the British cadastral survey of the 1930s both reconfirmed the existing situation (cf. Shryock 1997a) and became a sort of self-fulfilling prophecy. By simultaneously registering property to discrete individuals, effectively putting a stop to raiding and then distributing titles, government jobs, and education to many of those same individuals, the British almost certainly tended to ossify social distinctions, labor relations, and property rights.

16. My neighbors told me that according to the *sunna* (the sayings and actions of the Prophet Muhammad), it is permissible to pick fruit from any fruit-bearing plant on anyone's land as long as it is eaten immediately and not taken away.

17. Mitchell (2002) provides an excellent account of the British cadastral survey of Egypt's Nile Delta in chap. 2 of *Rule of Experts* ("Principles True in Every Country"), which emphasizes similar sensibilities.

18. Controversies over the privatization of communal lands tend to receive only passing references in the English media (Ziad Abu Rish's 2012 interview with Tariq Tell in *Jadaliyya* is typical). For a sympathetic account of the government's position, see Rania Al-Hindi's (2012) article in *Ar-rai*, "Business Man Releases Road Map to Solve the Problem of Communal Lands." For a more cynical account, see the unattributed article on Gerasa News (2012), "What's the Story of the Lands That the Kuwaiti Ambassador and the Brother of Kilani [president of the board of the Amman Municipality] Bought!!"

19. For more discussion of the greater license extended to women who are beyond childbearing age (especially widows), see Granqvist (1935, 319–324).

20. Although Bakhtin (1981) specifically concerns himself with the development of these processes in "the various histories of generic heterogeneity in the European novel," the distinction is artificial and should certainly include the literature of all western Asia—not just Europe—and North Africa. His extensive use of *The Golden Ass* and Augustine's *Confessions* merely emphasizes the narrowness of his focus on Europe; both works were written by North Africans. Likewise, his discussions of medieval chivalric romances could be compared profitably with coeval *udhri* (chaste) romances of Arabia and Persia like *Layla and Majnun*. The basic plot of *Layla and Majnun* concerns a semihistorical figure who falls deeply in love with a girl named Layla. His infatuation leads him to loudly and mawkishly proclaim his love for Layla in poetry—mentioning her by name. People begin to talk about his strange behavior and label him crazy (*majnun*). The epithet sticks. When he proposes marriage, the girl's father cannot abide the idea of his daughter marrying a crazy person. Growing out of the oral culture of the Arabian Peninsula, the story reaches its point of greatest elaboration in the Persian court culture of the thirteenth century in the able hands of the poet Nizami, who draws out its mystical themes by highlighting the parallel between Majnun's devotion to his

beloved and the ascetic's devotion to God. Nizami's Majnun wanders the desert and encounters Layla only in secret but chaste encounters. When her husband dies, Majnun is so focused on his idealized image of her that he runs away and she dies of grief (Seyed-Gohrab 2009). For a discussion of visibility, invisibility, interiority, and exteriority in the earlier Arabic version in *Kitab Al-Aghani*, see Ruqayya Khan's (2000) "On the Significance of Secrecy in Medieval Arabic Romances."

21. Because weaving was effectively dead as a local pastime in the various areas I have lived and worked in Jordan, I can access this history only through interviews with old women and the work of other ethnographers. However, Brinkley Messick offers a fascinating account of "world construction in weaving" (1986, 221).

22. In *Colonial Effects*, Joseph Massad (2001) shows how the British government and, subsequently, the Jordanian government sought to use the provision of military jobs to Bedouins as a tool for sedentarization and the creation of Foucauldian national subjects. Massad is particularly reliant on the paper trail surrounding the exploits of a British administrator by the name of Glubb Basha. To this day, the man enjoys a good deal of renown across Jordan where, by all accounts, he established himself as a sort of stranger-king for years at the interstices of the British Empire, the Hashemite Monarchy, and the upheaval of World War II before being thrown out of the country by the late King Hussein in 1956.

23. The use of a male gendered pronoun here is purposeful and reflects the gendered assumptions of those who invented the category of the "individual owner-builder," as discussed in the "Private Housing Suppliers Survey" of the *National Housing Strategy* (Shelter Unit 1987, 10–26).

24. Based on years of conversations about house construction, I was confident I could do it for JD 4000–5000, which is what it ended up costing.

25. The other bids were JD 800, 850, 900, 1,200, and 1,500. The latter bid was fully premised on the buyer having a whole year to collect the money to pay. In effect, it was a loan as much as an offer to work as a contractor. The JD was equivalent to about $1.41 at the time of research.

26. Our need to pay for the initial materials on an installment plan was related to a complicated mix-up with my US bank, which decided to cancel my ATM card without informing me. Harun was able to cover some but not all of the shortfall because he did not have a lot of liquid assets. However, such headaches are probably typical when people need a lot of cash at once. It may be difficult to coordinate all factors without such debt. In any event, there was nothing more ordinary than one's building projects eventually involving Abu Hashim—although I should emphasize that it was very generous of Abu Hashim to offer Harun and me credit on such good terms.

27. The only question of design that came up while working with the Egyptian crew was where to put the wall between the hallway and bathroom. Harun simply used his foot to draw a line in the debris on the ground, and the block-layer's assistant cleared a path for the wall.

28. An extended family that I was friends with took this metaphor to its logical conclusion and talked about "dressing" (*labisa*) the house by adding a stone exterior.

29. High-quality limestone is harder and does not turn brownish gray over time like the cheaper, softer stone.

30. Shryock (1997*b*) and Massad (2001) offer the fullest monograph-length accounts of the relationship and tensions between those from the East and West Banks from the perspectives of the former and latter, respectively.

31. We finally succeeded in obtaining the permit in November despite the fact that Harun had been cultivating the surveyor for years with food, free tanks of water, and small "loans" of a few Jordanian dinars. Harun finally got the house registered by showing up at the surveyor's office at the municipality building and insisting that he get in Harun's truck and go to the governor's office to sign off on the paperwork. This is apparently typical because my more subversively minded friends at the HUDC (on learning about my exploits in construction) responded, "Sure, you managed to build a house last year. That's easy—but did you manage to get the building permit yet?"

2

The Housing Market

THE 1970S AND 1980S CONSTITUTED A CRUCIAL MOMENT IN the development of housing policy in Jordan. Large swaths of tribally controlled land were transformed into partible commodities that could be bought, sold, and circulated because of a sophisticated regime of registration, zoning, and infrastructure provision. This process of commoditization is at the heart of this chapter. Adopting a sort of "methodological fetishism" (Appadurai 1986), I will show how this particular regime of value came into being by focusing on an international group of planners who sought to fix what they perceived as Jordan's housing problem.[1] To do this, I will draw on Appadurai's dialectic of singularization and commoditization because I find it deeply consonant with what these planners were attempting. I begin by reviewing some of the literature to clarify how these organizations operate and how I became involved with them and their reports. Next I will explain how the interaction between their policies and the political tensions between Palestinian refugees and the residents of the East Bank were crucial in catalyzing a shift in the dominant regime of value in relationship to land, building materials, and, ultimately, housing.

IN SEARCH OF THE INDIVIDUAL OWNER-BUILDER

Needless to say, the Jordan of the reports would be almost unrecognizable to most Jordanians. As Michael Goldman (2005) makes clear in his ethnography of the World Bank, *Imperial Nature*, knowledge production at the organization is largely beholden to the requirements of providing

global financial markets with guaranteed high-yield credit-based investments. The bank has neither the time nor the resources to focus on anything other than generating returns for its investors in the most efficient
way possible. Thus, major divergences between bank reports and anything that local people might identify as reality should not be at all surprising. The oral historical register in Jordan at the time of research, for
example, was largely dominated by this narrative of tensions between
Palestinian refugees and their Jordanian hosts. The country's 1987 World
Bank–financed National Housing Strategy made a point of denying that
it was wading into the controversy while making proposals that would
ultimately transform the relationship between the two groups.[2] In the
discussion that follows, I will rely heavily on Goldman's (2005) account
along with James Ferguson's (1994) widely respected study of World
Bank development discourse in Lesotho in the 1980s, *The Anti-Politics
Machine*, to understand the bank's actions. There is no particular reason
why events in the 1970s and 1980s in Lesotho (or southeast Asia) should
have any particular bearing on events in Jordan.[3] The countries are vastly
different and separated by thousands of miles—not that this would be
particularly apparent from the reports, which essentially seem to have
used the same framework no matter where they were applied.

The Shelter Unit

As Goldman (2005) and Ferguson (1994) argue, it is really beside the
point that these reports inevitably turn out to be internally inconsistent
and factually inaccurate. Ferguson writes, "The statistics are wrong, but
always wrong in the same way; the conceptions are fanciful, but it is
always the same fantasy" (1994, 55). At times, however, little bits of interesting and insightful work are simply included along with the steady
stream of the conventional wisdom of development discourse of the
1980s. Most notably, the report itself (once one dives into the minutia)
draws on some perceptive work by indigenous planners working in the
HUDC, Ministry of Planning, Ministry of Municipal and Rural Affairs,
and Urban Development Department. These planners had already realized the need to model house construction as the work of households
long before the invention of the fantasy of the "individual owner-builder."

One could even argue that Jordanian planners were performing crucial interpretive labor as they assisted consultants and World Bank officials in facilitating the conceptual slippage between the patriarchal household and the idealized individual owner-builder.

Ferguson focuses on the ways in which World Bank reports, as the gold standard of development discourse, inevitably seek to depoliticize problems by reframing them as technical challenges that can be met through particular "projects," which consist of supposedly technical solutions: "roads, markets, and credit" (1994, 71). The myopic focus on these things helps to stifle discussion about the role of labor, property, and space in promoting and sustaining the existing formations of political power by shunting many of the most contentious questions about them into the "private" realm of the household and, oddly enough, the market. By pretending that property relationships are a concern of the household and the market and outside of the government's "public" purview (something any Palestinian, Syrian, or Iraqi refugee would have some opinions about), these organizations can help rule out certain kinds of political contestation by stipulating submission to putatively apolitical "market" forces, which are, in fact, nothing of the sort.

When I arrived at the HUDC in 2010, I had initially intended to study a royal initiative called "Decent Housing for Decent Living," which sought to build one hundred thousand housing units in five years. When I returned with grant money in 2011, hoping to continue my study of this project (which seemed to be primarily designed to convince Jordanians to take out bank loans to buy houses), I found that the project had been canceled. Of the first 8,000 units, they had sold only about 2,500. Luckily, I resisted the urge to panic and continued to spend time at the HUDC, arranging meetings and talking to people about what they were doing. Around this time, through conversations with people in the policy department, I learned that the HUDC maintained a library under the tutelage of Abu 'Ali, a man who would turn out to be a most gracious host. In that library, I found shelf after shelf of English-language reports.[4] They had been prepared by numerous different groups of government planners in conjunction with the World Bank and the United Nations. For the employees, these were artifacts from the golden age of the HUDC when, flush with money from the World Bank, they exerted a powerful influence over Jordanian society. The reports in question attempted to document the struggles over housing policy of the 1970s and 1980s in minute detail.

These reports may claim to comment on the struggles of the 1970s and 1980s, but the important thing is that they can be studied as indexical traces of those conflicts. It is essential to emphasize what Ferguson calls "the complex relationship between the intentionality of planning and the strategic intelligibility of outcomes." Ferguson continues, "Outcomes that at first appear as mere 'side effects' of an unsuccessful attempt to engineer an economic transformation become legible in another perspective as unintended yet instrumental elements in a resultant constellation that has the effect of expanding the exercise of a particular sort of state power while simultaneously exerting a powerful depoliticizing effect" (1994, 20–21). An ad hoc workgroup of planners known as the Shelter Unit searched for a hedonic index that would quantify the value of every constituent part of the home. This group created the persistent (if largely fictitious) figure of the individual owner-builder, who later became the imagined beneficiary of a generation of housing policy. The World Bank–sponsored Shelter Unit is merely one constituent of a more diverse set of actors that have worked together to help land and building materials achieve the "commodity candidacy" (Appadurai 1986, 15) that continues to elude the homes of so many Jordanians.

Technologies of Speech

In the mid-1980s, the Shelter Unit was one of many ad hoc groups of international consultants that helped set housing policy at that time in Jordan and was tasked with writing Jordan's first National Housing Strategy. Despite the seeming importance of the title, it is hard to say how much of an effect it had. The report advocated the same things that English-language reports stored at the HUDC had been advocating for decades. Fitting in with the Reagan–Thatcher era, the report discouraged housing projects in favor of more laissez-faire policies. The report was especially focused on issues like ending rent controls, simplifying building codes, encouraging more high-density construction, providing infrastructure, and making it easier to get formal credit.

On the one hand, the people I interviewed at the HUDC clearly continue to be flummoxed by these issues: the municipalities refused to subdivide plots, people did not want formal credit, and red tape remained. On the other hand, it is hard to know how much more the housing situation would have been dictated by these sorts of forces if it were not for the persistent orientation toward a specific agenda, which the compilation of report after report helped engender. In either case, the report fits in with the shift away from large-scale public housing projects of the 1970s.[5] Those would continue until the short-lived royal Decent Housing initiative of 2008. What made this particular report notable was that it involved a household survey, which helped formulate the concept of the individual owner-builder as the imagined beneficiary of Jordanian housing policy. It also created a rationale for focusing the Jordanian government's limited resources on engineering a housing market instead of actual housing. As the previous sections on homebuilding imply, this was a strange feat that required the household to be collapsed into the figure of an individual and the web of reciprocal exchange relationships between households to be ignored. At the same time, the house and its constituent parts would be made commensurable and interchangeable through their inclusion in an overarching regime of value for commoditized things.

To understand the emergence of the individual owner-builder, it is useful to follow Matthew Hull in studying not only development discourse's "division of the world" or "denotational content" but also its various "speech genres," like the survey (2010, 258). The very method of interpellation of the *household* survey helped overdetermine the result: an image of a self-sufficient rational individual actor. As Hull points out, the roles of interviewer and interviewee are social roles that must be taught and that depend on an elaborate series of assumptions. In "Democratic Technologies of Speech," Hull provides an analysis of a specific survey conducted by the Ford Foundation in India that is highly suggestive. This discourse of social betterment through the practice of survey can easily be read into the planning and implementation of the Shelter Unit's Private Housing Supplier's Survey and echoes a lively genre of stories about how "backwards" (*mutakhallif*) people respond to such surveys. There was a tendency to view the survey as a variation on a "school exam." People resisted or simply could not comprehend the attempts of interviewers to access their innermost thoughts. Notably, there was obviously a belief on the part of some respondents that their responses would "lead to actions of the researcher's institution directed specifically toward the respondent" (Hull 2010, 268).

My interest in this particular survey began quite innocently with an offhanded comment to Harun and his brothers. Harun asked me about my day, and so I began to tell him about the documents I was reading at the HUDC. I started talking about some suspicious figures I had been looking at in volume 13 (Shelter Unit 1987, "Housing and Residential Land Affordability"). Reflecting on all of the inter- and intrahousehold provision of assistance during the various local building projects I had witnessed, I asked Harun if it seemed credible to them that only between 5 and 15 percent of builders in rural areas received assistance from their relatives during the 1980s. They recounted their own participation in the construction of various houses in the area that were built during that time period and estimated that, perhaps, all but 5 or 10 percent of people in rural areas relied on their relatives for assistance.

Then Harun continued, "Oh those surveys and reports are all lies! They bring the nice girls from the university here. Then they go and talk to the old woman (*khitiyara*), and she thinks that the state (*ad-dawla*) wants to help her, and she says she's poor and needy (*miskin*) and no one will help her. But it's all lies. She thinks the state wants to buy her a house." Surprised by Harun's statement, I recounted a conversation I had the previous year with an employee at the Department of Statistics who proudly told me that their interviewers were all women because women did not lie to each other. Everyone seemed to think this was hilarious. Harun countered, "They use them because they're girls, so they don't have to pay them a real salary. He's messing with you. Don't pay any attention to him." Harun's analysis highlighted the fact that interviewees could often fail to grasp the generic conventions of the survey (e.g., misconstruing a request for information as an offer of assistance). As I delved deeper into the documentation surrounding the survey, though, it became clear to me that the specific problem that Harun described was by far the largest preoccupation of the planners. There was extensive discussion throughout the report of households' tendency to underreport income with the belief that this would lead to government assistance and all of the strategies planners devised to overcome this tendency. One might even question why they insisted on asking questions when they were so instinctively skeptical of the answers.

However, a different kind of misunderstanding also seemed to be in play. Although the Shelter Unit conducted what was, at heart, a household survey, it interpreted the responses as if they offered insights into thoughts and experiences that were "radically individual and even interior" (Hull 2010, 268). The confusion was derived in part from the unit's attempts to answer a specific set of questions about "the housing market" as cheaply and easily as possible. As such, the sample frame, personnel, and many questions were borrowed from the Department of Statistics' household survey initiatives. The survey begins by requesting basic demographic information about the various members of the household before turning to a detailed series of questions about the house itself. Then, around the twentieth question about the house, the interview script slips into the second person:

> 215–Have any improvements to the following been made since 1980?
> 216–What following improvements does the housing unit require?
> 217–Which of the Following appliances do *you* have?
> 218–Is it possible to reach the following by foot within 15 minutes from *your* house?
> 219–Are *you* satisfied with *your* house? (Shelter Unit 1987, 18:53–54; emphasis added)

Because the only copy of the survey I have found is in English, I have no way of knowing whether the "you" is singular or plural—much less what the people conducting the survey would have actually asked respondents in Arabic or how respondents would have interpreted the pronoun (if at all). In the context of centuries of various states and empires encouraging families to choose a single older male as their collective representative (as we will see in chap. 3), it probably makes little difference.

Even if interviewees were eager to provide comprehensive, correct information, it would be hard to know how to respond to questions like, "What were the sources of financing?" or "Did any family member help in the construction?" When one is already speaking on behalf of one's family, what would it mean to ask if a "family member" assisted? Would these be family members outside of the household or outside of the community from which the interviewee was drawn? In either case, only 279 of the 2,246 respondents reported receiving assistance from relatives with the building process. Ultimately, it did not matter from the planner's perspective. Even this direct participation of other people can be subsumed within the model of the individual owner-builder. If one looks beyond the Executive Summary of the report (Shelter Unit 1987), a careful reading of the Housing Suppliers Survey reveals that, according to the report's actual (if incredibly difficult to locate) definition of the individual owner-builder, "he may even contribute his own labor or skills or those of his family or relatives" (9:5). No matter what the case, within the World Bank's ontology, there were markets, market actors, and commodities that circulated between the market actors in the markets. The rest was extraneous data, and because the World Bank could afford to finance the research, it exerted a lot of influence over the research agenda. Within this agenda, the individual owner-builder became a mere placeholder for an abstracted market actor.

The Hedonic Index

The erasure of the household as a living, hybrid assemblage of people, labor, property relations, and space, with its replacement by the abstracted individual owner-builder, is in keeping with "the conceptual polarity of individualized persons and commoditized things" (Appadurai 1986, 64). In Appadurai's processual framework of commoditization and singularization, anything can achieve "commodity candidacy." The issue is what objects take on these characteristics, under what circumstances, and for how long. The oral historical register in Jordan is replete with stories that describe the odd paths and divergences through which various things (particularly land) became commodities long before the era of government in the 1920s and the later initiatives of development organizations. I will return to this theme in the following section, but for now, one example will suffice.

Harun explained that Muath's grandfather Ahmad had a racing horse he would take to weddings and circumcisions back in the days when they had games and races. It was a beautiful horse, and he would always win. Suleiman's uncle Saleem asked to buy the horse, but Ahmad was clever. He said he wouldn't think of selling it. He said that "this is a racing horse" and "look how beautiful it is." Then Saleem's brother started talking to Ahmad about buying it. Ahmad was clever though. He knew it was really the brother asking. So he kept saying he wouldn't sell it. Finally, Ahmad sold the horse to the man for thirty-two dunum of land (thirty-two thousand square meters). That's all the land west of the village! The horse died in the snow that winter, but in the end, Ahmad had to sell it all because of girls.

Confused, I said, "What?"

Harun continued, "Well, in those days, if you didn't have any money, you could give land as *mahr*. So he had a lot of sons and nephews, and every time he wanted to marry one, he would give away some of his land to her father until he had almost none left."

The story was meant as an object lesson in shifting regimes of value and as a none-too-subtle way of impugning the neighbors. The story is part of a moralizing genre of oral history that recounts how land, which would now be incredibly valuable, was appropriated by cunning rather than right—only to be lost before the trickster figure could derive any real benefit. Although Harun intended to highlight the naïveté and cupidity of his neighbors, the story also reveals that we are not dealing with some precommodity age of innocence. Land could be bartered with none of the sentimentality of romanticized ideas of gift exchange. People were perfectly ready to use every bit of cunning to swindle their neighbors—even if they never got the opportunity to become million-aires, thanks to the surge in land values at the turn of the twenty-first century.

As the story makes clear, land was not the same kind of commodity that it is now. In the story, the line between singular people and com-moditized things is blurred. Land and livestock (much like people) are viewed as a bundle of overlapping rights and responsibilities (cf. Strath-ern 1985; Weiner 1992). This is all the truer when discussing other peo-ple's familial relations. Ownership is perhaps an anachronistic concept in this instance. One does not have recourse to the state to challenge other claims. One merely has the opportunity to defend various rights against other takers. Ahmad (like so many others in these stories) is able to seize property. Unfortunately, just as he takes it, it slips through his fingers as his various family members make all manner of claims on it.

In contrast, a hedonic index is an exercise in market research that seeks to understand individuals who independently control things in relationship to those things using a precise, numerical scale of value. It would be easy to dismiss the exercise as pointless—people could relate a horse to land, for example, in precisely those numerical terms decades before the World Bank was involved. However, the index is almost a distraction; even the Shelter Unit did not really believe the results. It was the far broader conceptual work of singularization and commoditization that was truly transformative.

During the latter part of the twentieth century, the World Bank, the United Nations, USAID, and the Jordanian government all worked to house a Bedouin population that was rapidly becoming more sedentary and a large population of displaced Palestinians. They formulated the problem as one of creating an efficient housing market, which would provide the credit necessary to meet demand. However, land and (by extension) anything on it were anything but the freely circulating commodities that the bank assumed they were. Likewise, people were not the fixed, autonomous, and grounded individual owner-builders that the bank assumed they were dealing with. As long as property rights were in question, people would be forced to see property through the lens of communal defense.

Reflecting this sensibility that wealth is worthless without people to defend it, I was taught the proverb, "The proliferation of men is better than the proliferation of wealth." With many people loath to move away from their families or use land as collateral (not just for religious reasons but also because of familial disapprobation), the dream of an efficient, frictionless housing market was a fantasy. As we will see, the Shelter Unit and its backers found themselves dealing with the fact that large amounts of marginal agricultural communal (*musha'*) land claimed by a large tribe known as the Bani Hasan were sitting next to rapidly growing refugee camps. An organization that asks squatters and people who see themselves as inhabiting ancestral lands how much their house is worth may appear to be getting ahead of itself. Nonetheless, the Shelter Unit and its backers exerted an outsized effect on a key aspect of Jordanian-Palestinian relations by getting deeply involved in the registration of land. In fact, they seem to have tacitly participated in the legitimation of the refugees' efforts to permanently settle in Jordan—all while generating profits for global financial markets.

CONSTRUCTION AS SEIZURE

For centuries, construction (the material transformation of the landscape) has been one of the primary means by which people in the Middle East construe and establish property claims. Until now, my ethnographic description has focused on the area west of Amman in the transition zone between the Jordan valley and the semiarid steppe. Further east toward the Amman–Zarqa corridor, a giant, unplanned, and at times illegal construction project emerges that involves the successive waves of refugees who have sought shelter and legal recognition in Jordan. Amman rises from the limestone bedrock as it is ground up into concrete, pressed into cinderblocks, and marketed to families that dream of stable sanctuaries where they may safely dwell and prosper. As fathers seek to help build homes for their sons and grandsons, the network of concrete structures becomes denser and more interconnected. Male kinship relations and community are materially instantiated in the built environment as each successive generation builds homes for the next generation around the existing structures. However, the assemblage remains partial, incomplete, and vulnerable to seizure: unfinished structures litter the landscape, aspirational concrete pillars jut out from people's roofs, and locals frustrate wealthy interlopers by making off with the plumbing in the night. Construction is important, but it must be defended, lest other imagined futures begin to manifest. In this next section, I use a combination of oral historical and archival data to illustrate how the HUDC and its collaborators at the UN, the Shelter Unit and the World Bank have facilitated and shaped all of this construction in subtle and unexpected ways. By and large, the focus has been relatively singular: the creation of a housing market.

"Land Was Free"

As I have argued, there could not be a proper housing market until land had become a different kind of commodity—specifically, one that could be defended as property by an individual with access to the repressive apparatus of the state. In other words, it had to become private property. In this section, I will interweave my own oral historical data with that of Omar Razzaz, whose doctoral dissertation *Law, Urban Tenure, and Property Disputes in Contested Settlements: The Case of Jordan* (1991) I take to be the definitive contemporaneous account of events. Razzaz would later go on to teach at the Massachusetts Institute of Technology, to run the World Bank's Lebanon office, and eventually to serve as prime minister of Jordan. His account will help illustrate how this novel idea of public and private was imposed on Jordanian conceptions of land. This transformation of land into private property has, at least temporarily, caused cash to loom in importance while the role of communal defense in securing housing has diminished. If cash continues to be the final arbiter of what kind of housing younger people can obtain, then they will likely continue to think favorably of the transformations in the gendering of labor, property, and space described in chapter 1. The status of land and the nature of property as private prerogative or object of communal defense remains open to contestation.

The fiercest contestation over land in the western part of Jordan near the valley (where I was based during fieldwork) happened in the 1930s when the British performed a cadastral survey and registered agricultural lands. Both Ottoman law and local practice conferred property rights conditionally on continued use and improvement of the land, and the land near the valley received enough rainfall to ensure that someone would be regularly availing themselves of it. This practice was and is increasingly difficult the further east one goes. Traveling east on the road to Zarqa, the landscape shifts from green to brown. In Zarqa, it was not even possible to farm the land for three consecutive years—the minimum required to register land under the *musha'* system (often understood as communal property). Elements of this system outlived the Ottoman and British empires and passed, largely unremarked, into Jordanian property law. With the postindependence explosion in the size of the state's bureaucracy (especially in the capital of Amman), the construction of a large military installation in neighboring Zarqa, and the influx of wave after wave of refugees, this land went from wasteland to some of the most valuable real estate in the Middle East in a matter of decades.

The current pattern in Jordan involves men hailing from the East Bank (especially in rural areas) who have been absorbed into the security services, where they continue to act out a sort of defensive role but now serve new masters (the state rather than their family). In return, they have been able to shore up their individualistic control of property through both the system of private property ownership and their differential access to cash (due to their government jobs). As this rural Jordanian middle class of government employees has emerged, more traditional forms of female labor in agriculture and animal husbandry have increasingly been taken up by foreign migrants. Women have become increasingly confined to the home as the older rationales for their movement throughout the community disappeared. Meanwhile, communities of various refugee groups have tended to cluster in urban areas while men travel to the Gulf and send back remittances or, increasingly, administer the use of Gulf capital within Jordan itself. This shift can be summed up in the widespread notion in rural Jordan that a Bedouin is a man who lives in a house with no door and that, by such a measure, there are very few Bedouin left. Men "these days" can be seen as "barnyard hens... well fed, but domesticated and ripe for the slaughter" (Shryock 1997a, 45).

Key to this dynamic is the notion of seizure. In the moralizing genre of stories about land, there was always an incredibly heavy taint of illegitimacy. This is to be expected because shifts in property relations tended to track closely with social upheaval. New interlopers were disruptive. Such disruptions were inevitably reconceptualized later in terms of the emergent Jordanian state in relationship to its geopolitical allies and competitors. The stories I recorded had a geographic as well as a moral logic: From the east came raiders and extortionists—this was a reference to the fact that during the 1930s, certain Saudi tribes would decimate the herds of southern Jordanian Bedouins and then take cover underneath the British defensive umbrella.[6] From the west came swindlers and loansharks—useful villains for a nationalist rhetoric that claims "Jordan for Jordanians" to the exclusion of Palestinian refugees. This example from the moralizing genre of oral historical accounts of land sales is typical.

Mahmud began, "I remember stories from those days in the past but not clearly. It's like a dream to me. I grew up hearing about these things in the 1970s. So people would come from Palestine and people would buy all sorts of stuff with land. Dates, olive oil, *halawa* [a sugary sesame paste], finely embroidered underwear." I cannot reproduce the uproar that followed, but it was clear to me that one of my neighbors' ancestors had actually traded land for underwear—despite the fact that it seemed like the height of folly in retrospect.

Mahmud continued, somewhat more seriously now: "Land back in those days was basically free (*balash*), and the people were hungry. People would die from hunger. So these traders would come from Palestine with dates, olive oil, preserves, and *halawa* [a sugary sesame paste]. Imagine if you were dying of hunger and someone brought you a tank full of *halawa*. You'd be beside yourself, right? The [neighboring tribe] sold so much of their land for *halawa*." Once again, in keeping with the moralizing genre, it is always about other people, and the narrative is driven by a combination of licentiousness, venality, and cunning on all sides.

The imputation of great cunning on the part of the Palestinian merchants is consonant with a tendency within Jordanian nativism to see rural East Bank dwellers as hospitable and naive in relationship to the depredations of interloping Palestinian city folk (Shryock 1997*a*, 1997*b*). I remained skeptical. I tried to imagine things from the perspective of the traveling merchant. Operating somewhat beyond the reach of the state, in possession of luxury goods, what were his options when the locals wanted things?[7] But from the perspective of the rural East Bank, Harun explained:

> You see, these traders were like [a particular figure that neither man had much respect for, who was once the *mukhtar* (village head) and also the *murab* (moneylender)]. See, he had a store and he would lend money and not harvest the debt (*yidayyin wa ma yahsid*). Then he would wait for a bad year and ask for the money. They wouldn't have anything to give him but their land. Isn't that *haram* [forbidden, sinful]? But there was a Palestinian who did this even more. His name was [so-and-so] Al-Nabulsi. He would let the [neighboring tribe] buy on credit, and then suddenly he would ask for his money and take the land as payment. Isn't that *haram*? He ended up with 400 dunum among the [neighboring tribe]! He had three sons and they divided it between them. One of them was a drunk in Madaba who sold all of his, but the other two still have all of their shares.

Based on generic conventions, it is only a matter of time until some misfortune befalls the other two or, at the very least, some more of their descendants. But Al-Nabulsi and the village head (along with their descendants) would probably have to rank as some of the luckier traders in history. If they had taken possession of such lands at any other time, it would have been the best solution to their disagreements with their customers, but they would not have reaped such outsized rewards. They would have either been absorbed into the community as the land was redivided to cover all manner of social obligations, or they would have simply been pushed off by someone more aggressive with more local support.

The Proliferation of Men

Land is not necessarily valuable. What is the use of having dry, unpopulated space with no electricity, roads, or sewerage? There is a popular origin myth about the Bani Hasan (who will figure prominently in the next account) that tells how the people were hungry and thirsty and begged a man from the Bani Hasan to help them find water for their crops. He told them that he would find them water: his cow would walk until it found the nearest well. But in return, he would get all of the land between the spot on which he stood and that well. That, I have been told, is how the Bani Hasan came to own the most land in Jordan—the most land, perhaps, but also the most useless land.

So imagine their delight when a city suddenly began to spring up around them after the waves of Palestinian refugees arrived, and then consider the sense of deep betrayal they must have experienced when the government not only tried to stop them from selling their lands to the settlers but actually challenged their ownership claims. This struggle is at the heart of Razzaz's account, along with his insight that the very undesirability of this land made it so cheap and thus attractive for those aspiring to join the middle class. At the time, 90 percent of legally available residential property was zoned for large upper-income plots that could not be legally subdivided any smaller than one thousand square meters (Razzaz 1994, 16). Meanwhile, the government had built Yajouz Road to connect the two cities of Amman and Zarqa, providing a transportation connection to a large swath of arid steppe with questionable ownership status. This helped underwrite the massive expansion of the

Jordanian middle class and a particular gendering of labor, property, and space. Ironically, as the land was connected to infrastructure, zoned, and registered, it became the kind of commodity that could be traded by global financial institutions. As a result, it was increasingly valued by those institutions at levels far beyond the reach of a typical soldier, bureaucrat, or labor migrant.

Razzaz, my oral historical data, the records at the HUDC, and my conversations with employees of the HUDC all agree that people began to build houses along Yajouz Road sometime in the 1970s. The materials could be moved into place by vehicle, people could bring in generators for electricity, and there was already a network of water trucks because the water grid was overextended. Sewerage could be handled with septic tanks. Members of the Bani Hasan enthusiastically sold plots to all takers using a sale contract (*hujja*) without the government title (*sanad*), which has been required since the Ottoman Tanzimat reforms. The Jordanian government objected vociferously to such sales, but the Bani Hasan were unrepentant. They watched as tribesmen in the west made millions selling land that was registered, zoned, and provisioned with water and electricity. Razzaz records one man who reasoned, "Islam tells us . . . if an unjust father treats his sons differently, feeding one and starving the other, the hungry son is permitted to seize his share, even if he has to steal it from his unjust father to survive. This is all we are doing" (1994, 18). When the government tried to demolish the houses of the Bani Hasan in 1983, they took up arms, shot at the security services, and burned military vehicles. When tribesmen were rounded up, their families rioted outside the jail. Various attempts at reconciliation followed, and building and demolition continued but with a new rule: if the roof was finished, the house was to be left intact.

By 1985, the area was in the middle of a building boom. People would wait until Thursday afternoon when the police went home for the weekend. If they could finish the roof before the police returned, the authorities would allow the structure to stand. Razzaz reports that people clustered together, often based on kin ties or common place of origin. He gives the example of a "Hebron" (Al-Khalil in Arabic) community that would take up a collection to bring in more gravel for their road every year.[8] Razzaz emphasizes the sense of security that living together engendered. There was also a major emphasis on the host–guest relationship. The "hosts" from the Bani Hasan made promises to continue to help the buyers defend their rights long after the sale had been made. One tribesman explained to Razzaz, "We do not think of a *hujja* as a regular sales contract. It is more like a marriage contract, binding both the buyer and seller for good" (1994, 24). This was no substitute for the certainty that came with official registration and title deed (*sanad*) in addition to the more traditional *hujja* or sale deed; nevertheless, it was some assurance.

Razzaz understood the concerns of the government perfectly. He reports that discussions with officials inevitably devolved into "a barrage of anecdotes." Razzaz noted that "the situation was always described as chaotic, a 'grave threat to law and order,' a 'potentially explosive situation where disputes between neighbors, heirs, and contesting claimants, could turn bloody and set the place on fire'" (1994, 26–27). In contrast, by initially learning about the conflict through development reports, it was hard for me to even explain what I was reading about to the veteran HUDC employees who regularly invited me for tea and coffee to discuss my findings. Based on the World Bank reports, I had zeroed in on the question of property rights and putatively apolitical initiatives for housing market "rationalization."

I wanted to ask them about squatter settlement standardization, but I struggled to even figure out the Arabic word for *squatter*, which I could not find in any dictionaries. I asked a friend and sociologist who worked down the hall from me in the HUDC, "What do you call someone who builds on land they do not own?" This led to a conversation about land tenure that I could not really follow because it was my first real encounter with the Arabic technical vocabulary of property law. What was clear from his perspective was that (no matter the law) land was there to be developed.

After being told by a number of bilingual friends that there was no Arabic word for *squatter*, someone suggested the word *'ashwa'i*. With connotations of informality, spontaneity, and randomness, it soon became apparent that *'ashwa'i* was the Arabic word that the HUDC had used to describe Yajouz Road. Once I told my friends at the HUDC that I was interested in *sakin 'ashwa'i* (chaotic housing), they had a lot to say and began explaining the whole process to me as one of "straightening out the lines," "widening the roads," and "organizing things." The property relations were an afterthought. These were increasingly dense settlements with no road signs, unreliable roads, and no services. To make matters worse, they were inhabited by people who disobeyed the government. The settlements were closed off and inscrutable and, especially with then-recent memories in mind of Black September and the expulsion of the Palestine Liberation Organization from the camps surrounding Amman, this worried employees at the HUDC. The World Bank stepped into this breach. Everyone increasingly accepted that the Palestinians were not leaving Jordan and would expand beyond the refugee camps and eventually fill in between Amman and Zarqa. The World Bank offered the following solution: Jordan would take out a loan from the bank, subdivide all plots in the squatter settlements, officially register the plots, provide some infrastructure, and then make the residents repay the loans.

The Bani Hasan could sell their land; the government created all sorts of jobs and opportunities for patronage; and, whether or not any given individual could pay back the loan, there was a delimited commodity asset that could be seized as collateral to either encourage repayment of the loan or sell to clear the balance sheet. As a veteran of that era in the organization recalled, "it was great for everyone . . . except maybe the people who are still paying off the loans." From another perspective, this land was the last within physical reach of regular employment opportunities in the capital that was sheltered from global commodity markets given its questionable ownership and zoning status and lack of infrastructure. Increasingly, Jordanians must compete in the same housing market as oil sheikhs, technocratic nouveau riche, hedge funds, and even their upper-middle-class neighbors who have high enough salaries to pay off a mortgage while still having enough money left over for food.

CONCLUSION: THEY WILL TAKE IT

In tracking changing conceptions of public and private in Jordan, I have tried to parochialize the division and simultaneously point to the fact that much of what Jordan's young-skewing population thinks of as "traditional" gender roles (with men working outside the home to house women within it) are in fact more fleeting. I have tried to connect this to shifts in labor, property, and spatial relations to emphasize the shortcomings of essentialist explanations and the superior explanatory power of more constructivist approaches. To avoid any impression of a unilineal evolutionary or teleological conclusion, it is useful to consider the Decent Housing for Decent Living initiative that first brought me to the HUDC. This view highlights the cracks and fissures in this status quo model of gender relations.

As I argued in the introduction and throughout the previous chapter, a certain sort of masculine ideal emerged in Jordan that valorized a certain kind of public man (Carver 1996). He could singlehandedly go out and earn the money necessary to provide for his household and thus assume a sort of sovereign control that came with differential access to cash and full confidence in the state's willingness to defend his property. In some ways, this ideal was unprecedented. Many ties entailed by older notions of property relations were sundered. Housing became stationary and suddenly switched from being women's wealth to men's wealth (although, as we will see in part 2, women often continue to own the furniture). Most notably, for the first time, large numbers of previously impoverished men suddenly discovered that they could afford to provide housing and food for their wives and to obviate the necessity that the women circulate through the community. In this, they began to partake in a classic premodern marker of nobility across the Eurasian landmass. However, it may not last much longer.

The global financial crisis did little to cool down the Amman real estate market. With profits from historically high oil prices working their way into the economy through remittances, banking, and direct investment (Parker 2009)—not to mention the likelihood that cement and steel will continue to be expensive because of high energy prices— there is little reason to believe housing will get any more affordable. This was the context in which the Decent Housing initiative emerged. When the Jordanian government first announced that it would provide one hundred thousand housing units that could be purchased on JD 100-per-month installment plans, demand was extensive. More than sixty thousand applications were distributed in two days. Applicants were required to be older than eighteen years old, make less than JD

1000 per month, and not be a beneficiary of any other housing project. Once they had received their new dwelling, they would not have been allowed to sell or rent it (Ghazal 2008).

The program was beset by problems from the beginning. The government was never entirely clear about how it planned to finance the program. When the program was announced, the government made it clear that it would only provide JD 15 million of the JD 5 billion project from its own treasury (Petra 2008). In 2009, the popular newspaper *Al-Ghad* published accusations of corruption or, in the subtler phrasing of Jameel Al-Nimry, "a 'conflict of interest' between public responsibility (*masu'uliyya 'amma*) and private benefit (*manafi'a khasa*)." After a twenty-five-day bidding period, the contract for the project was awarded to a company with close ties to the minister of public works. Its director was given a monthly salary of JD 8,000—a princely sum, even for an American manager. Because of the resulting outcry, the offending minister was removed from his position—and placed in charge of the Foreign Ministry (Al-Nimry 2009). By the time I was in Jordan doing fieldwork with the HUDC's marketing department, the government was offering mortgages for apartments that would cost from JD 110/month for an 88-square-meter home to JD 168/month for a 133-square-meter home.[9]

The marketers understood what a tough job they had in front of them. A member of the team told me, "We're not just selling houses. We're trying to change the mentality." Her coworkers quickly agreed: "They don't want a mortgage." "They all want to live on the ground floor." "They want to have a lot of kids." "They want to have a garden." "They don't want to live next to strangers." "They don't trust: they want to build it themselves so they know it is done properly."[10] At the end of the day, even with the government providing land and subsidizing the loans by paying part of the interest and offering guarantees to the banks, the initiative still required households to pay half of a soldier's income for housing when many homeowners already struggle to provide their families with chicken more than once a week. In return, applicants were being offered close quarters in four-story apartment blocks on the edge of town. By the time I returned in 2011, the problems with the project were widely known and everyone had an explanation. Employees emphasized the problems with the banks ("the bank has no heart"), and others argued that the lack of infrastructure and services (no mosques, no schools, no stores) had rendered the housing uninhabitable and that "we have to build communities—not just houses."

As I discussed the issue with one engineer, I got a much more jaundiced answer. I began to lay out my concern that the entire model of the Jordanian household that I had come to know seemed completely unsustainable: with salaries so low, a large percentage of the population could only hope to sustain their current lifeworlds by avoiding the need to pay rent; the only way to avoid paying rent was to continue occupying whatever sort of diminishing familial patrimony they had left. With the country becoming increasingly crowded and with more outside capital pouring in, higher property values seemed inevitable for the foreseeable future. This was presenting couples with a choice of postponing marriage and house construction—possibly altogether for many—or accepting serious downward social mobility by choosing to rent or take out a mortgage. In fact, with women now making up the majority of university students, it seemed like the ultimate solution was that women would start working in large numbers to defray the cost of housing.

Engineer Samir smiled at the prospect and said, "They do not like it, but they will take it." He began to enumerate all of the complaints I have already listed, adding plenty of his own, like "they don't want to walk up the stairs." He lingered on the politics of women joining the workforce before concluding with "they do not like it, but they will take it." At the time, it seemed logical enough to me that when faced with a choice between celibacy and downward social mobility through debt and renting, along with women's increasing involvement in the workforce, "they will take it." In other words, households will devote more of their time and money to pay for housing, and women going to work will be a big part of that. It seemed like I was doing salvage ethnography of the same patriarchal breadwinner model whose demise has long been heralded in Europe and the United States. It is also possible that patrilocal clustering to defend a shared patrimony (with force if necessary) could provide an alternative future. This is ultimately a political and social question before it can be purely economic. The sad reality is that if experiences in neighboring countries are any guide, great power machinations may well prove more decisive than local initiative. War and conflict tend to incentivize the older model of male defense of women and property that decades of (relative) peace and stability have begun to obviate. Either way, as Jordanians again transform their gender relations, the notion that gender relations used to be simpler is unlikely to go anywhere.

NOTES

1. These planners moved among private consultancies, various ministries, the HUDC, the Amman Municipality, the Housing Bank, USAID, and the World Bank.

2. The official position of the executive summary of the National Housing Policy on the "Palestinian question" deserves to be quoted at length: "Whether or not there is a resolution of the political question, refugee camps in urban areas at least, are clearly becoming permanent features of the housing stock. Government should therefore consider policies for upgrading refugee camps with the view that they will continue to function as permanent urban areas even if a large number of their present inhabitants were to leave" (Shelter Unit 1987, 32). What I find revealing here is the tenacity with which the Shelter Unit attempts to shield property relations from the contagion of "political questions."

3. The one notable and important exception is the proximity to a white settler colony. This fact is studiously ignored by the bank's discourse on both Jordan and Lesotho, despite its outsized impact on everything under discussion. As Ferguson (1994) argues, it would be silly to give an ecological account of why the Bronx is poor in relationship to Manhattan. However, ecological accounts abound when discussing Jordan or Lesotho. The fact that the residents have been pushed off of the more desirable land is treated as incidental.

4. I could never get over the fact that the reports were produced on American letter-sized (8.5 × 11-inch) paper and not A4. Were they produced in and shipped from the United States? Or did they have to find a printer in the eastern hemisphere with American paper? Although the reports were written in English, it is important to remember that most people at the HUDC spoke only Arabic and did not usually need any English for their jobs; some key English-speaking department heads in the office were sufficient for the corporation's operations to run smoothly. In fact, when I had finished studying the 24-volume National Housing Strategy from 1987, some colleagues asked to see my notes, since they did not have time to read such a long document in a foreign language.

5. The exemplar of this era is the thriving middle-class suburb in West Amman known as Abu Nusayr, which is now home to seventy thousand people. When I visited, residents claimed their community was very desirable, with high property values and few vacancies. They cited the great infrastructure (*binya tahtiyya*) and services (*khadmat*) like 24-hour street cleaning as particular enticements.

6. Alon (2007) weaves together oral and textual evidence to provide an account of the conflicts that defined the relations between Jordanian and Saudi tribes during the British Mandate.

7. Other scholars have also gleaned evidence that traders used to employ precisely this calculus when operating on the margins of state authority. For instance, Mundy and Smith report that, "One Irbid trader . . . facing fearfully the prospect of managing land . . . [in 1936] asked that his plots be consolidated. . . . He had bad relations with the [other] side of the village and, not being of or in the village, stated that he could protect neither his oxen nor his crops" (2003, 235).

8. Hebron (Al-Khalil in Arabic) is the name of a Palestinian village in the West Bank that has been occupied by Israel since 1967.

9. Some of these mortgages were offered by "Islamic" banks, which used financial instruments that have been certified as "sharia-compliant" by particular religious authorities.

10. In light of the pervasive concern about corruption in Jordan at the time, the lack of faith in the structural integrity of the dwellings was especially salient. It was a common concern when people I knew explained their lack of interest in the Decent Housing initiative. Far from a vague sense that a corrupt government would build corrupt (*fasid*) houses, a lot of people were incredibly explicit and specific about their concerns. I also know I was not alone in hearing such suspicions because an engineer at the corporation once told me (without prompting) about how he had personally made sure that the correct quantity of steel rebar was in place when the cement was poured—precisely the kind of precaution one would take at a time when steel was trading for JD 600–700 per metric ton.

Part 2

The Proposal: Making Persons and Other Moral Agents

3

The Delegation

THE DRAMA OF COURTSHIP AND MATCHMAKING HAS LONG preoccupied scholars working on gender and marriage in the region. In particular, women ethnographers have excelled in this field, often offering rich, highly textured accounts of people's emotional lives and the tough choices that they must often make (Adely 2016; Conklin and Nasser El-Dine 2015; Granqvist 1931; Hart 2007; Latte-Abdallah 2009; Ozyegin 2009; Tapper 1991; Walker 2013; cf. Antoun 1967). As a male ethnographer who is very much aware of the intensity of the separation between the genders (see chap. 1), I read these accounts with a sense of bashfulness, as if I am transgressing on realms to which I should not even be privy. One might argue that my positionality (particularly my gender) makes me wholly unqualified to discuss such topics, insofar as both the scholarly literature on marriage and local ideology assume women to be the privileged holders of this sort of knowledge. However, recent work has highlighted how even women must contend with fundamental gaps in their knowledge, either because of the inherent difficulties of "managing marriage uncertainty" on the economic margins (Walker 2013, 65–86) or the ambiguity that emerges amid the complex, overlapping (and often quite convergent) interests of young people and their elders (Hart 2007).

In this spirit, I have decided to focus on the arranging of marriages despite the inherent gaps in my knowledge. In this regard, I follow historians of science Robert Proctor and Londa Scheibinger in engaging in an *agnotology* of Jordanian marriage practices, highlighting the crucial role of ignorance in such arrangements as both an "active construct" and a "strategic ploy" (2008, 15). Rather than taking my ignorance to be a mere absence of knowledge and seeking to explain how marriages are "really" arranged, I focus on the generative role that male anxieties about the imponderability of marriage negotiations play in the constitution of dominant notions of kinship and personhood through the ritual pageantry of marriage. In this context, the information practices of the Sharia courts (with its intensive focus on transparency, documentation, and individuation) may seem radical in comparison to the cherished traditions of the village proposal delegation that they increasingly displace. By tracking the shifting relationship between these two rituals, I seek to bring together debates about the relationship of agency, knowledge, and intentionality that have blossomed in both science and technology studies and Middle East women's studies, arguing that both approaches can learn from each other.

A proposal delegation or *jaha* is, at least in theory, a relatively straightforward affair. The delegation from the groom's family would all pile into cars and drive to the home of the bride's family, where the two kin groups would meet.[1] Each contingent might be as few as thirty people or, in some cases, hundreds of people. On arrival, the delegation from the groom's family would divide by gender. The women would head for the *muharam*, and the men would be ushered into a guest room or tent that had been rented for the occasion. A line of men from the bride's family would be waiting to greet the guests. Each guest from the groom's family would move down the line shaking hands and exchanging greetings with each representative of the bride's family. They would then take their seats in facing rows of chairs and wait for the rest of the guests to file in. When everyone was settled, the representative of the bride's family would offer a cup of coffee to the representative of the groom's family. Demurring, the latter would rise and declare his family's interest in entering into a marital relationship with the family of the bride by marrying "what's her name?" or "your noble daughter" or some other circumlocution to avoid saying her name. After agreeing to a *mahr* payment (which is envisioned as a sort of alimony should the marriage end in divorce or the death of the husband), the representative of the bride's family would respond by accepting the offer. As the culminating gesture in the pageantry surrounding the delegation, the representative of the bride would again proffer a small cup of coffee to the representative of the groom's family. By drinking the cup of coffee, the representative of the groom's family would seal the agreement. Then those assembled would recite the opening verse of the Quran. With that, coffee would be served for all attendees, followed by tea, soda, and sweets. The ululation of the women would erupt in the *muharam*. When the delegation was finished, the groom's family would file out, shaking the hands of the greeters once again, and return home—often to the sound of celebratory gunfire.

The delegation is about distribution, with cognition, agency, and, ultimately, personhood itself being parceled out across the extended kin group and divided between two parallel rituals along gendered lines. From here, amid taboos around naming and cloistered goings-on happening in separate rooms in parallel, agency and personhood are aggregated (on the male side) in the figure of the senior male at the peak of the ritual's drama and then dissolved once again as the ritual moves on to shared commensality, mutual leave-taking, ululation, and celebratory gunfire. Increasingly though, with the expansion of Sharia courts into Jordan over the course of the nineteenth and twentieth centuries, the *jaha* is not the only ritual for the creation and recognition of marital bonds. If the delegation is about the distribution of cognition, agency, and personhood through an elaborate set of ritual acts, Sharia court procedures tend to exert an individuating influence by becoming increasingly concerned with recording the ostensibly uncompelled volitional acts of embodied individuals. For the most part, the antithesis between the two procedures produces little concern or cognitive dissonance. Often the rituals are concurrent, with a court-affiliated notary waiting in the next room at the *jaha* to conduct the contract-signing ceremony while the delegation waits. When legitimating marital bonds, most Jordanians will use all available rituals. However, the delegation and court procedures construct different kinds of moral agents. When these different moral agents come into conflict, the results can prove downright explosive.

My concept of a moral agent is heavily indebted to two sources: Donald Mackenzie's (2009) idea of the "economic agent" and the Sharia court's concept of the *wakil* (agent). In the case of the tribal delegation, these are the two "sheikhs" representing the bride and groom, respectively. What I hope to maintain by echoing Mackenzie is the assemblage's materiality, its emphasis on distribution, and its at times cyborg-like dimensions (Haraway 1984). Mackenzie's theorizations of economic agents tend to highlight the mechanical extension of the human while leaving open the possibility that the machines are taking over. I emphasize the tension between what I call the *embodied individual* and the sort of corporate bodies that emerge through practices like house construction (see chap. 1) and, as we will see, marriage proposals. Another important dimension of the comparison is that these agents have purpose. Whereas Mackenzie's agents are unproblematically economic (they seek to make money), mine seem to serve different purposes: they all make claims on people's reproductive powers in the name of collectives founded for the provision of mutual aid to people joined by bonds of (more or less) indissoluble kinship. This may not exhaust the category of the "moral," but it fits within it and furnishes a relatively transparent analytic category that could be easily translated back into Arabic.

In chapter 3, I contrast the different ways in which delegations and court procedures distribute agency, cognition, and personhood. The first half of the chapter will focus on the preparations and pageantry surrounding two delegations I witnessed during fieldwork, focusing on the collective familial ritual effort necessary to produce a legitimate marital bond. The second half of the chapter will draw on a combination of oral history, participant observation, archival records, and statistical analysis to show how the Sharia courts came to introduce form marriage contracts and other bureaucratic technologies into Jordanian marriage practices.[2] I will argue that the construction of moral agents through marriage proposals changed over the course of the twentieth century, as the information infrastructure around the proposal came to rely more and more on the individuating technologies of the Sharia courts. Turning to the work of historians of Islamic law, I note that this tension between the courts and extended kin groupings evinces a number of continuities with our understanding of premodern Islamic jurisprudence—implying that although these newer bureaucratic technologies certainly have consequential intrinsic qualities, many of them also extend and deepen the reach of preexisting tools of Islamic jurisprudence and administration.

In chapter 4, I will map out some of the ramifications of the specifically Islamic aims of the information infrastructure that has emerged to collect and disseminate information about marriage in Jordan. I will show how this information infrastructure has become an active participant in the production of new types of moral agents while working to dissolve older types of moral agents associated with the delegation. The Sharia court's procedures and—increasingly—its statistics are reifying specific categories of individual moral agents who are endowed with new forms of individual and collective voice that enable them to articulate new forms of social criticism. In narrating an unfolding struggle over the ritual template of the marriage proposal, I hope to show that the more familiar individuating ritual template of the courts is no more or less a logistical feat than the tribal marriage delegation. In Jordan, both continue to coexist in productive tension.

"The Problem Is Women"

I was sitting with my friend Abu Rizq the night before his son Rizq's delegation and *khitba* (engagement party) trying to gauge his feelings about his son's impending engagement and marriage. We sat on the roof of his son's future home drinking tea as Abu Rizq fielded phone calls and made final preparations. Such negotiations are, of necessity, fraught with mistrust, awkwardness, and the potential for humiliation. From the beginning, I had seen how this stage of the process had weighed heavily on Abu Rizq. When he was building a magnificent house for the future couple, he was in his element as he considered every possible detail down to the colored nightlights ("for sex," he said). Now, however, his son's marriage required negotiations over *mahr* (which is normally divided in two: the "prompt" *mahr*, known as the *muqaddam/ mu'ajjal*, and the amount to be paid in case of divorce, known as the *mu'akhkhar/mu'ajjal*). Marriage also required engagement festivities— not to mention determining the suitability of the girl herself. Aside from his ongoing concerns about the *mahr* and arrangements for the various festivities (balancing contractual aspects with verbal agreements), he explained that such a genealogically or geographically "distant" marriage required a lot of sensitive inquiries: "She could be blind, she could have a genetic disease, she could have bad morals. We had to ask around a lot."

It is no accident that the French sociologist Pierre Bourdieu (1977, 58) was moved by his study of North African Berbers to compare matrimonial strategies to a game of cards. Given the potential for embarrassment and generally *muharam* (protected) status accorded to women, no one person completely comprehends the situation. As an anthropologist, I shared many of the cognitive challenges faced by Jordanians themselves as I attempted to interpret the events unfolding around me. For the most part, marriage negotiations happened in closed family spaces that I rarely visited. Furthermore, because of my desire to be hypercorrect, I tended to avoid using women's names in conversation, preferring to use various circumlocutions instead.[3] For instance, I could figure out where someone's wife came from by asking a man about his *nasa'ib* (in-laws) and figure out where his mother came from by asking about his *khawal* (maternal uncles). Women were also somewhat removed from the discussions occurring on the men's side. The result was a potentially large number of side agreements emanating from every match, especially when multiple intermediaries were involved who did not even know each other. I did not record any concrete instances of the sorts of ruses through which men in Granqvist's (1931, 49–53) Palestinian village of the 1920s were tricked into marriages against their will; however, such anxieties were ubiquitous and not wholly ridiculous. Given how much remains tacit and diffuse, a certain degree of partitioning or distributed cognition (Hutchins 1995) becomes essential to facilitating a marriage.

Abu Rizq told me that the match had been made by one of his wife Umm Rizq's maternal aunts. This aunt had a friend and coworker in the school where she taught (who happened to be her paternal aunt) who told Umm Rizq that their paternal aunt had a daughter in university ready for marriage. Following this initial contact, a number of discrete meetings had taken place to arrange the details. He made a point of telling me that unlike the old days when the *mahr* was negotiated at the actual delegation, this had all been arranged in advance and would be purely a formality. Just then, he got a phone call from the father of the bride. After an exchange of effusive praise, they began to discuss the arrangements for the delegation. Abu Rizq complained that he was doing his part to keep the event "simple." He had invited only his relatives on his father's side and not those on his mother's side. However, he claimed he was unsure if anyone was coming, since various people were inevitably mad at various other people and/or upset that various other people had not been invited. It quickly became apparent that they were arguing about who would be responsible for the all of the different expenses associated with the delegation. Abu Rizq had already agreed to spend JD 100 on sweets and soda for the event. The family of the bride wanted him to contribute more for chairs. Abu Rizq responded by listing everything he had already bought to facilitate the marriage (focusing on the house) and complaining that, given the nature of his work in construction, he was unsure how his family would survive through the winter when such work was unavailable. He openly considered doing what would be *haram* (unlawful, forbidden) by taking out interest loans to facilitate the whole thing.

The father of the bride tried to defend his position by focusing on what he had spent. Abu Rizq was none too impressed. When the father said he would be renting a suit for JD 100, Abu Rizq snapped back, "I could *buy* a suit for that much." When he got off the phone (having agreed to pay for more chairs), he seemed more incensed by the consumer habits of his future in-laws than the financial imposition. "The problem is women," he said. I pondered the seeming non sequitur and stared back at him waiting for an explanation. As I suspected, there was a whole extra layer to the dispute:

> She wants to spend JD 20 on a slip. Do you understand? JD 20 for underwear! I've never paid any attention to clothes.[4] What's the point? If you buy nice clothes, they're worthless after a year anyway since the style is always changing. But these women get together and they all ask each other [adopting a feminine voice], "oh and where did you buy that? How much did it cost? What Salon did you go to?" "Oh, I went to a salon in Shmeisani [a wealthy neighborhood in the capital city]. I went to *al-bassa al-na'ima* [the Sleeping Kitty]."

Abu Rizq's complaints about his future in-laws, with their effete and feminized urban consumption patterns, emphasize the complexity of the exchanges that surround any match and the ways in which they inexorably draw a wide range of family members into more or less onerous relationships.

This account will only continue to drag in even more actors as Abu and Umm Rizq's son Rizq and his future wife become even more incidental to the story. The delegation and the two "sides" it constructs are sprawling *agencements* (Callon 2005; MacKenzie 2009) in which agency is highly distributed.[5] At first glance, the whole ritual seems to work to bolster the position of the most senior male. However, further investigation shows that many people can occupy that position only through an almost complete surrender of self. Following MacKenzie, it is necessary to avoid "focusing exclusively on what one might call action's glamorous agential peaks" (2009, 22). Instead, I seek to understand how these agential peaks involve more subtle forms of erasure and compensatory ritual elaboration.

The Procession (Al-Farida)

The next afternoon, we assembled at 2:45 p.m. to prepare for the trip to the bride's house to make the request. Despite Abu Rizq's dire predictions, about 25 men were soon assembled and even more women and children were sitting in their area. Abu Rizq had rented a bus for the women who could not fit in the cars. The procession involved the bus, two vans, and about eight cars. As the procession began to move, the women began clapping and singing. It was hard to make out exactly what the words were, since the voices of the children tended to overwhelm the older women who actually knew the songs, but it was clear that they mostly consisted of lightly risqué teasing of various men.[6] This was most clear when a girl began one of the verses "and bring Geoff," only to have everyone halt abruptly to consider the propriety of the previous statement. Her father chimed in and they continued with the song—switching next to sing about him.

On arriving, the guests filed into the tent that had been set up for the occasion. We were situated on a hill overlooking high-rise apartments on all sides in a relatively open area. After we were all seated, Abu Yehea (the most senior representative of the community) addressed the representative of the bride: "The messenger of God (peace be upon him) said, 'A woman is normally sought as a wife for her lineage, wealth, beauty, or religiousness, but choose a religious woman and you will prosper.' We are from [the such-and-such tribe] and we have come to you [the such-a-one tribe] to ask for—what's her name, Abu Rizq?"—"Noor."—"Noor . . . to

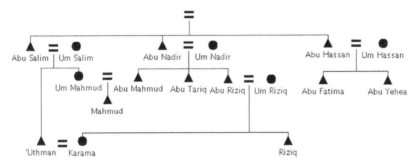

Figure 03_01. An abbreviated family tree showing the relationships between those involved in the various marriages discussed in this chapter.

marry our son Rizq." With that, the representative of the bride's family stood up and asked, "Do you accept the *mahr* and terms we agreed on?" Abu Yehea nodded and drank the cup of coffee he had been poured to signify his acceptance. With that, they recited the opening verse of the Quran and began pouring coffee for everyone. Soon the house erupted with the women's ululation, and the male relatives of the bride began passing out *kunafa* (a sweet cheese-based pastry) and soda. I made small talk with my neighbors (who quizzed me on what had just happened to make sure I had grasped the significance of each part in the ritual) and was soon put into service entertaining Rizq's army buddies, who were relative strangers at the event.

Within an hour, we were hurrying out to the car for the ride home. There was some shifting of places such that my friend Abu Rizq's sisters ended up riding with their brother Abu Mahmud and me. We also ended up with the drum—ensuring a festive ride home. As we began to move, we heard celebratory gunfire in the background as Abu Rizq's sisters sang songs about their brothers and me, highlighting their traditional matchmaking roles as sisters and female relatives. When they weren't singing, they were pointing to every nonveiled woman on the street and saying, "Look. There's your girlfriend, Abu Mahmud!"[7]

"He Came to Me Like a Thief in the Night"

The *jaha* seemingly distributes agency and cognition while having a hyperindividuating effect on a handful of older male figures. Such a man is called a sheikh, *wajh al-jama'a* (the face of the group) or simply *al-kabir* (the big man). In the ethnographic literature on Melanesia, the concept of the "big man" has come in for some useful reconsideration and critique. Roy Wagner describes an outdated view of the big man as "an emperor of social friction who uses society against itself to reinstate the essential individual at the top of the heap" (1991, 163). It is indisputable that some men are able to live up to this ideal. However, I appreciate how Wagner seeks to draw our attention to other ways of thinking about the relationship between the individual and the society or collective. He argues that we must keep in mind the possibility of a genealogical view of personhood in which "person as human being and person as lineage or clan are equally arbitrary sectionings or identifications of this enchainment, different projections of its fractality" (163).

I found little evidence outside the delimited bounds of the *jaha* that Abu Yehea in his role as "sheikh of the such-and-such tribe" was more than a projection of other agencies. Abu Yehea had no ability as a mere individual to find a suitable match for Rizq, much less marry the couple. In fact, he could only take on his position as sheikh through his surrender of self to the judgment of the group. This fits with a larger pattern in which people are defined relationally rather than as bearers of distinctive and coherent identities.[8] Relevant here is the tendency of Jordanians to refer to each other as *Abu* (father of) and *Umm* (mother of) their eldest son. At the same time, Jordanians tend to refer constantly to their membership in groups named after particular apical ancestors—from each of whom buds a distinct *shajarat al-'a'ila* (family tree). Consequently, personhood itself is distributed—for example, a fight between Abu Yehea's grandson and a neighbor angry with the boy for peeping into his house was described to me by the neighbor as "the problem with Abu Yehea's house."

When we arrived home, I went to greet Abu Yehea's brother Abu Fatima who had been unable to attend the delegation. We soon turned to discussing the engagement and the finer points of matchmaking in Jordan. This conversation was interesting in the way in which it focused on the need to keep women from the same family together through repeated exchanges. Whereas Abu Rizq was proud of having pulled off a "distant" match, Abu Fatima emphasized the need for marriage exchanges to ultimately be reversed (a family that gives a wife to another family should, eventually, also take a wife from them), preferably repeatedly. He pointed out a very practical reason (at least from a male perspective) for such an arrangement in which families pursued a series of marriage exchanges involving related women. Given the patrilocal settlement patterns that predominate in Jordan, he reasoned that "if the mothers are all sisters, then our sons will be able to go into any house they want and not be ashamed."

We went over to join the festivities at Abu Rizq's house—so much for his earlier claim that he wanted a "simple" delegation and no engagement party at his own house. Because the party was exclusively for the family, the in-laws would likely never be the wiser. The men were once again seated on the roof of his son's house chatting, smoking, and drinking tea. I took the opportunity to engage Abu Rizq in conversation about the whole affair. I began by asking about the *hadith* (saying of the prophet) that his cousin Abu Yehea had used to make the proposal. However, Abu Rizq made clear to me that that was not the *sigha* (formula) that he would have used. He continued, "Abu Yehea is older so I couldn't say anything. If I were making the request, I would have said, 'We'd love to request a pony from you. But a pony which eats with her hand—not a pony which eats with her mouth.' But there are many of these formulas. They all mean the same thing. There's no difference. It's like 'welcome,' 'hello,' and 'good morning'—they're all greetings. How would you make this kind of request, Salameh [Abu Mahmud]?"

Abu Mahmud instead explained the history of his own marriage and what his older brother Abu Rizq had said to his bride's father (their father's brother): "Abu Rizq said, 'He doesn't have a house, he doesn't have a job, he doesn't have any money, and he can't give you any *mahr* but you can have him if you want." Abu Rizq explained, "Salameh [Abu Mahmud] is a troublemaker now, but he's not like before. Salameh was a wild animal. He would go and sleep in the caves. He would do whatever he wanted. He was like February: hot/cold, hot/cold. He's a lot like that young man over there." At this moment, Abu Rizq pointed to Abu Mahmud's brother-in-law 'Uthman, a young man who was obviously courting Abu Rizq's daughter and would later marry her (see the family tree in fig. 3.1). Abu Rizq continued, "'Uthman came to me like a thief in the night." Abu Rizq smiled as he adopted a groveling, sycophantic tone and, looking at 'Uthman, said, "How are you doing, uncle. I'd like to marry your daughter, uncle. I don't have any money, uncle." Everyone laughed at this, but nobody laughed harder than 'Uthman himself.

The conversation soon took an unexpected turn as people began to enquire more about the family of the bride. Abu Rizq mentioned that "ten years ago, there was nothing in [their rapidly developing neighborhood in Amman]. Now you see how it's all built up, right? Well, that old man has a lot of land. The men will get five dunums each (five thousand square meters)." This raises an interesting question about the degree to which the vagaries of the Amman real estate market are driving marital strategies. Is this an opening gambit by Abu Rizq meant to give one of his younger daughters the option of marrying someone with tens (or more likely hundreds) of thousands of dollars worth of property and, by extension, ensuring some of his grandsons a place to build their homes?

The forces driving the marriages of young men like Rizq, Uthman, and Salameh far exceed the men themselves—or even the senior men who act out the "agential peak" of the ritual drama surrounding the delegation. This applies, differentially, in distant marriages like Rizq's and genealogically and geographically closer marriages like Uthman's and Salameh's. Although the latter two matches obviate many of the cognitive challenges posed by Rizq's (i.e., the women and their families were well known to the senior men), they also introduce higher stakes for various relatives and junior men, who may have their own reasons for promoting a particular match. Women may want to ensure they marry in such a way that they can reside with close kin who can serve as allies. Young people may develop intense affective bonds and demand that their families accept their choices. Entire families may decide a close marriage is preferable because it obviates the need to observe higher standards of modesty and/or preserves family property intact. More distant marriages introduce different economic considerations (e.g., the possibility of acquiring land and titles through savvy marital strategies) but also might be shaped by many of the same considerations as a close marriage. Nevertheless, motives become more opaque as the number of interested intermediaries between the two families increases. No matter what the arrangement, it is hard to imagine such a ritual for the creation of a marital bond as an exchange between individuals (whether the couple or the senior men) operating with full information and the absence of constraint.

"I Would Have Spit in Their Faces"

This type of marital rite is an exchange, nonetheless. As such, it seems important to, following Marilyn Strathern (1988), ask about *The Gender of the Gift*. Continuing with some of the Melanesian literature on personhood, it is important to note that "the multiple, partible nature of persons' constitutions is revealed in its internal relations. In the mother's case, this is made explicit in (say) the further contextualization of herself within enveloping male exchanges. It is only in retrospect that identification with the mother can be revealed as having had an effect on the life of the nurtured object of her regard" (Strathern 1988, 321). The key point is that gender is less an identity and more of a relationship. This relationship can involve bodies, it can involve things, and it can involve relationships themselves; marriage itself can become gendered. In the conclusion of the previous vignette, there was a focus on patrilineal (agnatic) parallel cousin marriage (the matches between Abu Mahmud and Umm Mahmud and Uthman's impending marriage). The following vignette will focus on a matrilineal (uterine) marriage involving Abu Fatima's daughter. Notably, the sheikh's claim to speak on behalf of the group becomes far more contentious on the men's side when the marriage is designed to strengthen female kin bonds. For some, the ritual's near failure calls the entire legitimacy of the match into question.

We arrived at 6:45 in the evening to await the arrival of the visiting *jaha* at 7:00 p.m. At about 7:30, we were informed that they were still a good hour away—probably more with the traffic. I did my best to try and figure out the relationships between the attendees, quickly ascertaining that the bride and groom were cousins through the mother's side. Finally, at 9:00 p.m., the guests arrived. This was late even by Jordanian standards. Everyone stood as the dignitaries filed in, and the younger men stood in the doorway and greeted the guests. For the life of me, I could not tell who the groom was supposed to be. We sat down and Abu

Yehea (the elder brother of the bride's father), welcomed the guests and poured them coffee. Attention focused on two elderly men who sat at the far wall facing the door. The man in charge took the coffee and said, "OK, let's get on with this. We're here to discuss the marriage of [name of groom] and . . . what's her name?" A number of people quickly said, "Fatima." The old men then began to talk about all manner of unrelated things: the weather, goats, and similar pabulum. At some point, Abu Yehea interjected, "We still haven't discussed the *mahr*." The old men asked, "How much are you asking for?" I was pretty sure this was not how it was supposed to work. Abu Yehea told them JD 3,000, and they protested that it was too much and began trying to negotiate.

The tension was so thick you could cut it with a knife, but it was also sublimated beneath a polite veneer. One of the other guests joked that he had asked for far less for most of his daughters—with the exception of the one who married through the matriline (for whom he required far more). Most people looked uncomfortable. Nonetheless, soda and sweets were passed around, and the trills could be heard in the distance. The gathering dragged on to the point where I felt like I was being rescued when my friend Abu Tariq beckoned toward me from the doorway. When I went to visit Abu Tariq's house the next day, he said not to write anything about it because it was completely wrong. I protested that sometimes people can learn a lot about what's right from what's wrong. Abu Tariq began to enumerate the shortcomings of the delegation for me. He noted that the other side arrived late and tried to negotiate the *mahr*. He said that if he had been in his cousins' places, he would have spat on their faces and kicked them out. He also claimed that the blame should go to his cousin Abu Yehea, who, as the family's representative, was responsible for the debacle. Intrigued, Abu Tariq's sisters (who were sitting with us) asked for more details. When Abu Tariq added that they talked about goats, everyone roared with laughter. I would later realize that there was more to Abu Tariq's displeasure than mere felicity to the ritual template. The way Abu Tariq saw it, Abu Fatima, with two daughters and no male heir, was allowing his wife and her family to take land away from the family. Abu Tariq said, "Abu Fatima's wife is laughing at him. She's just happy he has some goats to keep him busy, but there's no *natij* [product, productivity], so he can't marry another woman and have a son." As he conceived of it, at least half of his land and other assets would go back to Abu Fatima's wife's family through his daughter when he dies.[9]

It is useful to enquire about the "gender of the gift," but I must strongly emphasize that the Melanesian comparison can be taken only so far because what these authors oppose to the "Melanesian" conception of personhood (the so-called Western conception of the person as individual) finds its own forms of expression in contemporary Jordan in courthouse procedures. In this section, I have described the *jaha* in relative isolation from any sort of Islamic context because the delegation or *jaha* is a continuation of a pre-Islamic ritual, practiced today by Muslim and Christian Jordanians alike. In many ways, the *jaha* fits uneasily with an increasingly articulate and textually based Islamic revival that has produced zealous advocates for concepts like the individual, the collective, and society. Energetic adherents of the Aristotelian tradition, they see their most cherished ideas as anything but hegemonic as they fight what they perceive as a prevailing culture of *jahiliyya* (ignorance) and *shirk* (polytheism). Saba Mahmood describes adherents of the Islamic revival as providing an "account which privileges neither relational nor the autonomous self so familiar to anthropologists . . . but a conception of individual ethics whereby each person is responsible for his or her own actions" (2005, 173). The *jaha* and the cultural logics it represents and instantiates must contend with forces like the Islamic revival that seek to exert an individuating influence. For members of the Islamic movement, individual choices take on a moral weight that they are seen to lack in either a purely tribal context or the laissez-faire, anything-goes, individualistic context they perceive to be emanating from the West. Nonetheless, in Jordan, the Sharia courts are often foremost in counteracting tribal forms of moral agency, like those constructed through the delegation, with their emphasis on individual responsibility.

COURT AND CONTRACT

The Jordanian Sharia courts have grown out of a certain kind of a search for order. Yet their attempts to exert an individuating influence, to clarify the terms of marital agreements, enumerate the *mahr*, and prevent the eruption of open tribal conflict have never been completely successful.

To the degree that the courts have had this effect, it is a result of concerted effort over a long period of time. From Ottoman times to the
present, courts have insinuated themselves more and more deeply into
people's lives. Once an arbiter of last resort, Islamic courts now have
their representatives interact with virtually every married couple in the
country. To quote Ian Hacking (1982), the Islamic regime of enumeration, record-keeping, fact-finding, and arbitration has also had "subversive effects" because "enumeration demands *kinds* of things or people to
count. Counting is hungry for categories. Many of the categories we now
use are byproducts of the needs of enumeration" (Hacking 1982, 280). As
the marital exchange has been abstracted into a relationship between
embodied individuals over a numerical quantity of *mahr*, it has yielded
new moral agents. Aided by a new kind of artifact (the publicly stored
contract that records a legally enforceable alimony payment), the marriage contracts of the Jordanian Sharia courts have become entangled in
conflicts between the types of collective moral agents constructed by the
delegation and the various embodied individuals that court procedures
tend to reify. In the next chapter, I will track the ever deeper and more
systemic ways in which the information infrastructure of the contemporary Sharia courts influences Jordanian family life—especially as new
procedures for the aggregation, storage, and circulation of data about
marriage produce their own novel forms of collective voice and social
criticism through statistics.

Contracts on the Margins

Jordan's marginal status in the Ottoman, colonial, and postcolonial periods has shaped the development of its Sharia courts and their techniques
for the legitimation of marital bonds and the collection, storage, and
dissemination of information about those relationships. Historically,
the courts repeatedly came into conflict with tribal marriage customs,
embodied in the delegation, as they expanded their geographic jurisdiction to encompass Jordan in the late nineteenth and early twentieth
centuries. Rather than abating, such conflicts have continued as the
courts have expanded their reach more deeply into the lives of Jordanian
citizens. For instance, using itinerant notaries to encourage people to

register their marriages represents both a compromise with local custom's constructions of gendered space and a challenge to those constructions. The greater problem for the courts has always been enforcing their writ when conflicts emerge. The courthouse's ability to construct new kinds of moral agents does not mean those moral agents will win out against older ones. Although such conflicts between differently constituted moral agents are not necessarily the norm, they can range from the mundane to the spectacular. Such conflicts provide an opportunity to better understand the conflicting forms of moral agent produced by these contrasting procedures for the social recognition of marital bonds.

Sharia courts have generally taken considerably more interest in individuals in general and in women in particular than tribal proposal delegations like the ones I have described. In certain urban centers in the Middle East, the practice of writing marriage contracts goes back to pre-Islamic times. Highlighting such continuities between pre-Islamic and Islamic contractual procedures, the historian Amira Sonbol (2008) uses contracts and other court records to great effect to show how women in what is now Egypt were treated as legal persons in ways that Western women would not be for more than one thousand years.[10] She portrays women representing themselves in court and often winning against recalcitrant husbands. Her archive of marriage contracts shows that women often stipulated elaborate conditions in their marriage contracts, which provided grounds for divorce and the payment of the *mahr*. Working closer to Jordan with a focus on Ottoman Syria and Palestine, the historian Judith Tucker (1998, 2008) notes that jurists saw themselves as continuing a reformist project epitomized by the teachings of the Quran and the Prophet Muhammad.

Arguably, key aspects of this reformist project (especially in the realm of marriage) were aimed at preventing abuses by powerful senior men and extended kin groups against figures like girls of marriageable age, who were perceived by jurists as particularly vulnerable to exploitation. These jurists "took the notion of consent seriously" (Tucker 2008, 43) and worried extensively about the malign influence that senior men might have on a woman's marriage prospects (Tucker 1998, 40–52). One of the four nineteenth-century Palestinian jurists who Tucker profiles in *In the House of the Law* "waged a campaign of sorts" (1998, 54) against the various ways in which rural women often saw their *mahr* eaten up by their families and, especially, by senior men.

Once married, jurists place the responsibility for the provision of the wife's maintenance (*nafaqa*) squarely on the husband. If the husband was unable or unwilling to pay, the court would go so far as to empower the wife to borrow money on his behalf in the market and then compel him to pay it back (Tucker 1998, 58–62).[11] Palestinian jurists in Ottoman times also took aim at more explicitly tribal customs that "reduced women to chattel, whose sole worth lay in their usefulness to immediate family honor or gain" (Tucker 1998, 70). Among the more frequent targets in this regard were "marriage by capture," "bartering brides," and attempts to annul marriages on the grounds that a bride's broken hymen invalidated her claim to virginity (Tucker 1998, 67–69).[12] In each case, a vulnerable individual becomes the rationale for checking the prerogatives of the broader kin group and its members.

The situation was somewhat different in Jordan, at least until the end of the nineteenth century.[13] Going to the trouble of recording a marriage with the courthouse in Jerusalem (about half a day's journey on foot from the westernmost point in what is now Jordan) must have seemed a bit superfluous to people living across the river in Jordan where, by most accounts, the Ottomans could not even seem to prevent brigandage, tribal warfare, and extortion. From the sixteenth to the late nineteenth centuries, a single Ottoman Sharia court in Jerusalem was theoretically responsible for all of what is now Jordan. Nevertheless, one could go to a courthouse and have one's marriage recorded using a simple formula explaining that "so-and-so in the presence of their legal agent (*wakil shari'i*)" was present for a marriage involving some amount of *mahr*. Much like Sonbol's (2008) Egyptian contracts, the contractual arrangements in the Jerusalem registers could be quite detailed for important people. However, even after new courthouses were built in Salt, Ajloun, and elsewhere, there is little evidence of a rush to take advantage of them. Even with the consolidation of the courts in the 1920s under British colonial rule, they seem to have merely continued their visible but by no means ubiquitous presence in the marriage process (unless one believes that there were only about four to five thousand marriages happening every decade in central Jordan in the 1920s and 1930s). During this period, the courts worked primarily through a system of itinerant notaries known as the *ma'dhuns*.[14]

For some families, the *ma'dhun* may have seemed like a wonderful way to conduct the marriage contract without requiring the women of the house to leave the *muharam* or protected space; however, not everyone has been so sanguine about the process. These men were (and are) respected members of the community, recognized for their piety and learning. In general, employees at the Sharia courts explained that the more *muhafiz* (conservative) families preferred to use the *ma'dhun* rather than take a female family member to the courthouse. Even here, however, sensitivities were involved that continued to cause friction at the time of fieldwork. For instance, while the contemporary courts have tried to introduce a rotation for the *ma'dhuns*, I often observed in my fieldwork that people would discard the business card they had been given by the courts and choose a *ma'dhun* who was a friend of the family. In doing so, families challenged the state's attempt to mandate that female members interact with a strange man of the state's choosing. In one case, a man boasted to me that his family was powerful enough to get married using the *ma'dhun* with whom they had a preexisting relationship—despite the fact that the most recent enlargement of the Greater Amman Municipality had pulled them into a completely different administrative district from the courthouse with which the notary was associated. There was one kin group in particular that was widely understood to share a collective familial dislike for the entire concept of the *ma'dhun*: the Saba'awi tribe from Bir Saba' in Palestine. As members of the group and others in the community told me with striking regularity, the family preferred to go to the courts rather than bring a representative of the government into their homes. Most Saba'awi who heard about my research with the courts (including a court employee) proudly explained to me that their family had not even used the courts until the 1980s.

Even members of groups that were quicker to adopt the use of government-issued paper contracts expressed some skepticism about the whole process, implying that it was invasive, coercive, and infringed on the family's independent prerogatives. One man suggested that it was the introduction of public services like schools in the 1950s and 1960s that made the marriage contracts so important: "You take your child to school and the principal asks, 'Where is your family notebook (*daftar al-'a'ila*)?' You go to the Interior Ministry and they ask you, 'Where is your marriage contract?' Then they send you to the Sharia Courts."[15] Here, three postindependence state building projects conspired to push families to incorporate the Sharia courts into their marital arrangements: the move toward universal compulsory schooling, the 1951 Jordanian Law of Family Rights (the basis for the revamped contract form), and Law 32 of 1966, which established the contemporary Civil Status and Passport Department and the system of family notebooks for which they are responsible. Over time, most families have responded by opting to get official marriage contracts. Even the earlier Saba'awi practice of going to the courts for a certificate (*tasdiq*) of marriage to obtain the family notebook has fallen into disuse.

Graphic Artifacts

The contemporary marriage contract is far more than a mere record of marriages. The contract is a preprinted form that, to quote Matthew Hull, "precipitate[s] the formation of shifting networks and groups of people inside and outside the bureaucracy" (2003, 291). There is much to be gained by studying *sajjals* and marriage contracts as what Hull has called "graphic artifacts." Hull argues that, for too long, there has been a tendency to treat bureaucratic documents as merely more stable instantiations of the spoken word without paying attention to the broad diversity of genres of bureaucratic communication. He notes that "each genre has its own pattern of use, distinct formal discursive characteristics, orienting frameworks, interpretive procedures, temporality, and sets of expectations through which readers produce and make sense of it" (292–293). This is to say nothing of qualities of the document-like size, shape, and way in which it is allowed to circulate. Following Hull, it is useful to inquire about local "graphic ideologies" that, like semiotic ideologies (Keane 2003) and language ideologies (Silverstein 1979), have constituted Islamic court documents as socially meaningful artifacts. The degree to which the courthouse is largely a site for the production, storage, retrieval, and interpretation of graphic artifacts suggests that *sajjals* and marriage contracts play an important role in catalyzing these new forms of moral agent.[16]

The moral weight of court procedures and their ability to produce new kinds of agents became apparent to me long before I arrived at the courthouse. When I expressed an interest in marriage and social change in Jordan, I was repeatedly told by men of the increasing prevalence of *zawaj 'urfi* (literally, customary marriage)—or the related term, *zawaj friend* (note the code-switch to the English "friend").[17] The terminology reflects the shifting familial dynamics and assumptions about governance that this chapter is meant to interrogate. *Customary* in this sense simply refers to the fact that no copy is registered with the government. In the context of rapid urbanization, sexual revolution, and the decreasing power of the extended family in certain quarters, the meanings attributed to different kinds of archival procedures surrounding contracts are not the same as they would have been 100 years ago. I was told that both customary and "friend" marriages, while ostensibly Islamic (with witnesses, a contract, etc.), were fundamentally exploitative because, crucially, the signing was conducted in secret and the contract was not registered with the government—giving the woman little recourse if her "husband" grew tired of the relationship.

There is increasing polarization in terms of what such a relationship looks like. Customary marriage stands in for the threat of tribalism leading to women's exploitation, whereas friend marriage stands in for the threat posed by liberalization and westernization. With customary marriages, it is assumed that couples are not registering their marriages with the state because of illiteracy, suspicion of the state, or adherence to patriarchal values. Regarding the threat posed by friend marriages, two relatively novel scenarios figure prominently—both of which could be taken directly from a racy Egyptian soap opera. I heard frequent impassioned denunciations of these relatively cosmopolitan marriages that were either secret or merely unregistered. My interlocutors differentiated between two types of cases. The first was described as "something that happens among the 'open-minded' (*infitahi*). You have college students and a kind of love story (*qissat-habb*) and they want to have relations so they make an agreement with their friends acting as witnesses." The second was described as "a form of exploitation. You have a boss who wants to have relations with his secretary. But he's married and he's afraid of his wife so he won't marry the secretary. But he also doesn't want to commit adultery (*zina*). He wants to ease his mind so he makes her sign a piece of paper. When he's tired of her, he can tear it up. He thinks he can laugh at our Lord, but really he's only laughing at himself."

For residents of a highly bureaucratized society, it is easy to take for granted the idea that a piece of paper could bring the repressive powers of the state to bear on a recalcitrant husband—or forestall the imposition of those repressive powers. That is likely part of the appeal of a secret marriage contract that can be pulled out should the couple be discovered. In Jordan, as elsewhere, this has been accomplished only through a long period of negotiation as various precedents have emerged for understanding the complex entailments of court documents. Even government-backed legal documents may prove no match for the prerogatives of the extended kin group. The anthropologist, sometime intelligence officer, and sometime opposition politician Ahmad 'Uwaid 'Abaddi offers one example of this process of negotiation in his self-published doctoral dissertation:

> In the summer of 1980, a Bedouin (A) became betrothed to a Bedouin girl (B) for a stated bridewealth (*mahr*). The contract (*aqd al-nikah*) took place according to shari'ah law (which made her legally his wife), but the *mahr* was still as yet unpaid to her father (C), so according to the *'awayid* [customs] they were still unmarried).
>
> (A) had sexual intercourse with (B) while she was living at her father's home before the wedding had taken place. After a few months it appeared that she was pregnant. Her father was furious, and, went to the civil courts to complain. They rejected the case since it was within the shari'ah's jurisdiction. The shari'ah refused to hear the case, since (B) was legally (A)'s wife. (C) finally went to the *Muhafiz* [Governor] of Amman to report the incident. The *Muhafiz* took action to prevent the dispute from getting out of hand, and referred the case to three arbiters. By chance, I was in his office for my fieldwork. He invited me to act as the fourth arbiter. The final decision we arrived at was that:
>
> > although A's action was theoretically legal, correct behavior is not to have intercourse with the fiancée until after a public wedding (*urs*). . . . Since (A) committed this act secretly at (C's) house, (A) must pay all the outstanding *mahr* and should send a big *jahah* to (C) and make a feast of conciliation, with food, contributed by the notables of the two parties. He also had to pay a fine of 300JD for *hurmat al-bayt* [inviolability of the

home] of C. He was required to swear an oath that he had not had sexual intercourse with (B) before the marriage contract was signed, so as to secure her and her sisters' reputation, otherwise the sisters chances of marriage would suffer because of his action. (A) must take B to his house, as a wife, immediately after the *Jahah*. (Al-Abbadi 2006, 103)

A few things are striking about this passage. First, the bureaucracy appears completely uninterested until the matter rises to the level of a threat to public security. Once activated, government officials are forced to contend with the gap between "theoretically legal" and "correct behavior." A whole string of obligations and entailments involving various networks and groups of people emerge: the *mahr*, the wedding, the father's sense of entitlement to *hurmat al-bayt*, and the sisters' reputations. As late as 1980, these were ultimately determined not according to Sharia but rather by an explicitly tribal framework that relates these prerogatives to the enactment of nondocumentary, as opposed to documentary, rituals. When faced with a potential riot by the outraged family of the bride, the governor was quick to rule that the wedding and the transfer of *mahr* take priority over the paperwork.[18]

Even when I was conducting fieldwork in 2012, the governor's office continued to serve an integral role in solving problems for which the documentary procedures of the courts were ill-equipped. One of the most notable sources of tension was the court's requirement that a female virgin must have her legal guardian (*wali al-amr*) present to sign his consent to her marriage on the contract.[19] The early twenty-first–century system for the creation and legitimation of marital bonds is striking for its individuating tendencies and the ways in which it keeps the extended family in check. The Islamic regime of marital obligations highlights individual consent: without the consent of both bride and groom, there can be no marriage. The contract works to constitute explicit, undeniable indexical linkages (signatures, thumbprints, and stamps) between all concerned parties and a written rendition of the agreement.

The codification of male privilege remains through the requirement for the consent of the *wali al-amr* but in a much more limited sense: once a woman has ceased to be a virgin, she can act on her own behalf, as her father no longer has any legal standing. Even as a virgin, the broader prerogatives of her extended family are completely unrecognized. For a virgin to marry, she needs nothing other than the consent of her guardian (*wali*). Although a woman is supposedly represented (if at all) by the nebulous figure of the sheikh in the delegation, the *wali* is a well-delimited figure in contemporary Jordanian law. As Afaf Jabiri (2016) explains in her recent study of Jordanian guardianship, a woman's guardian is, first and foremost, her father. In the absence of her father, article 14 of the 2010 personal status code states that the guardian is reckoned "according to the order of al-'asaba [male blood relatives] as established by the Hanafi school" (Jabiri 2016, 15). This means, as is further spelled out in article 223, the father's designated custodian (often a brother), then grandfather, then her grandfather's designated custodian, and so forth. Reform-minded Muslims envision the guardian as defending the woman's rights by checking the excesses of a preexisting tribal order that they view as backward and oppressive toward women.[20] Nevertheless, difficulties may emerge when a woman and her guardian disagree about her marital prospects. Without this concurrence between the woman and her guardian, the Sharia courts generally refuse to become involved, necessitating intervention of the governor's office.

I met Muhammad (an employee at the governor's office) while visiting with a friend from the Sharia courts. He immediately drew the connection between my interest in marriage and his office. As everyone knows, the governor's office is where people go when they want to elope. We sat together discussing the basics of the procedure: "If you want '*zawaj shari'i*' [both a Sharia marriage and a legal marriage], you need the permission of the girl's guardian (*wali al-amr*). But sometimes, a boy and a girl run away from their parents and they come to the Office of the Governorate, and the governor marries them to prevent a tribal conflict. Then they have to leave and go live somewhere else. They're married, but it's not an Islamic marriage." Another guest was incredulous, but Muhammad explained, "See, she's already been opened [lost her virginity]. Then they come to us, and we try to fix the problem before it widens."

KHALID: But it's not *shari'i* [legal and Sharia-compliant]?
MUHAMMAD: No. It's not. [Turning to me] Who told you about this? Did [Muhammad's cousin] tell you about this?
ME: I mean, I've seen it. This one time I was sitting with Hussein [a notary and key consultant] and he got a phone call. There was a case like this at the

Governorate office. There was a problem between the families, but the father had agreed to come and give permission, so Hussein hurried over to give them a *shari'i* marriage. Maybe you remember this case? It was a few months ago.

MUHAMMAD: Yes. I do.

ME: So how many people marry this way every month?

MUHAMMAD: It differs. We get more when the weather is hot. It warms the blood.... I'll give you an annual rate: 8–10 per year.

ME: Only in Madaba? What about other places like Amman? It must be more, right?

MUHAMMAD: See, you have to remember that this is a tribal area. Amman is different. It's more like America with autonomous families. In Amman and Zarqa, they have different procedures (*ijra'at*). Normally, there, a girl will go with a man for a while. Later she wants her rights, and she goes to the police and says he raped her (*ightasabha*). Then it's a case of rape (*ightisab*), and it's a criminal case and it has to be solved using criminal procedures. Here if, God forbid, there was a rape, it would widen quickly. The whole tribe would stand up. There would be killing. So we have to solve the problem quickly. If a girl disappears, they go to the police immediately. The police come and they talk to her mother. Normally, the mother knows who her lover is. The father doesn't know, but the mother does. Then the police go and find her lover. They bring him to the police station and talk to him. Then we bring the two to the governor's, and we marry them. It's not a legal solution (*hal qanuni*), it's an administrative solution (*hal idari*). To give you an example—if, God forbid, someone from the Shawabkeh [tribe] *khatafa* (kidnapped/eloped with) someone from the Azaydeh [tribe], there would be tribal clashes (*mushajara 'asha'iriyya*).[21] We would have to find them quickly before the problem widened. Each area is different with it's own customs and traditions, and so the procedures of each governorate is different.

Unable to accept certain tribal mores but not powerful enough to suppress them, the Sharia courts are forced to yield some of their jurisdictional prerogatives to the governor's office to this day. The attitude of Muhammad and the governor's office more generally is at odds with that of the courts insofar as it elides or outright dismisses concerns about individual consent (of the woman but also her father and her prospective husband). This was viewed by such officials (whatever their religious commitments) as a necessary compromise with the regime of personhood epitomized by the *jaha*. In this case, the Jordanian state reveals itself to be unsure as to whether (and to what degree) every group member's sexual liaisons are a collective concern.

CONCLUSION: "THE STRONG AMONG
US ATE UP THE WEAK"

Such tribal sensibilities are far from hegemonic in the Jordanian context. In fact, plenty of people find them constraining and backward in relationship to what they see as a progressive and empowering Islamic revival. For most Jordanians (and most contemporary Muslims in the Arab world), Islam does not exist in a void: it enters the world historically in a context of extreme ignorance while promising avenues for progress. As I will argue in part 3, in the language of the contemporary Islamic movement, this pre- or un-Islamic world is a world of *jahiliyya* (ignorance), defined by male forms of desire, aggression, and sociality run amok. In Jordan especially, tribalism is an especially salient manifestation of this *jahiliyya*. In contrast, the Islamic golden age of the Prophet Muhammad and the rightly guided caliphs is taken to represent a particular historical moment that transcended the base injustices that came before and after it. Ja'far ibn Abi Talib, one of the companions of the prophet, famously described the shift like this:

> We used to worship idols and eat carrion flesh; we practiced fornication, we disregarded family ties, we neglected the duties of hospitality, and the strong among us ate up the weak. Thus we continued until Allah sent us a Messenger of our own number, of whose descent we know, and whose truthfulness, faith and chastity are unquestioned. He summoned us to Allah, to believe in Him as One God, to worship Him, and to repudiate what we and our fathers worshiped apart from Him in the way of stones and idols. He bade us tell the truth in our conversation, observe good faith in ties of kindred, be faithful to our hospitable duties, and refrain from eating the forbidden foods and blood. He forbade us to practice fornication and to use false speech, to eat up the property of orphans and to slander chaste women.

In quoting this passage, the Muslim Brotherhood thinker Sayyid Qutb adds that because this description was uttered in the presence of two envoys from the Quraysh (the foremost tribe among the erstwhile persecutors of the early Muslims) and they did not object to Abi Talib's account, "this must be a true and reliable description of the former state of affairs and of the new" (1953/2000, 174).

It is no accident that the passage turns on the repudiation of what "we and our fathers worshiped . . . in the way of stones and idols." As early as Al-Kalbi's eighth-century scholarship on pre-Islamic religion, *The Book of Idols*, Muslims have drawn a strong connection between pre-Islamic idolatry and tribalism. According to this account, Mecca was a market town and cult center that hosted a number of tribal totems representing the various patrilines.[22] Given its religious association, it was supposedly a sort of island of tranquility in the middle of a Hobbesian war of all against all. The world of the "Age of Ignorance" was, I have been told repeatedly, a world in which families would bury their newborn daughters alive lest they suffer the shame of having them kidnapped and raped in subsequent raiding. In the stories that contemporary proponents of the Islamic Revival tell themselves about themselves, the Age of Ignorance was an era of male privilege run amok that could be corrected only by divine intervention in the form of God's messenger Muhammad.

For those who support the contemporary Islamic revival, ignorance is a recurring problem that must be defeated once again. Just as Al-Kalbi narrates the devolution of Abrahamic monotheism into a perverted and exploitative state of perpetual warfare, Qutb and other contemporary Islamic activists see themselves as heirs to a luminous Islamic tradition that has become tarnished over the years and needs revitalization. As we will see, employees at the Sharia courts took this duty to protect the weak (defined as women and children) quite seriously. The system of guardianship is deeply paternalistic, but its proponents justify it as a necessary response to the realities of power differentials within existing family structures. As employees of the courts made clear to me, women and men may be equal before God, but the exigencies of their lives require that the courts treat them differently. In promoting such a rationale for the formation and expansion of Sharia courts, the production of increasingly abstract and individuated moral agents like the virgin and the guardian continues to challenge and be challenged by the forms of personhood that the delegation embodies.

NOTES

1. When people describe rituals to me as are supposed to happen (rather than as I witness them), I use what I like to call the "ritual subjunctive"—as opposed to the "ethnographic present" (Fabian 1983)—to highlight the inevitable gap between the ritual ideal and particular instantiations.

2. My engagement with statistics and my attempts at statistical analysis are merely a dimension of my participant observation. As with my engagement with oral history and archival sources, my engagement with statistics takes its cue from the knowledge practices of those I hope to understand.

3. Respecting a woman's *muharam* (protected) status requires a complex set of avoidance rituals involving the gaze (minimize looking), the hands (no touching; instead of shaking hands, the hand is placed over the heart), and the voice (avoid using female names, limit conversation to essential business matters). Such rules were generally relaxed so long as there was a significant age gap and I was well known to the family. Nonetheless, to utter a woman's name among her male relatives expresses social closeness—to which one might or might not be entitled and about which I was inclined to exercise caution.

4. Generally, the groom's family is expected to provide the bride's clothing. In some cases, it gets counted as part of the *mahr*. I have seen a number of recent contracts that listed JD 500 for clothing as part of the prompt *mahr* payment. At the same time, I have also noted resistance among the employees of the Sharia court to including it, although they said there was no rule against it. In my experience, unless the families were of high social status, applicants were counseled that "the clothes are between you."

5. I acknowledge that the word *agency* carries a fair amount of baggage with it, but I can think of no less problematic alternative term. I would ask that the reader remember that I, following Saba Mahmood, use the term with the understanding that "it is crucial to detach the notion of agency from the goals of progressive politics" (1995, 14). For a more thorough discussion of issues of agency and resistance among Bedouin women, see Lila Abu-Lughod's (1986) *Veiled Sentiments: Honor and Piety in a Bedouin Society*.

6. There are divergent opinions on whether various wedding songs have sexual connotations. For instance, some people think there are sexual overtones to the women's song about getting ready for "the Indian needle," whereas others say it "doesn't mean anything at all. They're just words to fit the meter of the song."

7. The diagram is highly abbreviated and is meant only to display relations between people mentioned in the ethnographic vignettes in this chapter by name. Siblings are ordered from youngest to oldest (left to right). A full family tree of the descendents of the wedding participants' forefather "Musa" would include upward of seventy people. "Karama" is a name used out of respect on printed materials like wedding invitations to avoid writing the name of an unmarried girl. Here, I use it because, while all names have been changed, I want to highlight the fact that I was never directly told certain people's names.

8. In *Intimate Selving*, Suad Joseph (1999) gives a broader illustration of this phenomenon based on fieldwork conducted in Beirut. She shows how brothers and sisters come to see themselves relationally through a long process of socialization in the home environment.

9. Assuming his wife outlived him, it would be more than half because his wife would also be entitled to a share, according to Islamic law.

10. A number of scholars have argued that the introduction of French legal theories both through direct colonial rule under Napoleon and later indirectly through the late Ottoman system and particularly the Tanzimat (reorganization) reforms of the nineteenth century weakened the status of women. Amira Sonbol notes that "this mention of 'giving' the bride's 'body' to the groom constitutes the most important

difference between French and Islamic contracts" (2008, 109). Likewise, Kenneth Cuno argues that it is only because of "scholarly neglect" of nineteenth-century legal reforms that many Muslim women's legal disadvantages could be seen as holdovers from Islam. He concludes that "these [new] rules were particularly disadvantageous to women, yet women's use of the legal system to protect their rights shows that they were not mere victims, neither silent nor constrained" (Cuno 2009, 4–5).

11. Tucker (1998) argues that precolonial Palestinian court officials were exacting in their attempts to uphold women's rights to maintenance. In contrast, Kenneth Cuno has argued that, especially with legal reforms in the twilight of Ottoman rule in Egypt, women became increasingly unable to receive the maintenance they were supposedly entitled to in return for obedience (2009, 18).

12. Similarly, Antoun reports that the local *ma'dhun* in the Jordanian village where he based his research dramatically reduced the incidence of *tabadul* (sister-exchange marriages or "bartered brides") in the early 1960s. This involved two fathers marrying two of their respective sons to two of their daughters, using the daughter herself as the *mahr* (1980, 457). Reviled by the Islamic legal guilds for its denial of a woman's right to her *mahr*, this was nonetheless a widely attested kinship ideal historically in Jordan and Palestine—although not perhaps one that was always so widely practiced (see also Granqvist 1931, 109–119; Mundy and Smith 2003, 136–143). For a sense of how widespread these mores are, see chap. 7 of Nancy Tapper's (1991, 141–156) study of marriage practices in Afghanistan, *Bartered Brides*. She argues that "the exchange of women between two men indicates a mutual recognition of status equality, while the single transfer of a woman by one man to another for brideprice [*mahr*] indicates the recognition by the wife-giver of the potential or actual status superiority of the wife-taker" (1991, 141).

13. Lynn Welchman's (1988) review of Jordanian family law draws attention to a number of key divergences between the Jordanian and Egyptian cases in the twentieth century. Strikingly, it turns out that the Jordanian Law of Personal Status (JLPS) lacks a number of the colonial-era practices that Sonbol critiques (i.e., with regard to preventing women from adding stipulations in the contract and being compelled by the state to obey their husbands): stipulations are not only allowed but have a dedicated space on the contract form, and ideals of female "obedience" (*ta'a*) are unenforceable. At the same time, Welchman observes, "there appears to be an interesting tendency, in the JLPS in particular, towards achieving equality of the spouses under the law with regard to the claims they may raise, although this takes the form, paradoxically though it may seem, of provisions benefiting the husband rather than the wife" (1988, 872).

14. My understanding of the history of the itinerant notaries comes from a mixture of oral history and the documents themselves. Many notaries come from families that are still respected in the area to this day. For a few, I can even track their peregrinations from village to village as they move along discernible circuits that I continue to use to travel. Antoun's (1980) work on Sharia courts offers a compelling contemporaneous account of these important "broker" figures in an earlier era, as they struggled to reconcile court procedures with what they encountered in the village.

15. When children are born, they are added into their father's family notebook. On marriage, they are moved from their father's family notebook to a new family notebook for the newly formed family.

16. All of this begins to paint a picture of the *sajjals* and contracts as a tantalizing source of data for social history that, nonetheless, defies a naïve reading. As Beshara

Doumani (2003, 173–200), Heather Ferguson (2003), Annelies Moors (1995, 7–8; 1999), Fatma Gocek (2003, 78–79), Iris Agmon (2003, 201–220), and Judith Tucker (1998, 11–22) all argue, court records cannot be taken at face value. Dror Ze'evi writes that the *sajjals* are "carefully constructed legal narratives in which the legal aspect, although invisible to the reader, is still the essence of the record" (1998, 38). This legal aspect is itself open to investigation because there is no reason to believe that a uniform set of precepts prevailed across the Ottoman Empire and much reason to suspect hybrids of Islamic law and parochial custom (Layish 1991). Ze'evi explores some problems with various methodologies for studying contracts. Quantitative methods are problematic because we have no way of knowing what kind of sampling of the larger population they provide. Most important, numbers like the amount of *mahr* and age may actually reflect public perceptions of what court officials want to hear—not the details of actual historical marital arrangements between families. The use of court records to construct narrative history is at least as problematic. The *sajjals* and contracts provide a sort of factual Rorschach test—a series of disjointed bits of information that verily cry out for narration. Unfortunately, as most experts agree, we can be fairly sure that the various scraps of data that we find in court records were carefully curated to construct a "legal narrative," the conventions of which we almost certainly fail to comprehend toady. Yet Doumani argues that with sufficient attention to a particular set of court records, patterns emerge to the point where the astute historian can come to appreciate the "symbiotic relationship" between courts and local populations "to the point that no easy distinction can be made between actual disputes and legal strategy" (2003, 183). For instance, drawing on contemporary fieldwork, Mir-Hosseini observes that it is even difficult when witnessing disputes in person to determine people's actual socioeconomic status, noting wryly of litigants in court that "great efforts are made by each party to appear poor and needy" (1993, 29). At this point, much like the court officials who made the record, it becomes possible to predict the relevant details before one encounters particular cases because they all reflect a common conjuncture of court procedure and widely existing social tensions (in the case of Doumani's eighteenth century Nablus and Tripoli data, widespread resistance to—and insistence on—the inheritance of immovable property along Islamic lines).

17. Hasso (2009, 2011) argues that these new forms of marriage reveal the instability of gender regimes at a time when a range of transnational flows are connecting people, ideas, products, and practices in radically new ways.

18. This persistent disjuncture between courthouse and village norms (and its accommodation) is also at the crux of Antoun's (1980) ethnographic account of Jordanian Sharia courts. In this, he is participating in a much longer-running debate about the significance of Islamic jurists' widely noted tendency to accept and even encourage certain deviations from the legal norm. Hussein Agrama's (2010) recent ethnographic work on fatwa councils in Egypt also addresses these debates, but he faults earlier accounts for focusing more on their ability to instill flexibility and adaptability within Islamic societies while neglecting their ethical dimensions. In this way, he argues that what is essential is that, from the perspective of the believer, it is always better to do what is hated *makruh* rather than what is forbidden (*haram*) and what is merely permitted (*mubah*) rather than these "most reprehensible of permitted acts" (Agrama 2010, 11; 2012). This is not merely limited to matters of Sharia either. So-called tribal law continues to trump criminal courts in certain instances to this day (Hughes 2018; Watkins 2014).

19. Sonbol (2008) notes that a difference of opinion exists on this point among the various schools of Islamic jurisprudence: Malikis and Shafi'is require a male guardian's consent for all first marriages, whereas the Hanafi school allows women to marry on their own behalf once they have reached majority (*bulugh*). This difference is one of a number of ways in which, as Welchman (1988, 873, 877, 879) notes in a number of other regards, Jordanian family law has moved away from its Ottoman era Hanafi roots to embrace aspects of Maliki and Shafi'i law (see also, Antoun 1980, 464)—often to the detriment of women's ability to make their own independent decisions.

20. Sonbol's (2008, 87–94) treatment of pre-Islamic marriage contracts and her convincing arguments about the continuities between pre-Islamic and Islamic contracts in what is now Egypt seriously problematizes this characterization.

21. As Cynthia Werner (2004, 2009) has argued based on her study of similar customs in Central Asia, "a number of ambiguities make it difficult to determine whether or not a kidnapping case is 'consensual' or 'nonconsensual.' There is no single question that gets at this issue" (2004, 82). This issue becomes more pressing in the context of ongoing debates about Jordan's article 308, which historically allowed an accused rapist to avoid prison by marrying his accuser. Some women's groups finally succeeded in changing the law in 2011; however, others argue that changing the law will take away women's ability to lose their virginity in order to force their parents to accept a particular match that they would otherwise oppose (Hattar 2012). In the final vote, members of Parliament rejected amendments that would have made exemptions for consensual sex and cases where a man "seduces a virgin over 18 years of age with the promise of marriage and caused her to lose her virginity" (Husseini 2017), raising questions about the degree to which those on the two "sides" of this issue can even agree on the terms of debate.

22. Leila Ahmed (1992, 41–63) and Ghada Karmi (1996) have challenged this mainstream view of pre-Islamic Arabia, arguing that there was a diversity of kin forms before the advent of Islam and that Islam catalyzed a shift away from matrilineality and matrilocality.

4

The Courthouse

WHERE THE TRIBAL DELEGATION SEEMS PICTURESQUE AND unfamiliar, the procedures at the courthouse might initially appear quite mundane and commonsensical to those otherwise familiar with bureaucratic state societies. However, a closer examination reveals the deeply subversive effects of the contemporary system for the collection, storage, aggregation, and dissemination of information about marriage.[1] Whereas the previous chapter considered the individuating tendencies of marriage contracts and court procedures more broadly, this chapter is focused on the ways in which the knowledge practices of the courts array these individuals in a precise configuration that enables the emergence of different kinds of people. The knowledge practices of the Sharia courts have tended to replace the more or less chimerical figure of the tribal sheikh with that of six key individuals (the legal guardian, the wife, the husband, two witnesses, and the *ma'dhun*) and a particular kind of paper trail. The technological shift from the *jaha* to the written and government-stored contract has further enabled the aggregation of information about marriage in the form of courthouse statistics. These statistics, in turn, have aided and abetted the abstraction and elaboration of particular categories of person. Over time, courthouse officials have developed an increasingly specific analytic vocabulary for talking about participants in marriage contracts and related knowledge practices. As these knowledge practices themselves have helped reify such categories of person (inciting the production of ever more research, statistics, and analysis), they have helped enable the construction of new forms of moral agents endowed with new forms of individual and collective voice.

TOWARD A TEXTUAL POLITY

Drawing on an analysis of 877 marriage contracts from central Jordan concluded between 1926 and 2011 and the more than one hundred marriages I witnessed in a Jordanian courthouse in 2012, this chapter continues to contrast the tribal delegation with the emerging regime of enumeration and record-keeping around marriage. After a discussion of the spatial layout of the courthouse and the office of the contract writer, I will explain the ritual template associated with the contract. This idealized ritual template will then be contrasted with oral historical, archival, and ethnographic examples that highlight the particular kinds of infelicities (Austin 1975) associated with extended kin group family dynamics that contemporary court officials seek to overcome. As in Brinkley Messick's (1993) *The Calligraphic State*, these court procedures are implicated in the foundation and perpetuation of a sort of "textual polity" that remains in productive tension with the kinds of politics embodied by the tribal delegation. In the latter half of the chapter, I will show how these textual practices produce radically new—not to mention unexpected—grounds for political contestation. Dissident intellectuals associated with the Islamic movement are increasingly using the court's own statistics to call into question the legitimacy not just of tribal forms of marriage but also of specific court procedures and the Jordanian state itself.

"Put Your Hand in the Hand of Your Father's Brother": Court Procedure in Theory

Of many contrasts between the tribal delegation and court procedures, there is one I would like to caution against: a simple opposition of orality and literacy (cf. Goody 1986; Ong 1982). To follow Messick (1993) in exploring the ways in which Sharia constitutes a "textual polity" means attending to the material and embodied dimensions of both the spoken and written word in ways that, until recently, Western scholars have resisted. Such a political assemblage requires "both a conception of an authoritative text, involving structures of authorship, a method of instructional transmission, institutions of interpretation, and modes of documentary inscription, and a pattern of textual authority" (Messick 1993, 6). Scholars like Goody and Ong (who rely on a parochial teleology in which Euro-American textual conventions represent the developmental apex) mistake Sharia's practical concerns about felicity for evidence of a cultural time lag. In fact, as Messick (1993) argues, Sharia's suspicion of writing as somehow lacking has direct analogues in the logocentrism of the Western canon stretching all the way from Plato to Saussure to Ong himself. Perhaps a language like Arabic, which relies on a script without vowels (known as *harakat*, or movements), might exaggerate this by emphasizing the interpretive labor of recitation—but only slightly. All written languages force the speaking subject to make editorial decisions to some extent as she vocalizes and thereby animates the text (Messick 1993, 25–26).[2] What makes Sharia distinctive is the way in which the legitimacy of a text tends to be constituted through its relationship to particular kinds of face-to-face interactions and complex practices for modulating presence and absence as well as proximity and distance in response to sophisticated readings of gendered and age-based power dynamics within families. To fail to attend to the hybrid oral-literate character of court procedures (or to see them as necessarily part of a social configuration that represents an intermediate stage on the path to full literacy) is to fundamentally lose the plot.

The local courthouse was tucked away near the marketplace on a quiet side street in a large two-story concrete structure faced with white stone. The first floor consisted of a series of mostly empty storefronts with only the one on the far right being used (two retirees sold forms and photocopied documents there for a fee). To access the court, citizens would mount the dark staircase in the middle of the building, passing an ashtray and arriving at the second floor. They would be greeted by a guard from the public security forces sitting at a weathered wooden desk in a small foyer. The room was bathed in the glow of fluorescent lights reflecting off of walls painted an institutional shade of white. The courthouse itself consisted of a single long corridor with rooms branching off on either side. Two narrow doorways defined the foyer where the guard sat. To the right, there were (moving clockwise) the break room; the head scribe's office; a storage closet overflowing with files; the accountant, charged with collecting fees; the storeroom (*al-mustawda'*) for the contracts; "the pen" (*al-qalam*), where the scribes worked; Head Judge Sayyid's office; the office of the accountants in charge of executing inheritance cases; and Judge Ahmad's office. To the left of the foyer there were rooms for (again moving clockwise), Judge Abdullah's office, the head accountant's office, more storage, the head of implementation's office, and a room where the female guard passed her days sitting behind a desk next to a black cage that was perhaps two meters long and three meters wide. The court was a strikingly self-contained disciplinary apparatus, with a mixture of tools for working on both the individual body (e.g., the prison cell and the guards) and the population as a whole (through the collection, storage, and reproduction of documents and aggregate information about the community).

Those hoping to marry were expected to arrive with the groom, the bride, her father, two witnesses (optimally one from each "side"), ID cards for all involved, the family notebooks for the two sides, the results of medical tests for genetic risk factors, and a marriage request form from the storeroom on the first floor.[3] Assuming a relatively standard marriage involving a virgin "girl" over the age of eighteen marrying a man with no other wives, there was no need to gain the permission of a judge or have a scribe write out special letters.[4] The couple and their families could proceed directly from the copy machines on the first floor to the office of the head scribe. There, a sheikh (in the religious rather than tribal sense) was ready to officiate. His office was somewhat spacious with a large wooden desk, computer, printer, filing cabinets, and coffee table. The walls were lined with armless pleather chairs. Normally, the sheikh would sit in the far left of the room behind the desk, and I would sit to his right. I would introduce myself, explain that I was studying marriage, and ask if I could observe. No one ever objected.[5]

At first, the sheikh would begin by filling out an elicitation form, which would later be painstakingly hand-copied by a scribe onto the actual contracts using his beautifully formed yet legible and precise penmanship. The documents themselves provided most of the relevant personal information (name, age, place of birth, place of residency, marital status, occupation, national ID number), but the sheikh would usually double-check.[6] One potentially touchy subject was the individuals' "social status": the sheikh would ask, "Have you been engaged?" If not, a man would be classified as a (celibate) bachelor (*'azab*) and a woman would be classified as a virgin (*bikr*). If someone had been engaged, it was up to court officials to determine if men were currently married, widowed, divorced, or divorced before consummation and whether women were widowed, divorced, or divorced before consummation. Unsurprisingly, any socially adept contract writer would try to make some sort of comment or joke about a few other aspects of the paperwork while filling it out to lighten the mood a bit and put everyone at ease.

With the basics out of the way, the sheikh would ask that the door be closed so he could begin the proceedings in earnest. He would usually ask the woman a number of times if she consented to the marriage, following the initial "do you agree?" with increasingly pointed formulations: "No one is coercing you?" "You're not being required to do this?" "You're sure?" If there was a large age difference, if the man had another wife, or if the woman was still in school, the sheikh would explicitly raise these as possible objections that the bride might have before moving on. Next, the sheikh would ask about the *mahr* and stipulations, making sure to note whether or not the *mahr* had been received. Then, the sheikh would instruct bride, groom, witnesses, and guardian to sign the relevant forms including the sheet for eliciting the details of the contract (blue ink) and the three copies of the official contract (black ink)—one for the woman's side, one for the man's side, and a "fixed copy" that would remain in the courthouse.

With that, the sheikh would begin to recite the formula (*sigha*) for marrying the couple. He would start with the verse from the Quran that now sits atop the marriage contract (30:21): "In the name of God the compassionate and the merciful: And of His signs is that He created for you from yourselves mates that you may find tranquility in them; and He placed between you affection and mercy. Indeed, in that are signs for a people who give thought." The sheikh would then transition to a popular *hadith*: "and the messenger of God (peace be upon him) said, 'A woman is married for four things, i.e., her wealth, her family status, her beauty and her religion. So you should marry the religious woman (otherwise) you will be a loser.'"[7] He would then ask the groom to "put your hand in the hand of your father's brother" so that the bride's father could repeat the following formula, the *ijab* (offer):[8] "I married you, my son [so-and-so], to my [virgin] daughter [so-and-so] for the agreed upon *mahr* and according to the book of God and the practices of God's messenger (Peace be Upon him)." Then the groom would be asked to repeat the following formula, the *qubul* (acceptance): "and I married your [virgin] daughter [so-and-so] for the agreed upon *mahr* and according to the book of God and the practices of God's messenger (Peace be Upon him)."[9]

After completing the formula, the sheikh (and I) would congratulate the men and shake their hands. The sheikh would tell the groom, "A thousand congratulations! Remember today's date: the date you cast off '*azubiyya* [bachelorhood/celibacy]." The sheikh would ask the couple if they prayed. Normally, the bride would say yes, and the groom would stammer out some sort of excuse. Sheikh Hussein (the contract writer with whom I worked most closely) was fond of seizing on this and chastising the young man by referring to a popular *hadith* that teaches "marriage is half of religion, but prayer is the other half."[10] Then, smiling and turning to the bride, he would instruct her, "You need to buy a whip and get him up every morning for the dawn prayer." As a final admonition, the sheikh would warn them that they were now married and that they should beware of divorce. He would explain that the contracts would be available for pickup the next week and then instruct them to pay a fee of JD 35 "for the state" and "whatever you want" for the employees.

Much of the court procedure is concerned with constituting and preserving evidence of the presence of the participants in fully embodied dimensions. The face, voice, and hands figure prominently. Messick's (1993) work on Yemeni court practices exaggerates and accentuates some constitutive features of the Jordanian case. He defines the *muwajaha* (the unimpeded face-to-face encounter) as the primary mode of governance in prerepublican Yemen. He notes a whole genre of social criticism that turned on derivations of the Arabic root *h-j-b*, with its connotations of seclusion, concealment, and, of course, veiling (*hijab*), to critique the tendency of rulers to grow distant from their subjects. Messick writes, "proper and just 'masculine' conduct is enacted through the regular presentation of one's face and through the secure medium of speech" as opposed to a "feminine" mode, which "relies on the concealment of the face and works through the dangerous medium of writing"

(1993, 173). This gendered structural opposition of the masculine seen and the feminine unseen also extended to types of evidence. According to Yemeni legal manuals and mirroring aspects of the distribution of cognition described by Abu Rizq in the first part of chapter 3, "contracts . . . conversion, witness evaluation and death" were the purview of men, whereas "female virginity, childbirth, menstruation, breast feeding, and [female] physical defects under clothes" (Messick 1993, 180) were part of the domain of women. Whereas Messick falls into the use of the English-language public-private dichotomy, it would perhaps be better to preserve the original Arabic vocabulary of *zahir* (seen) and *batin* (unseen) to keep close to the analytic categories of key social actors and, notably, the deeply embodied dimensions of that vocabulary.

Infelicities

What renders contracts believable and admissible as evidence under Islamic law is not some fetishistic regard for the written word but, to the contrary, recognition of the way in which a contract emerges from an agonistic and highly visible face-to-face encounter. The resulting contract carries with it the undeniable indexical linkages of stamp, fingerprint, handwriting, and/or signature that connect it to the bodies of known individuals and, by extension, the outward performance of volitional acts by the various principles (Messick 1993, 209–230). These, in turn, are connected to the hand that gives and the hand that receives. The best way to illustrate this orientation of court procedures toward the prevention of subsequent conflict is to focus on cases in which participants disagree openly and vociferously about the nature of their relationships. Such conflicts (which I refer to here as *infelicities*) help illustrate the powers and limits of court documents and procedures. J. L. Austin developed the idea of infelicities to understand how utterances like "I do" (e.g., in the context of a marriage ceremony) can actually "make it so" or fail to—given certain "felicity" conditions. A focus on infelicity highlights both the strength and the frailty of social orders in the face of various "abuses" and "misfires" (1975, 14–15). To borrow from a more materialist tradition, one could also look at these infelicities as "breakdowns" in the "information infrastructure" of the courts. As Susan Star argues, such infrastructure "becomes visible upon breakdown . . . the server is down, the bridge washes out, there is a power blackout. Even when there are backup mechanisms or procedures, their existence further highlights the now-visible infrastructure" (1999, 382). By focusing on tension, conflict, breakdown, and infelicity, it is possible to see the courthouse's antagonism toward the power of extended kin groups and their delegations and the ongoing coexistence of the two rival rituals for contracting a marriage.

At the most basic level, there were moments during fieldwork when the requirements of presence created more or less insurmountable obstacles to those hoping to marry. These ranged from the silly to the tragic. At the latter extreme was the case of the Syrian bride trying to marry a Jordanian man and escape the civil war tearing her home country apart. The Syrian embassy had sent her brother (her legal guardian) back to Syria to get some documents. En route, he was apprehended by the police and held incommunicado. The groom tried to put on a good face and initially told Hussein that "her father is dead, her brother is in Syria, but her cousin (father's brother's son) and mother are here." Hussein said that none of these would suffice. "Would you let your mother marry your sister?" he snapped. The man then snapped back, explaining the situation and ending by pointing to her (rather lanky) cousin in the hall, "They held that man for one month! He was one hundred kilos [220 pounds] before!" It was only by obtaining written proof from the Ministry of the Interior that she had no male relatives from her immediate family in the country that she could be married—"in the name of the court." At the more ridiculous extreme was the case of the man who declared that the woman's guardian was "really fat . . . too big to fit through the staircase." More intermediate were cases where fathers were far away on business for long periods of time. Mirroring the logic of the tribal delegation, families would generally try to cover up this discrepancy by multiplying relatives—as if a mother, two brothers, and a father's brother should make up for the lack of the father.[11] I never saw this gambit succeed.

The insistence on physical presence and face-to-face encounter is tied to particular assumptions about power relations and constellations of interest within the family. Men and women could encounter more or less coercive conditions in the setting of the contract. Although their presence in the courthouse (normally surrounded by mother, father, and other relatives) might not seem like the ideal context for judging consent, it probably opens up more opportunities for dissent than the setting established within the home for the traveling contract writer. A man once emphasized this to me by relating stories "from long ago" of families who dealt with reluctant brides by having a sister impersonate her recalcitrant sibling and consent to the marriage from behind a door or screen to fool the *ma'dhun* into believing the marriage was lawful. Such stories emphasize the fact that Sharia (much like other systems of law) must operate based on surface-level facts (the seen) while refusing to delve deeply into motives, intent, and the subtleties of indirect speech— thus Hussein's insistence that women loudly declare their intentions in contravention of other gendered ideals of feminine comportment. At times, Hussein would say, "Raise your voice, my sister!" Yet the system of guardianship still relies on the assumption that the interests of the bride and her guardian are aligned, if not unproblematically then at least more so than they are with any other figure who could be defined in the abstract for legal purposes.

No one believed that a woman's interests necessarily coincided with those of her guardian. In fact, employees at the Sharia courts often took it upon themselves to shame and cajole wayward guardians. Such men were often accused of "selling their women" and neglecting their financial obligations to them. Employees were aided in such (ostensible) activism by court procedures that required additional paperwork (i.e., threw up additional hurdles) for marriages that were known to involve a high probability of abuse and exploitation:[12] polygyny, young brides, and marriages involving foreigners. Despite their attempts to drag out the process and give women the opportunity to voice their displeasure, I never saw it happen. In fact, I remember a number of cases in which the male staff of the courthouse seemed much more scandalized than the women in question. In a particular case that sticks out in my mind, Hussein created hours' worth of paperwork for a particular guardian who had married one of his other sisters to a man who later proved to be quite abusive. In this case, however, the sister seemed happy to be marrying a wealthy old man who would likely be dead soon anyway—freeing her from her brother once and for all.

If the face, voice, and hands are intimately connected to the validity of the contract, so too are the conditions of its storage. The system of three contracts distributed among the two sides with a final fixed copy held by the court was designed to render documents like marriage contracts more convincing as evidence. However, as the following exchange illustrates, both employees and applicants of the court were quite nuanced in their appraisals of putative evidence.

Two women, a mother and daughter, walked into Hussein's office. The mother wore a flowing hood that draped down from her head to her stomach and a matching floor-length dress, all in a green floral pattern. Her daughter was about nineteen and wore a *hijab*. The daughter began, "There was a familial problem and they divorced me." Hussein replied "ignore it" (*la taruddi*; literally, "don't respond"). He then began to ask a series of questions to settle certain matters of fact while trying to put their minds at ease:

HUSSEIN: Is there consummation (*dukhul*)?
WOMEN: Yeah.
HUSSEIN: Is there pregnancy?
WOMEN: No.
HUSSEIN: What does your husband say?
MOTHER: He didn't say anything. But he only responds to his father.
HUSSEIN: Ignore it. Did you marry his father?
MOTHER AND DAUGHTER (SMILING A BIT): No.
HUSSEIN: Then ignore it. What's the *mahr*?
MOTHER: You had three thousand *mu'ajjal* (prompt) and five thousand *mu'ajjal* (deferred).
HUSSEIN: And you received it?
DAUGHTER: No. I didn't receive anything. Even the clothes!
HUSSEIN: If he divorced you, all of that is on his head.
MOTHER: But there are connections (*wastat*). . . . Can you make sure he hasn't already divorced her?
HUSSEIN: No, Hajji. There aren't any connections. That's impossible. No one can be divorced without knowing it.
DAUGHTER: I'm military. Thank God nobody is coercing me [to marry] (*fish hada yaghasibni*), but I have been engaged before—I divorced before consummation.
HUSSEIN: Don't be afraid. If you're a lawful woman and a woman of the people, don't be afraid.
DAUGHTER: How am I going to bring my possessions?
HUSSEIN: Ask. And if he doesn't respond, bring the police.

MOTHER: That will destroy everything. There's nothing without connections. . . .
HUSSEIN: What's his name?
MOTHER: _____
HUSSEIN: Oh. His relatives are in the pen [al-qalam; i.e., they are scribes]. Don't
   respond [la taruddi]. The judge won't respond to him. The judge only listens
   to the two partners.
MOTHER: But connections!
HUSSEIN: He's just a scribe. Don't be afraid of talk like that.

At this point, Hussein took the unusual step of talking to the employees who were related to the man in question (one of whom happened to be taking a sick day) and intimating that "with all of these corruption investigations" they should be careful and might want to consider getting a lawyer should they choose to involve themselves in this matter.

Even acknowledging such potential weak links in the chain of authentication should not mean reducing such documents to mere fetish objects with power that is merely a condensation of arbitrary social relations. Contracts are stored in bound books and numbered, making them difficult to remove or replace. The handwriting of the contract writer is distinctive, and it would raise eyebrows if different copies of the same contract were written in different hands or had signatures that looked markedly different from one another. Valid contracts must also bear official seals that, while perhaps more vulnerable to appropriation by wayward employees, are even harder for outsiders to forge. I should also emphasize how out of the ordinary this was during my months of participant observation at the courts, despite constantly being on the lookout for this sort of blurring of boundaries between formal and informal roles. The mere accusation caused a huge scene, the reverberations of which were palpable for weeks. However, I doubt this was due to the peculiar honesty of the employees (although they were fine people) but rather because of the elaborate safeguards I have described.[13]

More striking than the possibility of forgery is the notion that the contract can be understood as false in a certain sense about the prior particulars of the future arrangement (in this case, although the contract claims the mahr was paid, it had not been paid) but still be fundamentally valid. The reason is that, once again, assumptions about the felicity of documents in Islamic law are always conditional on the manner in which they emerge from face-to-face encounters. Although a contract might

In the name of God the compassionate and the merciful   Number

{And of His signs is that He created for you from yourselves mates that you may find tranquillity in them; and He placed between you affection and mercy. Indeed in that are signs for a people who give thought} Trust in God the Mighty

The Hashemite Kingdom of Jordan

The Sharia Courts in _____   Date of the Contract

Place of the contract _____

Stable Copy

		Name	Father	Grand-father	Family	Place and date of birth	Place of Residence	Citizen-ship	Reli-gion	Marital Status	Employ-ment	National Number
1	Groom											
	Bride											
2	Documents											
3	Bridewealth	Upfront										
		Delayed										
4	Payment of the bridewealth											
5	Those Present:											
6	Requirements											
7	Witnesses											
8	Agreement of the guardian or permission of the court											
9	Formula											

I am _____ [Judge] [Contract-Writer] in _____ I implemented this contract on the itemized side above after verifying the completion of the requirements and without prohibitions

Witness   Witness   The Groom or his Agent   The Bride or her Agent   The Legal Guardian   The Contract-Writer   Certification of the Judge

Figure 04_01. A translation of the contemporary contract form used by Jordan's Sharia courts.

be taken as sufficient proof of marriage (assuming no obvious signs of forgery), this does not mean that the particulars and especially the payment of *mahr* will be taken at face value. Nor will the acceptance of the fact that the *mahr* was fraudulently recorded on the contract as already paid invalidate the contract. Such moves, perhaps more in keeping with Anglo notions of contract law, would be seen as an unacceptable abridgment of the woman's rights—compounding the oppression (*zulm*) she suffered in being denied her right to *mahr* in the first place.

In short, the contemporary system of Sharia in Jordan is deeply concerned with establishing particular kinds of evidence of the agreement of particular individuals within a particular interactional context, and then registering that consent via indexical linkages that connect the document to the bodies of those present. The system then relies on the ability to securely store such documents and prevent their manipulation by relying on the assumed divergence of interests between the two sides to create a self-policing system in which neither the bride's nor the groom's side can alter the document without the other crying foul and immediately presenting compelling evidence to back up the accusation of forgery. The acceptance of documents as evidence, however, is always done with reservations. This should not be taken as a sign of backward enthrallment with the spoken word but rather as part and parcel of the jaundiced view of human behavior characteristic of Sharia practitioners that has been gained from over a millennium of hard-won experience.

CHANGING FORMS OF INDIVIDUAL
AND COLLECTIVE VOICE

As Messick (1993) emphasizes, Sharia is a diverse and often surprisingly polyglot legal discourse that is highly sensitive to time and place and endlessly adaptable. Crucial divergences exist between the historical context of the Jordanian case and that of the Yemeni case. Where Messick's interlocutors describe a deep history encompassed by what he calls *The Calligraphic State*, my own interlocutors emphasized the neglect of Ottoman rulers and the subsequent entry onto the political scene of the Hashemites and the British. More important, even during the twentieth century, there has been a good deal of change in Sharia court procedures. By focusing on the development of three fields on the marriage contract template in my archive spanning the years 1926–2011, it becomes apparent that Sharia courts have come to assert themselves more and more in the face of customs associated with the delegation. Whether focusing on the development of the field for the "agent," the *mahr*, or the "stipulations," the courts appear to be ever more directly and pointedly targeting many practices of extended kin groups that Islamic jurists have been criticizing for centuries. Foremost among these are questions surrounding women's consent to marriage, the payment of her *mahr*, and the insurance of her proper maintenance after marriage. As they problematize such issues, court procedures respond to and facilitate the elaboration of new forms of moral agent endowed with new forms of individual and collective voice. While these more individual forms of moral agent and voice assert themselves in the interactional space of the courthouse, the more collective forms of moral agent and voice tend to work through the aggregation and dissemination of statistics and the accompanying social commentary. In the past twenty years, the knowledge practices of the courts have contributed to the emergence of two new forms of moral agent: the spinster and the person divorced before the consummation of the marriage.

Genealogies of the Contract

The first form contracts in Jordan were introduced during the late Ottoman period in an explicit bid to conform more closely to Western notions of textual authority and bureaucratic administration. My systematic engagement with court records begins with the year 1926; however, my piecemeal and unsystematic knowledge of earlier Ottoman contract forms leads me to suspect that the trends I discuss hold true beginning somewhere around the 1880s.[14] Throughout this section, I recommend referring liberally to the image of the contract template and the accompanying translations. The early contracts are striking for how little involvement of the couple they evince. In many cases, there is no signature, stamp, or thumbprint from either bride or groom. For some, the consent of the two parties is not even mentioned: we merely learn of an agreement between the *wakil* (agent) of the bride and the agent of the groom. Even the earliest contracts attempt to elicit a fair amount of information about the various participants: name, age, place of residence, employment, and religion. The early contracts ask about the date of the contract, the witnesses, and the contract writer along with the *mahr*. Nevertheless, attempts to properly classify and enumerate nuptial exchanges have also had subversive effects as categories proliferate and, at times, come into their own as fully fledged moral agents.

Perhaps one of the most notable shifts in power relations catalyzed by court procedure is the change from *wakil* (agent) to *wali* (guardian) over the course of the twentieth century and the accompanying emergence of the bride as an indispensable party to the marriage contract. The earliest forms tend to downplay the role of the bride and make no mention of the guardian at all. The forms simply request that the contract writer record that the marriage was "accepted as legitimate as issued from" agents representing bride and groom. At the bottom of the earliest form, there are spaces for the "[agent of] the groom" and the "agent of the bride and receiver [of the *mahr*]" to sign.[15] This signified the assumption at the time that *mahr* would not go to the woman but rather to her agent. This intent was emphasized through the use of the formulaic phrase "received in the hand of the agent of the bride [so-and-so] with her permission" following the *mahr* in the majority of contracts.

My sample of 377 contracts from the Amman courthouse spanning the years 1926 to 1953 shows that in most cases, the agents were what would now be considered guardians. More than half of brides' agents were fathers. There are also a number of boundary cases in which the agent might have been what the contemporary court would consider the guardian, given the low life expectancies of the era: 21 percent of agents were brothers of the bride, 8 percent were father's brothers, 1 percent were grandfathers, and 1 percent of agents were father's brother's sons. In seventeen cases, the bride represented herself; in five cases, she represented herself, along with her father or brother acting in some sort of guarantor capacity. A sizable minority of contracts exist in which the agent clearly diverges from the guardian. In fully 11 percent of contracts, I can discern no relationship between the bride and her agent, despite the fact that every Arab name includes the names of the person's father and grandfather along with a family name. In addition, two contracts list the *ma'dhun* as the agent and six list the mother's brother—neither of which has ever had any particular standing in Islamic law. Even where the agent is listed as a relative through the patriline, there are clear examples in which the father appears in the contract as receiver of the *mahr* but not as the agent. Although the bride's role as an active agent in the contract process is muted in the early years, the groom's position has been more pronounced throughout the twentieth century. A full 88 percent of men in the sample of contracts acted as their own agent—clearly reflecting gendered assumptions about autonomy and consent.

A statistical approach and the discovery of regularities should not overly bias our understandings of the shifting role of the agent and the emergence of the guardian. Even if 90 percent of contracts involved the bride's guardian, her ability to marry without her guardian (for better or worse) is significant in understanding the grounds for the social recognition of marriage. Moreover, even a single contract can expand the definition of what is possible. In this regard, the most striking contract in my sample is contract number 12175. This contract concerns a young couple from Mahata (a village that was later incorporated into Amman) who married in 1952. The man was a twenty-one-year-old carpenter, and the woman was an eighteen-year-old virgin. No occupation is listed for her. Nevertheless, in this contract, she was listed not only as receiving her own *mahr* (a practice that was becoming more common at the time) but also as acting as her own agent despite being a virgin—a practice with which current court officials refuse to involve themselves. The presence of her father and brother is attested to, but, unlike other contracts, they served as mere witnesses. It is hard to know what circumstances led to this unique document's genesis, but it should serve as a reminder of how enumeration and record-keeping can create new social possibilities.

The *mahr* field of the contract shows similar tendencies of regimes of enumeration and classification to produce new categories and to help elaborate older sets of concerns among court officials about the status of emergent moral agents.[16] Up until the 1940s, the category of *mahr* is rather boring in the sample. With the exception of three contracts, it simply lists the amount of money or gold. The three outliers are "12 *'amm asuda'* [black headwraps]," "Plot of land worth 20 Palestinian Guineas and 15 head of goat worth 10 Palestinian Guineas," and "5 plots of land rented for 2 years at a price of 16 lira; 4 lira of wheat, 20 lira of labor." The amount of *mahr* paid was surprisingly consistent during the early years—suspiciously so. No matter the currency (Ottoman lira, Palestinian guineas, Palestinian lira), the amount of prompt *mahr* remained within a consistent and narrow band. It actually converged ever more closely on the number thirty over the course of the 1920s and 1930s before exploding in diversity during the 1940s. The recurrence of one number over and over in the contracts implies that the field was being treated by officials and applicants at court as pro forma and not taken seriously. In at least one case, I was able to find the son of a man who was a party to one such "thirty in *mahr*" contract.[17] Without any prompting, the man told me that his father "was an expensive man. He gave thirty-five *dunum* [thirty-five thousand square meters] of land as *mahr*." When I told him the amount of *mahr* written on the contract, he seemed unconcerned with the discrepancy ("a dunum was like a lira"). In fact, after looking through sixty-seven contracts involving members of a single local tribe, I found that every single one of them had the same *mahr* (thirty Palestinian guineas received in the hand of her guardian with her permission), and there was no evidence of the ubiquitous mentions of land transfers as *mahr* that I found in the oral historical record.

In the 1940s, everything changed, implying an explosion of interest on the part of applicants and court officials about *mahr*; suddenly, *mahr* payments are all over the map, and many include long and involved lists of home furnishings. The following entry is perhaps the most precise but also indicative of the era: "50 Guinea Wardrobe with mirror; 18 Guinea for 6 chairs; 40 Guinea Carpet; 10 Guinea Bed; 30 Guinea for 2 Wool Mattresses, 2 Cotton Blankets, 4 Wool Pillows, 3 small tables; 50 Guinea radio; 1 kilo" (I can only assume the contract writer got impatient at this point in the list of *mahr*). My initial hypothesis was that as the state grew in power, it would begin recording the arrangements of those outside of the cash economy—providing a record of "traditional" *mahr* exchanges. In fact, the early contracts show no such evidence.

When people do begin enumerating the *mahr* in detail, it is not peasants or farmers (those who it turns out are most likely to record thirty of something) but rather those members of the community most closely aligned with the market and the state: merchants, soldiers, and government employees. By the 1950s, this practice of listing the various objects had fallen out of fashion, but the new forms also introduced a new category: *tawaba'a* (nonmonetary *mahr*). These gifts were inevitably recorded in monetary terms (e.g., so many dinar for clothes, so many dinar for furniture, so many dinar for gold). There seems to have been an insistence that some amount of money be placed in the monetary field, which led to the practice of writing "one Jordanian dinar" in the field for monetary *mahr* and then enumerating the actual *mahr* in the *tawaba'a* field.[18] During my fieldwork, nearly a decade after the category of *tawaba'a* was abandoned, people were still regularly showing up to court and specifying "one Jordanian dinar" in addition to much larger amounts of furniture, gold, and clothing, implying the depth of the mutual adjustment between courthouse officials and applicants.

Much as with the *mahr* field, the stipulations field seems to indicate that people tend to abhor an unused or underutilized field on a form almost as much as they abhor an overly baroque field. The stipulations field appears with the 1950s revamp of the contracts and, to say the least, never made up a large percentage of the contracts—only 13 contracts involve stipulations in the primary Madaba courthouse sample out of a total of 355. In addition, a single contract from the Amman courthouse dated 1945 (before the introduction of a dedicated field for stipulations) involving a local trader stipulates "2000 Guinea [extra *mahr*] if they leave Amman." Counting this contract as an early attempt by applicants and a particular *ma'dhun* to add a stipulation to the contract, that makes a total of 14 contracts out of the overall sample of 877 involving stipulations. Nevertheless, the existence of the field seemed to exert marked effects. When I broached the topic of stipulations, men would often scoff that no one should marry someone if they trusted them so little that they felt the need to make such stipulations. Others felt it was an abridgment of their rights to marry four women or move around as they saw fit. However, the mere requirement that court employees ask about such issues obviously provoked intrafamilial discussion and influenced the course of events, as the following exchange illustrates:

HUSSEIN: How much is the *mahr*?

[Silence]

HUSSEIN: You agreed beforehand, right?

GROOM: Put one Jordanian dinar. . . . Five thousand dinars gold for the *mu'ajjal* [prompt *mahr*] and ten thousand *mu'ajjal* [deferred *mahr*].[19] . . .

WITNESS (A RANDOM PERSON FROM THE COURTHOUSE): Blessings, God willing.[20]

GROOM: Actually, I stipulated it. They said three thousand, but I said five thousand.

HUSSEIN: Stipulations?

[Silence]

HUSSEIN (NOT SURE IF THIS WAS SERIOUS): Should I put that he can only marry once?

UNCLE: Can you do that?

HUSSEIN: It just means that marrying a second wife would divorce him from his
  first.
MOTHER: Put "finish her studies."
HUSSEIN: She's in university? What year?
BRIDE: Fourth year.
HUSSEIN: Has the *mahr* been received?
GROOM: Not yet.

As this exchange shows, an initial impetus to enumerate and document *mahr* has, over time, dragged the government ever more deeply into internal familial dynamics while opening up new grounds for contesting the legitimate role of various moral agents.

The increasing interest of courthouse procedures regarding brides, guardians, *mahr*, and stipulations puts the courts somewhat at odds with the goals and aims of the delegation. The emergent courthouse procedures are designed to foster new forms of ever more individuated voice within the interactional setting of the face-to-face encounters that are central to all marriage contracts involving the Jordanian Sharia courts. Following on centuries of juridical commentary about the depredations that tribal customs are believed to inflict on women, court procedures increasingly fixate on questions of consent, the payment of *mahr*, and stipulations for the wife's appropriate maintenance after marriage. Whether or not brides (or their male guardians or grooms) are able to effectively articulate their individual aspirations through these voicing mechanisms represents another matter—one that I am hesitant to adjudicate. In many respects, it is impossible to do so without also looking at the forms of collective voice that emerge as data about marriage are aggregated through statistics and turned into fodder for new modes of social criticism. This allows those who mobilize such data to claim to speak on behalf of social categories constituted largely through court procedures themselves.

The Islamic Movement and the Reappropriation of Sharia Court Data

The impulse for enumeration, at times coming from applicants and at times coming from court officials, has slowly enmeshed the Sharia courts, the Jordanian state, and something we can only call "Jordanian society" within a system of accountability not fully of their own devising.

An Islamic nongovernmental organization called the Chastity Society (al-ʿafaf) epitomizes this trend because it uses the published statistics of the courts to highlight and develop two novel moral agents: the spinster and the person divorced before the consummation of the marriage. The Chastity Society's publications are filled with direct references to the statistics contained in the annual reports produced by the Sharia courts as the society seeks to raise awareness about what it sees as a crisis of marriage. The Chastity Society is quite willing to take statistics from anywhere to bolster its case—the Jordanian Department of Statistics, the United Nations, and the Sharia courts of neighboring countries all figure prominently in its bibliographies. But what makes this form of marriage crisis discourse notably different from earlier iterations is the way in which the Sharia court's system of record-keeping focuses attention on processes of governance and the state itself.[21] It also molds the terms of the debate into a more Islamic cast, and with the idea of a crisis of divorce before consummation, the knowledge practices of the courts become the condition of possibility for significant aspects of the emergent marriage crisis.

One of the first indicators that activists working with the Chastity Society tend to use in publications about this crisis of marriage is the annual number of marriage contracts. ʿAdal Badraneh's (2009) *The Guide: Indicators of Marriage and Divorce in Jordan* (*Ad-Dalil: Muʿashshirat Az-Zawaj wa At-talaq fi Al-Urdan*) is typical. He begins with the "First Indicator: General Rate of Marriage." This is calculated using the following formula: 1000 × (number of marriage contracts in a particular year / population in the same year). Beneath the formula, Badraneh credits his sources: "Sharia Courts and Churches." In the early years of the Chastity Society, the figures were quite compelling. In Faruq Badran and Mufid Sarhan's (1999) *Spinsterhood: The Reality, the Causes, and the Solutions* (*Al-ʿanusiyya: -Al-Waqaʿ -Al-Asbab -Al-Halul*), the first table details a secular decline from a rate of 10.1 marriages per year per thousand people in 1993 to 8.1 in 1998.

By 2009, when *The Guide* was published, the rate of marriage was increasing, and the political opponents of the Chastity Society were responding with their own reports. As I described in the opening pages of this book, I was warned early on that this "crisis of marriage" was little more than an attempt by the Muslim Brotherhood to make the Jordanian government look bad. These intellectuals were armed with their own numbers and argued that the crisis of marriage was a sort of ideological displacement of broader anxieties about social change in the region—specifically, relating to shifting gender roles, new technology, and economic challenges.

Keeping track of the number of marriage contracts makes it possible for outside groups to hold the state accountable in ways that would otherwise be unthinkable. The issue is more than the mere existence of an embarrassing set of figures here or there. The fact that activists from the Chastity Society continued to foreground the number of marriage contracts and the rate of marriage long after it ceased to unambiguously bolster their argument calls into question a simple reading of their appropriation of official statistics as opportunistic. Building on the earlier work of Jürgen Habermas, Michael Warner (2002) has proposed the concept of the "counterpublic" to describe the ways in which the circulation of media can help construct both communities and oppositional associations of critics. I would argue that contracts are one such media: the circulation of contracts helps construct various categories of moral agent (the agent, the guardian, the spinster, the person divorced before consummation, and maybe even the Jordanian citizen) who can then hold the state accountable to various Islamic standards.

It could also be argued that quantifying media like contracts (perhaps more than other media) can help create such moral agents. As Theodore Porter notes in *Trust in Numbers: The Pursuit of Objectivity in Science and Public Life,* "adequate measurement, clearly, means disciplining people as well as standardizing instruments and processes" (1996, 28). As Badraneh makes clear, the point of the exercise is to understand "the effect of economic and social factors in interpreting this phenomenon" (2009, 36). Without a state collecting such data in such a minutely disciplined fashion, it would be much more difficult to argue for the existence of a coherent economy and society that should be refashioned in accordance with a specific political agenda. In this case, it turns out that the state's systematic collection of data about the population serves a coordinating function for potential dissidents, political opportunists, and malcontents alike.

A second highly abstracted moral agent that owes even more to the court's knowledge practices is the person divorced before the consummation of the marriage. In recent years, the court's annual statistical report (*At-Taqrir Al-Ihsa'i As-Sanawi*) has included a breakdown of divorces into four categories: divorce before consummation (*at-talaq qabl ad-dukhul*), revocable divorce (*at-talaq al-raja'i*), and two levels of irrevocable divorce (*at-talaq al-ba'in*).[22] In this case, two things are striking: the increasing prevalence of divorce (representing a 25% increase from twelve thousand per year in 2006 to fifteen thousand per year in 2010) and the increasing precision with which people's social statuses are being recorded and taken up as sociological categories by both activists and relatively apolitical citizens. This is not to imply that the interest in social status is novel. To the contrary, despite the lack of an actual field for social status in the early contracts, my sample of contracts from the Amman Courthouse only includes thirteen contracts that failed to reveal some information about this topic. Of the 377 sampled, 348 used one of two terms: 270 brides are classified as virgin (*bikr*) and 78 are classified as previously married (*thayyib*). Nine are classified with euphemistic circumlocutions like "girl," "woman," or "woman of the house." What is striking is that of all 377 samples, only four women are classified as divorcees and only one woman is classified as a widow; these terms came into regular use in the 1950s. In another case, we learn that the woman was previously married to the same man.[23] The circumlocutions are gone now, but divorce before consummation has become a recognized social category since the late 1990s, joining the categories of *divorcee* and *widow* that came into wide use in the 1950s. All of them now appear in court documents and in everyday conversation. People who are divorced before consummation occupy a liminal status: they *could* have lost their virginity but claim that nothing transpired in the time between the signing of the contract and the wedding that never happened. Divorce before consummation is a new and growing category that is attracting attention and focusing broader and more diffuse anxieties; according to annual reports I saw in the courts, it made up more than 40 percent of total divorces in 2010.

The category of divorced before consummation represents a new stage in the ongoing negotiations between the ritual of the delegation

and that of the court-sanctioned marriage contract. Unlike the tempo-
ral dilation implied by the customary model, which creates a liminal
waiting period for the couple between the delegation and the wedding
when their social status is ambiguous, court officials are adamant that
the contract itself creates a marital bond. Nonetheless, court officials
continue to be forced to accommodate the practices of people who insist
on treating the wedding and consummation as the final constitutive act
forming the legitimate marital bond. To understand the significance of
this compromise, it is important to attend to the role of female Islamic
activists in working with the courts to construct those divorced before
consummation as the kind of moral agent endowed with a collective
voice that can make demands on the courts, families, the state, and society more broadly.

It would be a mistake to overplay the tensions between Islamic activists and the courts. Much as the proliferation of categories can be used
to critique the Jordanian government, the categories can also be used to
critique Jordanian society. In this respect, activists and the courts can
prove to be great allies. One example is Amal 'Abdeen's (2010) *Divorce
before Marriage and in the First Year of Marriage: Social and Psychological Causes and Effects (At-Talaq Qabl Ad-Dukhul wa fi As-Sana Al-Uwla
min Az-Zawaj: Al-Asbab wa Al-athar An-Nafsiyya wa Al-Ijtima'iyya).*[24]
Her study for the Chastity Society, which she makes clear was possible
because of the support of the Supreme Judge Department, attempts to
understand the troubling increase in the divorce rate and particularly
the increasingly prevalent phenomenon of divorce before consummation. After giving some background statistics from the usual sources, she
gives the results of her survey of fifty women divorced before consummation and fifty women divorced in the first year. According to 'Abdeen,
"the findings indicate that the most important reason for divorce among
the divorced is a bad match, followed by familial interference, then lack
of bearing responsibility, followed by subordination of the husband to
his mother or another member of his family" (17). 'Abdeen ultimately
advocates for "consciousness-raising" (*taw'iya*) through the media and
the relevant ministries, including more "guidance for willing individuals" from the courts "before the case gets to the Judge" (152) and more
research. Through her use of survey technology, she gives voice (after

a fashion) to the aspirations and concerns of a particular sort of moral agent, itself an emergent effect of the knowledge practices of the courts as they seek to come to terms with the local practices.

'Abdeen (2010) provides an eminently contestable diagnosis of the "problem" of divorce before consummation in Jordan, but her work involves a kind of contestation that has become thinkable only through long-term engagement with particular kinds of knowledge practices for enumeration, individuation, and data storage. The Islamic movement may try to position itself as a critical interlocutor vis-à-vis the state; however, it also seeks to position itself as a moral alternative to the "tribal" system exemplified by the delegation, which was described in the beginning of part 2. Islamic activists, like Islamic jurists, work to redistribute agency, cognition, and personhood itself within and outside of kinship structures. The goal of this chapter has not been to deliberate on the best distribution but rather to understand the practical, material, and embodied means by which various individuals, collectives, institutions, and political movements attempt to wrest people from their preexisting relationships and commitments and reconfigure their affiliations. In contemporary Jordan, these court and delegation rituals continue to coexist despite the obvious tensions.

NOTES

1. Following Foucault but also diverging from him, Hacking (1982) argues that Foucault followed a polarization in the governance of life between "anatamo-politics" (focused on the individual body) and "bio-politics" (focused on what Foucault called "the species body" of statistically enumerable human communities). Hacking cautions that the erotics of the former can distract from the mundane and subtle but nonetheless pervasive powers of the latter, which he describes in terms of "subversive effects."

2. Adding vowels to a written word can substantively change its meaning. For instance, the plaque in Hussein's office contained a special diacritic over the first letter lest people confuse *ra'is al-kuttab* (the head scribe) with *ra'is al-kitab* (head of the book). Such ambiguities are ubiquitous in Arabic, although context generally mitigates the problem.

3. In fact, witnesses were often drawn at random from the crowd of courthouse applicants, which would (under normal circumstances) make them quite difficult to find if the contract was ever called into question. This problem was ameliorated to some degree by the incredible standardization and precision of the contemporary court procedure and the more or less unassailable integrity of contemporary court officials, who are generally too distant from the affairs they handle to be considered interested parties.

4. In the parlance of the contemporary courts, *virgin, never-married woman,* and *girl* are synonymous.

5. People did, however, have interesting theories about why I was there. My favorite was, "That's the supervisor from the US embassy." Everyone involved was aware that US imperialism makes my research possible, but that did not mean that people were necessarily pessimistic about its outcomes. Most believed that my honest attempts to understand Islam could only have positive effects: perhaps it would increase cross-cultural understanding, help humanize the victims of US military aggression in the eyes of my countrymen, or even lead to my personal salvation by showing me the true religion.

6. I could go on at length about the various manipulations that documents prevent, but given space constraints, I will mention only the most notorious: lying about the bride's age, pretending the groom is gainfully employed when he is not (although this is still possible to some degree under the current documentary regime), and trying to mask the existence of particular individuals lest they become subject to taxation or conscription.

7. This is exactly the same formula that Abu Yehea used in the *jaha* (Muslim 2007, 119).

8. Although many men do marry the daughter of their father's brother, the employees at the courthouse explained that by marrying a man's daughter, all young men become their fathers-in-law's nephews.

9. The formula, while varying a bit from employee to employee and ceremony to ceremony, began with the *ijab* (offer) from the father, for example: *ana zawwajtak ya ibni fulan ila binti fulana al-bikr 'ala al-mahr al-musama wa 'ala kitab allah wa sunnat rasul allah salla allah 'alayuh wa'alihi wa sallam.* It was then followed by a *qubul* (acceptance), for example: *wa ana zawwajtu bintak fulana al-bikr 'ala al-mahr al-musama wa 'ala kitab allah wa sunnat rasul allah salla allah 'alayuh wa'alihi wa sallam.*

10. This *hadith* championing the importance of marriage, along with another in the following pages cautioning against high *mahr* payments, are both associated among my better informed interlocutors with Muhammad Al-Albani and his *Targhib wa Tarhib* (2000, 404–407). A self-taught twentieth scholar who positioned himself in opposition to the formal legal guilds, Al-Albani became a leading figure in the *salafi* movement, which seeks to purify Islam of later accretions. He settled in Jordan in his later years, where he was an influential figure. Ironically, neither of these purported sayings of the prophet are particularly well attested to by the earliest scholars.

11. For more on Jordan's system of guardianship, see Afaf Jabiri's (2016) *Gendered Politics and Law in Jordan: Guardianship over Women.*

12. Some projects aimed at implementing Sharia, like the Sharia Council set up by the Birmingham Central Mosque and staffed largely by women with backgrounds in domestic violence prevention (Bowen 2016, 123–142), are self-consciously grounded in an activist tradition. However, I would not want to exaggerate the altruism of Jordanian court officials or label them as "activists." They could also be difficult or lenient simply because they were in a good or bad mood or wanted to show their power (or just counteract the boredom of their jobs). Nonetheless, the dominant idiom for all decisions was the protection of the vulnerable (women and children), even if what happened in practice was nothing of the sort. Indeed, as Antoun noted in his study of the courts, in certain cases, "The remarkable fact is that legislation to protect women has been turned

against them" (1980, 463). In a fascinating analysis of the impact of colonial state policies on gender relations in India, Flavia Agnes argues that, despite a rhetoric of saving women, "The colonial interventions served to usher in a new patriarchal legal order that legitimized several traditional antiwomen practices and recast them into a new modernity through a complex interface of contest and collusion between colonial and local indigenous patriarchies" (2009, 20). Seeing such parallel responses to the changing role of women in society emerging among Hindus in colonial India should underscore that this phenomenon is not uniquely Islamic.

13. Agrama has argued (following Asad 2003, 124; 2004, 282–283) that modern liberal law is defined by a certain pervasive suspicion "that transforms the gap between law and its application into a constant problem in need of solution" (2012, 131). He contrasts this with strains within the Islamic tradition that have found ways of thinking about the nonapplication of law as a good thing (rather than a bad thing) (143–145). Whether or not my own suspicions about the application of Islamic law may have reflected my own previously engrained biases, I did not find the Sharia courts I encountered to be wracked by the sorts of suspicions I came expecting to find and that Agrama reported in his own ethnographic findings about the Egyptian courts (131–141). People were not blind or overly credulous, but their confidence in the ultimate robustness of the system seemed well placed. Even when it came to the widespread lack of faith in the veracity of the information about the *mahr* that was recorded on contracts, court officials were sanguine that it would be worked out should problems arise (although it would undoubtedly complicate things). The overwhelming sense I got was that everyone at the courts went home and slept soundly at night.

14. A number of Jordanians have kindly shared marriage contracts with me from their family archives that date back to the late nineteenth and early twentieth centuries that were issued by the Jerusalem courthouse. I also had an opportunity to look through the archives of the Salt Courthouse during my preliminary research where I found bound notebooks of contracts dating back to the 1880s.

15. In the earliest contracts, contract writers would add the word *agent* to the form above the stamp, thumbprint, or signature of the groom's agent as necessary. This changed with the revamping of the contracts in the 1950s and has remained the same subsequently; the form is now phrased, "the groom or his agent."

16. For more on how women in the Arab world have long pursued complex and intricate strategies to maximize their *mahr* and secure it for posterity, see the work of Martha Mundy (1979), Diane Singerman (1995, 109–121), Tomas Gerholm (1985), and Annelies Moors (1995). All emphasize the tendency of women to cede certain claims (e.g., their inheritance in land) to male kin in return for other forms of support— although there may be a coercive dimension to these decisions, and women can suffer consequences for violating these norms (Moors 2003, 104).

17. I often asked myself (and anyone who would listen), Why thirty, three hundred, or three thousand (the most common numbers)? No one had any idea. The number three shows up with alarming frequency for reasons no one can explain. Initially, I was convinced I must have been entering the data incorrectly. But after double- and triple-checking, I determined that the discovery must be an effect of the confluence of the peculiar knowledge practices of both the courts and myself. The number three does have a lot of significant resonance—the number of days of the wedding and the number of days one is expected to provide hospitality—but no one made those connections

without my mentioning them. Based on a similar mix of evidence, Mundy and Smith similarly report that the going rate in the 1930s along the East Bank was "between ten and thirty liras"—although the reality was always far more variegated and uneven (2003, 125). They argue that this was a transitional period in which cash was becoming the dominant medium of exchange, displacing the role of other goods like olive trees, clothes, furniture, and, for a brief time, land.

18. Annelies Moors (1995) discusses the emergence and divergent meanings of the "token" *mahr* payment of "one dinar" in *Women, Property and Islam: Palestinian Experiences 1920–1990*. She argues that the practice was embraced across the class spectrum but with very different meanings, with the wealthy seeking to constitute their relationships on the basis of gift-giving, whereas the poor framed the issue more as "taking one's chances" (Moors 1995, 106–113; 2008; 2011, 27–33). In seeking to combine both the token *mahr* and the enumeration of noncash "gifts" (although, ironically, often enumerated in cash), people express their ambivalence about the nature of marriage as "exchange." Moors observes that by registering household goods, "some sort of balance is achieved between showing disinterest in the material side of marriage (attempting to claim a higher status through registering a 1 JD dower [*mahr*]) on the one hand, and including some legal guarantees on the other" (1995, 125).

19. Here, the man used the same words that are used on the contract (*mu'ajjal* and *mu'ajjal*) as opposed to the more colloquial *muqaddam* and *mu'akhkhar*.

20. This seems like a none-too-subtle insult: in the words of one purported saying of the prophet that was in wide circulation at the time of research, *qallal al-mahr wa kaththar al-baraka*: decrease the *mahr* and increase the blessing (of the marriage). Although this is likely a bowdlerization of a somewhat weak *hadith* recorded in *Sahih al-Jami' As-saghir* (1182) that reads *a'zim an-nisa' baraka aysirhuna mu'ana* (Al-Sana'ai 2011, 503; cf. Al-Albani 2000, 405) and basically translates as "the greatest blessing for women is simplifying their provision," it nonetheless reflects the lengths to which some men would go to exert social pressure on each other to avoid inflating *mahr* payments— supposedly for women's sake. Most men told me not to pay attention to *mahr* at all. At the same time, women went out of their way to emphasize the importance of attending to *mahr*, and I never heard a woman complain about inflation in the cost of *mahr* payments.

21. In Hanan Kholoussy's (2010) *For Better, for Worse: The Marriage Crisis that Made Modern Egypt*, statistics are notably absent, which does not stop people from complaining about a crisis of bachelorhood or spinsterhood. Yet it seems to render the crisis more diffuse. As a result, the culprits seem more like the stuff of quotidian family dramas. The colonial state is largely ignored in favor of critiques of overprotective parents, feckless young men, and finicky young women.

22. Ironically, divorce before consummation has had a more successful career as a category in the courts' data collection system than the more formally recognized— although also incredibly controversial—category of *khul'* divorce. This form of divorce is initiated by the woman, who agrees to give up her *mahr* claims in return for immediate separation. As a form of divorce, it is widely attested to in the historical record of the premodern Levant. Forced through over the opposition of Parliament in 2001 during a period when the king had dissolved the body, this "temporary law" has languished as a political football, kicked back and forth between the upper and lower houses of parliament (Warrick 2009, 116–124; Welchman 2009, 138–144). If the Sharia courts keep

any statistics about *khul'*, they are not included in the courts' annual reports and are not widely available—although Warrick notes that an article in the government newspaper *ad-dustur* in 2006 alleged, without citing any sources, that 80% of divorce cases were *khul'* divorces (2009, 122).

23. Presumably, he divorced her, they separated, and he never completed the three utterances of the wish to divorce necessary to render it irrevocable. However, he did wait until the three-menstrual-cycle waiting period had ended to reconcile with his estranged wife, thus necessitating a new contract and a new *mahr* payment.

24. This work was originally written as a master's thesis at Jordan University before being published by the Chastity Society.

Part 3

The Wedding: Privatizing Joys?

5

The Feast

*Tonight we set up the tent. Tomorrow there is dancing and tea and coffee.
Then on Thursday we will have the procession (farida). We will drive
to ... the bride's house. The bride and her mother will come back to [our
village] with us. When she is here, we will shoot guns and there will be more
singing and dancing. Then we will have the groom's shower (hammam).
We will eat kunafa [a kind pastry made with phyllo dough, sugar and
cheese] and drink Pepsi (bibsi).*[1] *After the shower, we will go back to the
tent for more dancing and tea. Then comes the wedding procession (zifaf):
we will carry the groom to the women's area. Then he goes in and dances
with the bride. They go to his room. He sometimes serves her some food.
Sometimes some juice. Sometimes, they wait 3 days. Sometimes it happens
that night. Then, on the last day of the wedding, everyone eats mutton.*
—FARIS, DESCRIBING AN UPCOMING WEDDING
TO A FOREIGN ANTHROPOLOGIST

AS IN MOST TIMES AND PLACES, WEDDINGS IN CONTEMPORARY
Jordan serve as a rite of passage tied to the legitimization of marital
unions and the children those unions produce. Yet weddings in Jordan
are also increasingly used to embody particular sets of commitments to
competing visions of Jordan's future. The model of wedding described
by Faris (which aligns with objectified tradition and the prerogatives
of the extended family) no longer goes unchallenged. With the elite
leading the way, a growing percentage of urbanites from across the economic spectrum have come to prefer abbreviated two-hour weddings at
purpose-built wedding halls or hotel ballrooms. Meanwhile, participating in a trend in the broader Muslim world (Jad 2009), the Islamic charity
the Chastity Society has begun organizing mass weddings that are even

more pointedly and explicitly designed in opposition to traditional models of wedding. The emergence of new, competing models of wedding represents dynamism in what could be called, following Lamia Karim (2008), an "economy of shame" around weddings and marriage in Jordan, challenging not just the norms of hospitality at such events but the very essence of the relations that such events are supposed to produce. With the emergence of multiple, mutually antagonistic ritual frameworks for marriage, the grounds of social struggle and contestation expand from being primarily indexical (who has the most meat and the most guests) to encompass important choices about iconically representing one's allegiance to a certain vision of Jordan's future and accompanying networks of patronage, care, and mutual defense.

Unfortunately for participants, consciously pressing weddings into the service of such an ideological struggle carries certain hazards of representation (Keane 1997). For one thing, the necessity of actually enacting rituals like weddings ensures that all sorts of exigencies tied to their materiality can impinge on the consciously ideological projects that increasingly motivate them, like a can of Pepsi or a car in the midst of an otherwise rustic and traditionalistic tableau.

In Jordan, just as marriage proposals have been and continue to be large communal projects that create various kinds of social affinities, debts, and antagonisms, so too are weddings endlessly generative sites through which the social order either produces and reproduces itself or gives way to something new. In the case of weddings, the chief constraint is currently conceptualized as material.

Looking back at Faris's description of the wedding from the perspective of people who often make $400 per month or less, the extravagance of the event looms large: the tent, the tea and coffee, the gas for the cars, the bullets, sweets, Pepsi, and meat. Such commodities circulate globally and, in many cases, track global commodities prices closely: the prices of tea, coffee, gas, bullets, and Pepsi in Jordan are comparable to those in the United States despite the disparity in wages. Whereas even middle-class Americans might balk at the prospect of providing such hospitality for hundreds of people, the relative cost for most Jordanians is downright exorbitant. In some cases, most notably when it comes to meat, the high cost of food and land in Jordan conspires to make commodities far more expensive than they would be in the United States; the cost of local meat in the market in Madaba rose from JD 8 per kilo in summer 2010 to JD 13 per kilo in summer 2012 (or from $11.28 to $18.33: JD 1 was $1.41 at the time of research). As a result, the role of meat in weddings represents a powerful and often remarked-upon indicator of the economic restructuring that Jordan is undergoing. It is an effective metonym for the ways in which population growth, urbanization, refugee influxes, privatization, and austerity create a denser, more crowded polity in which the struggle for resources and survival demands ever more in terms of money, time, and energy—the struggle at the heart of part 1 of the book.

In the first chapter of part 3, I argue that in the context of this broader economic transformation, weddings increasingly emphasize ideological struggle and enter the mass-mediated realm of global public culture. Elites in particular participate in the elaboration of an "economy of shame" around weddings, through which older notions of honor and shame are "instrumentalized" (Karim 2008) to serve a novel, increasingly capitalistic order. In a cruelly ironic twist for the rural poor, those with differential access to capital are suddenly able to exceed their more parochial neighbors in their fealty to certain aspects of traditional standards of honor—both because they can afford it and because they can then use aspects of traditional standards of honor against those already marginalized. The proliferation of distinct, antagonistic models of wedding and the discourse around them indicates a high degree of self-consciousness about the ways in which weddings legitimate not just individual marital unions but an entire social, economic, and political order. The increasing focus on the wedding as a tool of ideological struggle may even magnify the hazards of representation associated with weddings, as it has with other forms of ritualized hospitality in Jordan (cf. Shryock 2004b). Just as promise and hazard are two sides of the same coin, so it is easy to see how the promise of welcome entails the hazard of trespass; the promise of affinity entails the hazard of antagonism; the promise of honor entails the hazard of shame; the promise of generosity entails the hazard of greed. When weddings are expected to legitimate not just individual marital unions but an entire sociopolitical order on an enlarged stage, the stakes are perceived as even higher, and any incidence of trespass, antagonism, shame, or greed is all the more explosive for its publicity. In chapter 6, I show how the Chastity Society has taken the wedding ritual as a relatively popular, grassroots phenomenon and reorganized it to draw out these very hazards and opportunities in a way that undermines the rural, tribal, traditionalist sociopolitical order with which it contends. But where the members of the Chastity Society portrayed themselves as freeing youths from parochial bonds of debt obligation, their detractors portrayed the society as nothing but a competing network of patronage. In this way, enactments of Jordanian weddings become a form of semiotic struggle over the future of their participants and Jordan as a whole.[2]

THE WEDDING AS SEMIOTIC STRUGGLE

To emphasize the sheer geographic scope of the shift in wedding practices, it is useful to contrast the changes unfolding in Jordan with a perceptive study of weddings among Greek Cypriots entitled *Tradition and Modernity in the Mediterranean: The Wedding as Symbolic Struggle,* which the anthropologist Vassos Argryou (1996) conducted in the late 1980s and early 1990s. He argues that Cypriot weddings "have been transformed from rites of passage to rites of class distinction." Argryou focuses on four major changes to Cypriot weddings: a shortening of duration, an increasing number of guests, the abandonment of the "ritual display of the bride's virginity," and a polarization of wedding types between two poles.[3] The rural and urban working-class "village wedding" is increasingly contrasted with a new truncated ceremony preferred by urban elites that is hosted in a hotel and eschews a full meal in favor of light snacks and beverages (Argryou 1996, 10–11). Both Cyprus and Jordan have a third type of wedding (favored by urbanites who aspire to join the upper classes) that mixes elements of both—normally involving an open celebration in a hall for one's acquaintances and a separate, more intimate gathering for the purpose of shared commensality. These changes are remarkably similar to changes in Jordan, arguably, for many of the same reasons: because wedding celebrations in Jordan, like Cyprus, increasingly express "antagonisms, mainly between social classes, but also between villagers and city dwellers, as well as between the generations" (Argryou 1996, 171). At least in Jordan, many of these antagonisms are both long-standing and have their limits—especially when they bump up against the continued necessity of maintaining older networks of clientage and the persistence of the wedding as a rite of legitimation and passage.[4]

My introduction to Jordanian weddings as part of that rural system of clientage was almost imperceptible. As a Peace Corps volunteer, I attended engagements and weddings on a regular basis from virtually the moment I arrived, as they were one of the primary venues for village sociality. I estimate that I have attended well over fifty Jordanian weddings in my lifetime. The vast majority have been large, outdoor weddings that lasted multiple days and involved hundreds of guests, dancing, pyrotechnics, and a lot of meat. Although such weddings are increasingly rare in Jordan, it is easy for a foreign anthropologist to end up at one: they are open events, they welcome all guests, and, most important, Jordanians immediately recognize them as the kind of event that an American visitor can and should be interested in.

Weddings exist along the border of a zone of "cultural intimacy" that produces a mixture of social solidarity and acute embarrassment vis-à-vis the potentially judging gaze of outsiders (Herzfeld 1997; Shryock 2004a, 2004b). Despite receiving invitation after invitation to such weddings, I am highly cognizant of the fact that they represent a dwindling minority of weddings as new commercial wedding halls have continued to open their doors on a regular basis across Jordan. It was much more rare that I attended weddings in such wedding halls (e.g., my sample size is four), which normally lasted a few hours. These ranged in size from 80 guests to hundreds. Aside from these two types of wedding typical among average working Jordanians, I attended one mass wedding, which I will discuss in great detail in the next chapter.

It is no accident that I, a foreigner, saw far more of the rarer outdoor weddings than the quotidian indoor weddings. The former are widely believed to epitomize what the Jordanian anthropologist Mahmud Na'amneh calls the country's "intangible cultural heritage" (2009, 31). Matching Professor Na'amneh's enthusiasm for weddings, colleagues, acquaintances, and near strangers frequently invited me to taqlidi (traditional) or sha'bi (popular) weddings—often promising me fulkur asli (authentic folklore). It would be easy to take aim at the authenticity claims of my hosts and point out the irony that these multiday outdoor weddings are becoming fodder or "local content" for what Andrew Shryock has called "a cultural interzone that, in Jordan, is framed and continually remodeled using concepts drawn from the English language and the globalizing policy discourses that flourish in it" (2004*b*, 44). However, it is more fruitful to follow Shryock's approach and try to understand the struggles, accomplishments, and even pleasures of Jordanian elites and commoners as they position themselves carefully in relation to this cultural interzone.

Emerging norms around weddings increasingly impose somewhat contradictory imperatives on Jordanians, demanding the display of proper deference to tradition before certain audiences (predominantly local, lower class) and space for ironic or analytic distance in relationship to other audiences (primarily upper class, cosmopolitan).[5] My own positionality as more of the latter than the former made me intensely aware of the balancing act people confronted in this regard. I begin by describing the kinds of promises and hazards of representation with which the lower classes contend (the life cycle, reproduction, bounty, and scarcity) and how these elements drive people to either have a multiday outdoor wedding or a brief wedding in a hall. I then turn to the outdoor weddings to which powerful families with rural political ambitions have invited me. Because I (like most of my interlocutors) have never been invited to a wedding in a five-star hotel, I will avoid discussing them in any great detail, although my primarily middle-class friends and collaborators tell me all manner of stories about the depravity of such weddings. Gender mixing, drinking, and fighting figure prominently in many of these accounts.

The goal is neither to capture the full diversity of Jordanian wedding celebrations (or opinions about that diversity) nor to fully elucidate the "normal" wedding, which is increasingly difficult as the class-inflected divergence of wedding practices continues apace. I cannot say much definitively about the sorts of weddings that I and my interlocutors are not invited to—five-star hotel weddings, Christian weddings, and weddings meant to be highly intimate and/or inexpensive.[6] All of these should be noted despite their absence in the following descriptions. Rather, my goal is to show how various forms of social antagonism have rendered a few discrete models of the ideal wedding as competitors for the status of ideal type and the legitimacy-conferring powers that such a status would entail. Given the task at hand, the modest achievements of most Jordanians will figure much less prominently than certain feats of ritual acumen and certain notable failures. For many Jordanians, weddings remain a joyous rite of passage tied to sexuality and hospitality and to individual and collective senses of honor, with the long-standing antagonisms and solidarities that entails. However, the very existence of competing models of wedding recontextualizes all weddings, rendering them ideologically charged no matter the intent. In this way, the wedding's power to exacerbate preexisting antagonisms and sunder old bonds and block the formation of new relations is greatly augmented.

"Slowly, Slowly"

At the time of research, a middle-class family needed thousands of dinar to approximate the traditional wedding immortalized by Bedouin soap operas and folklorists. Many middle-class families still did so. In the first example, much like the earlier description, the initial building of the tent was followed by a night of dancing on Wednesday and then the *zifaf* (wedding procession) on Thursday and a feast on Friday.[7] It would be easy to point to all the innovations as evidence of the wedding's invented-ness as tradition, and the footnotes will do just that. Nevertheless, some Jordanians still perform weddings that fully replicate older models both in broad form and substance—to embed the newly formed household within a preexisting matrix of mutual obligations by forming a multiplicity of exchange relations with a large number of people simultaneously. People can also have a lot of fun in the process, all while studiously reproducing the kinds of antagonisms that old men recalled as central to older weddings: antagonisms between patron and client, between guest and host, between the generations, and even between the new affines.

These recollections of weddings of the past were remarkably uniform and in keeping with the ethnographic record (see, e.g., Elizabeth Fernea's classic *Guests of the Sheik* [1965, 195–213] and Hilma Granqvist's *Marriage Conditions in a Palestinian Village* [1935, 54–126]). They also speak to a more general point that was at the heart of much structural-functionalist thinking about marriage within anthropology.[8] As Antoun notes in his study of the role of marriage in the life course in 1960s Jordan, "The crisis of marriage is not alone a reflection of economic factors. It is a structural problem" (1967, 297). This is because marriage represents a "personal problem" of identity that can be solved only by "a considerable rearrangement or at least re-evaluation of the important structural ties and norms held by a relatively large number of people" (Antoun 1967, 301). Such a rearrangement cannot help but leave its mark on other people's relationships and feelings.

The actual wedding procession (*zifaf*) occurred Thursday night. A group of about fifty people left in the afternoon and drove to pick up the bride from her home and take her and her mother back to the village.[9] Following a practice that the old men told me dated from time immemorial, the family of the bride did not attend the wedding—the logic goes, who could bear the thought of celebrating the loss of a sister or daughter to another family? On arrival, we divided by gender. I went with the men, and we were greeted by a delegation of the bride's male relatives, who sat with us and served us coffee and sweets. Soon we took our leave and, saying our goodbyes, left the bride's family. We drove away from her family's house to ululation, gunshots, and honking. Once back in the groom's village, his family commenced ululating (among the women) and celebratory gunfire (among the men). The men gathered in the tent, and our hosts (the family of the groom) served us coffee. Once all of the guests had arrived and the sun had begun to set, we went to groom's uncle's house for the shower (*hammam*).[10] As we walked, we sang "popular" rhymes like the following while the men hoisted the groom aloft:[11]

Daraj ya ghazali / Ya Rizqa halali
Daraj nuna nuna / 'Arustak Mazyuna
Daraj nuna nuna / 'Arustak hanuna

(Step O my Ghazelle / O lawful sustenance
Step slowly slowly / your bride is pretty
Step slowly slowly / your bride is tender)

Shin al-qalayla Shin al-qalayla
Allah Yil'an hathihi al-layla
Hana wa irbut bab ad-dar
Hata tatla' bint mukhtar
Ikhra' wa izra' bayt injan
Yil'an ras abu za'alan

Shamim rihat handaquq
Shila't qalbi hali fuq

(Start a little start a little
God Damn this Night
Here tie the door of the house
Until the daughter of the mayor leaves
Take off your clothes and plant eggplant
Damn the head of the angry father
Smell the scent of *handaquq* [an herb used in the wedding feast]
My heart has risen upward)

As with the description of a wedding that began this chapter, it is easy enough to analyze such a wedding as a classic rite of passage with its corresponding phases of separation (the bathing of the bride and the groom, parading the latter around the village), liminality (the eventual sequestration of the bride and groom alone), and reincorporation (during the feast the following day). One can even see examples of what Victor Turner would call "the reduction of culture into recognized components of factors . . . their recombination in fantastic or monstrous patterns and shapes; and . . . their recombination in ways that make sense" (Turner 1967, 106): the eggplant and the "head of the angry father" as phallic symbols, the gazelle as metaphor for an overeager groom, the "heart rising upward" as a euphemism for sexual release. However, there is no sense that there is a temporary embargo on the discussion of social antagonisms at weddings—as shown by the casual discussion of the bride's family's unwillingness to attend and, as we will see, the anguish the mother is expected to perform in recognition of the "loss" of her daughter. I emphasize these points because I want to make clear that I am arguing for a shift in the terms of social antagonisms rather than presenting the idea that weddings were once harmonious occasions before they became desacralized and key sites for ideological struggle and the expression of status distinction.

Under that older system of clientage, the wedding marked a major shift in social persona from girl/youth (*bint/shabb*) to woman/man (*mar'a/rajul*), which entailed a significant degree of freedom to operate independently of one's parents. Today the shift in the balance of parental authority is, admittedly, as gradual as it is interminable—even if most young people still do not leave home until marriage unless their

education or employment demands it. With the arrival of mass schooling and formal employment (not to mention rising marriage ages),
Jordanian youth now have a large number of smaller rites of passage
that they experience before and after marriage. Graduations, final ex-
ams, dorm life, first jobs, distant postings, engagement parties, working abroad, and promotions have all become major life events that now
compete with the wedding for significance in the lives of many young
people. However, the wedding remains important to people, as shown
by its size and expense.

This importance is significant because the wedding need not be
figured normatively as the most valued, costly, and elaborate rite of passage in a community's social life. For instance, Turner's (1967) classic
study of rites of passage focused on a puberty rite, which (ironically)
he found more significant in terms of how women worked through the
social tensions involved in marriage and their accompanying migration
to their husband's village than the wedding itself. Julian Pitt-Rivers
(2017, 270) reckoned that marriage was the third most important rite of
passage in Catholic Spain—after baptisms and funerals. In other parts
of the world, people deem funerals more significant than weddings,
reasoning that one might marry many times over the course of a life but
everyone dies only once. Richard Kisiara (1998) illustrates this vividly
in his work on the Luo of East Africa when he describes relatives who
must store their deceased loved ones in the morgue for months until
they can afford a proper burial. In this case, the crisis is not delayed
weddings but delayed funerals. Gillian Feeley-Harnik has taken this
even further, describing how funerary practice in colonial and postcolonial Madagascar came to constitute a whole "political economy
of death" (1984) as people turned to ritual to contest and make sense of
their incorporation into the global capitalist system. The question
of where to place the ritual emphasis within the life course can also
be subject to conscious elaboration as a form of social critique. For instance, Islah Jad notes in her study of the mass wedding phenomenon in
Palestine (discussed in more detail in chap. 6) that these weddings are
particularly appreciated for their ability to produce a "cycle of joy and
festivity . . . amid a grim political situation full of long days of mourning,
sadness, and humiliation" (Jad 2009, 50). Depending on the time and

place, any event from a baptism to a bat mitzvah to a confirmation to a quinceañera might prove more significant to the life of a given community (or individual) than a wedding. One could argue that the four-year liberal arts college experience represents one of the longest, most elaborate, and most resource-intensives rites of passage ever adopted on a mass scale.

While final exam scores, engagements, and promotions are also occasions for festivities, the amount of time and money a young person's family will invest in these celebrations pales in comparison to the wedding. Not even funerals come close to attracting the level of spending, discussion, and innovation that Jordanians have put into weddings in recent decades. This brings me to one of the central questions posed by this book: Why are weddings the rite of passage *par excellance* in Jordan? In the next chapter, I will take up this question in-depth and argue that Jordanian weddings loom large in importance because filiation remains fundamentally "biosocial" in Jordan and, as Morgan Clarke has argued, "legitimacy is a material component of filiation" (2009, 198) in this common formulation. Put slightly differently, "questions of substance" are inseparable from questions of propriety, and both must be worked out in specific ways through wedding rites.

In the middle of the second day of the four-day extravaganza, following a triumphant return, the men congregated at the groom's uncle's house, where they were seated in plastic chairs and served *kunafa* and Pepsi while they sat and talked.[12] When the shower (*hammam*) was over, some young men hoisted the groom on their shoulders and began to walk back, clapping and chanting as they went. They paused in front of the women's section on their way as more ululating and gunfire erupted. The groom's father's brother stood in front of the open gate such that the men were prevented from seeing inside the women's area by the high walls. After a bit of chanting, they quickly moved down to the tent. Everyone settled into their seats in the wedding tent, and the hosts served more rounds of tea and coffee.

At this point, the groom's father began sitting various relatives down with his son Ali to give him final words of advice. I was sitting to the left of Ali's uncle when his father seated Ali to his right. He leaned over and spoke for a while in hushed tones. He then reclined a bit and said, "slowly, slowly" (*shway, shway*). Ali stood, shook his hand, and walked away. Soon, I noticed Ali telling his father, "I'm ready." Calls went around that it was time for the wedding procession (*zifaf*). We stood up and began to gather together. Now under cover of darkness, Ali was hoisted aloft, and we took him up to the women's section once again. Here, the mother of the bride presented herself and there was a brief back and forth between her and the men (still chanting the same bawdy rhymes) as she acted out an acute expression of distress over the loss of her daughter. The men then set Ali down and virtually thrust him through the gate and into the women's section.

Such antagonisms are at the heart of the conscious and explicit archetype of the "traditional" marriage ceremony. The primary antagonisms expressed through such weddings and commentaries about them are those between the family of the bride and the family of the groom, as well as those between the generations and, as we will see, between hosts and guests and between patrons and clients. Nevertheless, these are the antagonisms of people who are intimately related to one another—not the antagonisms of abstract sociological types. They are also part of a heady mix of highly ambiguous and even contradictory emotions that accompany rites of passage like weddings: *farah* (joy, happiness, wedding) but also *huzn* (sorrow) and even *ghadab* (wrath).

As a general rule, the bride's family is not actually outraged by the prospect of their daughter marrying.[13] Rather, they were experiencing the same kinds of overwhelming and conflicting emotions that mark weddings in other parts of the world while engaging in prescribed activities designed to emphasize the bride's value to them and the great honor that her husband and his family should feel at being offered the opportunity to marry her. Far from dampening the potential for explosive conflict, however, the highly stylized nature of these expressions of emotions merely raise the stakes. These stakes were perhaps the highest when the rules of hospitality demanded acts of shared commensality. Nonetheless, it is important to emphasize that this rite involved a kind of antagonism that was both a product of intense social solidarity (among family members) and an impetus to further social solidarity: the creation of new families and family members to build new alliances against common foes while mitigating the potentially dangerous effects of unchecked antagonism. In doing so, such weddings engage with *karam*: the broader ethic of hospitality, honor, reciprocity, and generosity.

"Is Everybody Full?"

The next morning came the inevitable feast—the grand unifying gesture of reincorporation that ties together the whole wedding and its participants—and the sharing of "bread and salt" (*'aish wa milh*). These substances are widely reputed to create bonds of mutual protection and obligation through the act of shared commensality. Like a clumsy display of sexuality, a clumsy display of hospitality brings great shame, whereas successful displays bring respect and renown. Both represent major sources of anxiety, with the twinned necessities of displaying and hiding in order to increase the honor of one's group (thereby increasing the size of the group, the resources at their disposal, and their ability to perform acts of hospitality). However, it is important to note certain shifts in the discourse of honor and shame. Jordanian weddings have become an important site for the production of an "economy of shame" in which older notions of honor and shame are "instrumentalized" to serve novel, capitalistic ends (Karim 2008).

In this formulation, the discourse of honor and shame remains for many of the rural poor a "symbolic covenant with God" and "moral resource through which they view themselves as superior to rich and urban people" (Karim 2008, 10). Although the discourse of shame has always been a key "instrument of social control," it is increasingly useful as a repertoire of traditions and institutions (in the broadest sense) for powerful social actors working at the interstices between the kin-based patronage economy and the world of transnational capital accumulation. This shift has come at the expense of the power of the discourse of shame to serve as a leveling mechanism and a mode of redistribution. Elite actors increasingly co-opt the idiom of tradition and its ritual forms to "instrumentally violate local norms of cohesion and community" (Karim 2008, 7–9). Ironically, elite Jordanians can even bolster the grounds for their differential access to foreign capital through elaborate weddings (because of that differential access to foreign capital) at the same time that they can cast aspersions on the honor and authentic belonging of their more parochial neighbors. Much like the new systems of microcredit indebtedness that Karim studied in Bangladesh, the new economy of shame in Jordan around weddings produces distinct winners and losers and exacerbates the differences between them.[14] This process of transforming family honor into capital and capital into family honor in contemporary Jordan increasingly plays out through spectacles of commodity consumption like the wedding, which combine displays of generosity and modesty. This shift comes at the expense of other facets of the older discourse of honor and shame like the collective defense of land and organized feuding.

The men began arriving for lunch after the noon prayer on Friday. I took my place in line to greet and congratulate the host (in this case, the groom's father) along with the groom himself and a number of his uncles and brothers. I exchanged handshakes, kisses, and wishes of future success as I passed from one greeter to another. Following protocol, I slipped some cash (known as the *nuqut*, a wedding gift that, at the time of research, generally consisted of a JD 10 note) into the groom's hand as I shook it and kissed him on either cheek. The amount of money can vary depending on one's financial means, one's relationship to the family, and any number of possible strategies for the production and alleviation of social debt. In principle at least, the *nuqut* is a wedding gift to be returned at subsequent weddings—perhaps for the giver himself or his kin. I once went to a wedding where the groom's father emphasized this principle of reciprocity by joking that "you [bestowed *nuqut*] upon us. So now I have to come to your wedding and [bestow *nuqut*] upon you. But I'm an old man and I can't ride on an airplane, so you'll have to do your wedding here." The elite take this one step further: at the largest weddings, there is a man who stands next to the groom with a ledger entering the names of the various guests along with the amounts of their gifts.

Once assembled, the 150 or so men were treated to heaping plates of *mansaf*, Jordan's national dish of mutton boiled in a yogurt sauce served atop bread and rice with parsley and nuts.[15] A man took out a pistol and began to shoot it in the air to announce to everyone, far and wide, that lunch would be served. The brothers and cousins of the groom brought out about thirty to forty waist-high metal stands and knee-high plastic tables.[16] Then they placed four individual servings of bottled water atop each table.[17] Next, the men returned with giant platters heaped with meat and rice.[18] When the platters had been distributed among the metal stands across the length of the tent, our host exhorted us to eat until we were full. The men arose and clustered around the platters in groups of four or five. After saying "in the name of God" (bismillah), we rolled up our sleeves and dug in with our right hands, forming the meat, yogurt sauce, and rice into balls and then tossing them into our mouths. While each person limited himself to an equivalently sized triangular sliver of the platter, we pushed choice morsels on one another as we all ate rapidly. Had the women and small children been served yet?[19] Best to eat quickly just in case. Relatives of the groom's family circulated through the room, encouraging us to eat and offering bread and more yogurt sauce. On finishing, the guests signified their satisfaction by saying "praise God" (al-hamdulillah) and went to wash up. Meanwhile, the groom's father walked through the scrum of men waiting for soap and water, anxiously asking, "Are you full? Are you full? Is everybody full?" When the guests were seated again, the groom's brothers and cousins began serving tea and coffee as people slowly wandered off to other obligations, wishing the groom and hosts well as they left.

When I asked my hosts why they had chosen this type of wedding rather than the truncated indoor wedding, they seemed confused: why would they do anything different unless they were too poor to properly provision their guests? They simply saw their son's wedding as being the way any self-respecting man would mark such an occasion—with singing, dancing, and acts of generosity. However, it is hard not to interpret this wedding as making a number of powerful statements about the family's allegiances and commitments when placed in a broader context, which includes radically different models for weddings. Compared with other popular or traditional weddings, the primary mode of comparison is indexical: How many days? How many guests? Most important, how much meat? In the subsequent examples, whole new axes of comparison emerge. Increasingly, the wedding is not a simple index of one's honor and generosity within widely agreed traditional terms but rather an icon

of the hosts' adherence to or rejection of that tradition—as opposed
to other possible visions of Jordan's future that might give precedence
to nationalism, liberal capitalism, or Islam over older tribal patronage
networks.

"IN HIS FACE"

If middle-class families like Ali's struggle to continue having
reasonable—if modest—weddings along the same lines as their ancestors, the wealthy and the poor must also contend with various
challenges. When looking at what constitutes success and failure for
people from the socioeconomic extremes, it is important to note the
complex ways in which different kinds of weddings both take on and
subvert various class resonances. To do so will require that I overcome
a certain amount of "ethnographic refusal" (Ortner 1995) on my part.
I have received nothing but kindness and warm hospitality in my trav-
els across Jordan. All invitations should be cherished, and it would be
ungrateful of me to criticize my hosts—especially when they have such
humble means compared with my own. However, as Argryou points
out, traditionalist weddings and the honor that they can confer on their
hosts turn on the assumption of the existence of a kind of uncalculated
generosity that is all the more cruel because it "disregards economic
inequality and proceeds as if generosity and 'good heart' were the only
relevant factors" (Argryou 1996, 78). Yet a "good heart" is neither a necessary nor sufficient condition for a successful wedding. I will ask the
reader to imagine that, at times, I encountered young men who simply
lacked the means to perform the proper wedding. To the degree that I
can surface suppressed narratives of their marginalization within the
Jordanian wedding complex, one must imagine the even greater de-
grees of marginalization to which lower-class women and children may
be subject. Their silence in this chapter is intended to be unsettling.

To critique the system as a whole without casting aspersions on my
hosts, I will try to help the reader imagine a comparison of two brothers of humble means who chose radically different types of weddings (a
multiday outdoor feast and a two-hour event in a wedding hall) and then
lay out how their neighbors might respond. Next, turning away from

this mode of highly distanced, obscured writing on those who do not fit into the system, I will compare two large, outdoor weddings hosted by transnational elites with rural political ambitions to show the opportunities that such weddings promise. In providing the "local content" for Jordan's "cultural interzone," Jordanian elites and commoners are driven at least as much by the logics of consumer capitalism, with its global dreamscapes and prestige goods, as they are by their more parochial commitments. At its most cruel, this combination of kin structures and transnational capital accumulation can prove "toxically synergistic" (Karim 2008, 15), especially for the poor, who must conform more assiduously to its shifting strictures. This leads to all manner of anxieties as social actors seek out protected, legitimacy-conferring signs they can use to guard against attacks on the forms of legitimacy that wedding rituals must enact. These new forms of consumption fit seamlessly into the wider economy of shame, serving alternatively as shield or bludgeon.

"This Is a Simple Wedding"

Mahmud and Mu'tasim, despite being brothers, chose very different styles of weddings. Their parents divorced when they were children, and their father has not supported either them or their mother financially since. Even after their mother's remarriage, they were heavily reliant on their extended kin for support. Forced to leave school and support themselves from a young age, they went in different directions. Mahmud was drawn to agricultural labor, whereas his brother Mu'tasim worked primarily as a shop boy in various urban centers in Jordan.[20] Neither had much formal schooling, but Mu'tasim continued to work on his English and follow cosmopolitan fashions, developing a reputation as something of a dandy in the process. When the time came for the two of them to marry, they opted for markedly different weddings.

To be clear, neither brother could have carried out an elite wedding at a five-star hotel. Even if they had the money (which they did not), their relatives and friends would have been too intimidated to attend.[21] Working-class villagers across Jordan were unanimous on this point: "It's not comfortable," was a common refrain. One man wondered, "Can you smoke in a hotel wedding? I don't know. I would be afraid to smoke." Yet another asked, "What are you supposed to wear? If I was the only one wearing a headscarf and robe, people would laugh at me." Mahmud opted for the "village" wedding, whereas Mu'tasim opted for something different: he rented a wedding hall for two hours, and rather than serving his guests dinner, he served only coffee, Pepsi, and sweets. The two approaches provoked markedly different responses. Mahmud's attempt at a traditional wedding provoked mockery and condescension; Mu'tasim's wedding happened and was never discussed again. The comparison highlights the economic factors provoking what I call (to the amusement of my Jordanian interlocutors) the privatization of joy or the wedding (al-farah). Part of this change is about gaining the ability to better insulate oneself from the effects of social inequality. The other part is about gaining the ability to express one's uniqueness through wedding ritual.

When the subject of Mahmud's wedding was first broached, his uncle Abu Saleem was mostly annoyed. His first reaction was, "Mahmud doesn't even live here. When I invite people, they're going to ask, who's Mahmud?" Nonetheless, he and his brother Nasser agreed to host despite the huge amount of effort such a wedding entails. They brought a sound system, a tent, chairs, and plenty of tea, coffee, and assorted nuts and seeds for the guests. Mahmud brought two goats for slaughter, each of which must have cost him about a month's pay. The first night, no one danced and there was no poetry. The next night, I got home in the evening and found Nasser running behind schedule with the feast. They told me that there were men down in the tent and that I should go sit with them since "there's nobody from us down there." I arrived to find one of Mahmud's friends and one of their second cousins. I served them coffee and sat with them until we saw Mahmud's truck arriving with his guests.

As they approached, we looked around and realized the tent was in shambles. Some children had strewn the plastic tables and chairs about, and many of the tables were sticky and stained with tea from the previous night. We quickly set about rearranging the chairs and tables in preparation for the arrival of guests. The evening prayer was wrapping up, and the main contingent of relatives and neighbors was beginning to arrive en masse from the mosque. Mahmud's brother Mu'tasim tried to get him to sit in the appropriate seat on the edge of the tent so he could greet his guests, but he demurred. Perhaps he was starting to see how the celebration was going to turn out and could not bear to stay. In any event, I hardly saw him after that. Because dinner was running late, everyone spent a fair while sitting and drinking tea in preparation for dinner. In what would become the leitmotif for the whole wedding, guests repeatedly referred to the celebration as a "simple wedding," the condescension virtually dripping from their lips. Time seemed to drag on and on as the food failed to materialize. I felt flush with a shame as I imagined what catastrophes might be unfolding in the makeshift kitchen above.

Finally, the plates of food arrived—although it was painfully obvious that the hosts were stretching the meat to accommodate the fifty or so men assembled. Each platter had about four or five hunks of meat to adorn large piles of rice and yogurt sauce. Unfortunately, there were about six people per platter. As a host of sorts, I begged off offers to eat but relented under pressure from Nasser and Abu Saleem. I joined a platter with four other men and a child. Rolling up my sleeve, I dug in with my right hand, forming balls of rice and yogurt sauce and placing them into my mouth. Normally, it would have been incumbent upon me as a host of sorts to push the meat toward my guests and insist that they eat more. Unfortunately, there was hardly enough on the platter, and it would have seemed ridiculous to try. Instead, I watched the delicate dance of five people competing for four pieces of meat (I had already resigned myself to a meal of rice and yogurt).

Despite my modest sacrifice, there was no way around it: the poverty in the community was on display for all to see, and everyone was implicated in it. The father tore off pieces of meat for his son and reassured him, "Eat, eat. Don't be ashamed. Don't be ashamed." The father probably would have behaved in a similar manner if the platter had been overflowing with meat. Nonetheless, his repetition of *la tistahi* (don't be ashamed) rankled. Again, mindful of my role as host, I continued to pick at the rice (lest my guests be ashamed that they were eating alone) right up to the bitter end when the child was done eating. Who knows what was left over for the women and younger children. Then we washed up and came back for coffee and tea. Before I had even finished my cup, almost everyone had left.

The lack of meat was overdetermined by recent transformations to the pastoral economy that I described in part 1 of the book and that have contributed to the rising cost of local meat (from JD 8 per kilo in 2010 to JD 13 per kilo in 2013). Population growth has meant more demand for meat at the very moment when arable land (used both for grazing and for growing feed) is being given over to urban sprawl. As a result, many middle-class Jordanians have been reduced to eating chicken no more than once per week, and fresh sheep and goat meat are now almost exclusively consumed at wedding and funeral feasts.[22] There is some talk of using imported meat from Romania (JD 6 per kilo at the time of research) or the United Arab Emirates (JD 8 per kilo at the time of research), but people can taste the difference. The most obvious difference in taste appears to be the result of freezing the meat for shipping; it is also likely a result of the questionable diet of such animals. On top of concerns about the safety of the meat and adulteration, observant Muslims must ask themselves whether they trust butchers in far away places (as opposed to their hosts) to provide genuinely *halal* meat, which has been killed in a humane manner and bled fully from the jugular "in the name of God" (*bismillah*). Consequently, such products have had a hard time gaining traction in the Jordanian marketplace with most people saying something to the effect of "I would rather not serve meat than have my guests be unsatisfied with it."[23]

For the next week, I felt like people were going out of their way to bring up Mahmud's wedding and make invidious comparisons between it and the ideal type. The refrain was always the same: it was an *'urs basit* (simple wedding) for *nas basita* (simple people). One man called Mahmud a "needy youth" (*shabb miskin*) and referred to his family as "eating wind"—in other words, broke.[24] While no one explicitly mentioned the paucity of meat (I was probably too close to the hosts to hear a criticism that scathing), I heard plenty about the size of the tent and the small number of guests. Another man told me that a "real" Bedouin wedding might have "a thousand people" and "a hundred head [of goats]" (as opposed, presumably, to Mahmud's wedding). It was pointless to bring up the factors that overdetermined this outcome. Mahmud was not only uniquely unable to meet the minimum requirements of a traditional wedding due to a lack of parental support, but he also needed to strengthen ties with distant kin all the more urgently to compensate for the lack of parental support and to ensure some degree of protection against the vagaries of the agricultural economy, with its mix of unpredictable weather, landlords, and investors. Caught up in a toxically synergistic combination of kin obligations and entanglements with larger forces of transnational capital accumulation, Mahmud found himself spending all of his savings and going into debt while failing to succeed in impressing any of the people he needed to impress. Although Mahmud had set out to perform his newfound role as a generous man, it only emphasized to his neighbors that, wife or no wife, he was still a "needy youth."

In contrast, Mahmud's younger brother Mu'tasim opted for a brief, two-hour wedding. It happened, and I never heard a word about it again. It provoked some grumbling in the run-up, almost exclusively from his uncles—the same ones who had complained about his brother's wedding plans. The men had two criticisms of such weddings. The first was that a guest should be entitled to dinner if they were going to go to the trouble of congratulating someone on such a happy occasion. Second, the men claimed that putting the men's and women's sections so closely together often led to needless "problems" (in other words, fights). Otherwise, everyone simply stated matter-of-factly that the wedding would happen in a wedding hall. By now, the idea that people marry in wedding halls and do not provide their guests with a full meal goes without saying. This may violate people's cherished ideas about their own traditions, but it provokes little commentary at this point and no outrage.

Everyone drove to the village of Mu'tasim's bride dressed in their best clothes, picked her up, and drove in a loud procession with her family to a wedding hall, where they divided themselves by gender—the women inside and the men outside. The men lined up to greet the groom one by one. As the guests shook the groom's hand, they slipped him the *nuqut*—most likely JD 10 each. After greeting the groom, everyone took their seats and listened to the din of music from the women's room. As we sat, Mu'tasim's younger cousins brought us coffee, Pepsi, and store-bought *kunafa*. I took each and thanked them, responding, *fi 'ursak* (as in, "I'll repay this at your wedding") and the inevitable reply, *mawjudak!* ("You'll be there!"). An hour and a half later, we went home and, as I have said, that was the last I heard of it. Mu'tasim had, through his rejection of tradition and embrace of the privatization of weddings, successfully managed expectations and avoided public shaming.

Key to his success was the clear low-risk, low-reward proposition he was offering his friends, relatives, and guests through his adoption of the abbreviated wedding model. He was asking very little time of the guests and very little labor of his friends and family. The goal was less the kind of social extension and intensification of ties associated with the traditional model of wedding and more a sort of modest box-checking, which was qualitatively different. For disadvantaged young men like Mu'tasim who are working in the contemporary service sector in urban Jordan, much like their American compatriots, there is a growing need for the kinds of "weak ties" (Granovetter 1973) that they would never be able to afford if those ties had to be cemented through healthy servings of meat and rice. At somewhere between JD 8 and 13 per kilo, provisioning a substantial number of men with meat in the hopes of someday landing a precarious job paying JD 200–400 per month increasingly seems like a losing proposition, if not the height of folly. Today, the actions of people like Mu'tasim are increasingly reframing the abbreviated indoor model of wedding as lower class rather than cosmopolitan. At the same time, elites are increasingly the ones working to keep traditional modes of wedding ritual (and the patron-client relationships they entail) alive.

The Lieutenant

Admittedly, the preceding description is a somewhat extreme attempt to write about the shameful, repressed, and uncomfortable side of the Jordanian wedding complex within its own terms. It highlights the marginalization of subordinate men and hints at the kinds of cruelties that women and children may encounter in cases of divorce, abandonment, and illegitimacy. The fact is that economic conditions are militating for an increase in the number of these bad weddings that nobody and everybody wants to talk about. Nobody, including this ethnographer, wants to be directly associated with bad weddings. From the perspective of most Jordanians, if I knew a friend was having a hard time putting on a wedding, would I not be expected to lend him some money or take responsibility for some aspect of the wedding? It would make me a low and stingy person not to—the very opposite of the persona of generosity and *qalb tayyib* (good heart) that I ought to cultivate. While Jordanians from across the socioeconomic spectrum feel the increasing effects of poverty and income inequality within their own friend and kin networks, they tend to exteriorize and disavow the problem—much like the preceding account. The acknowledgement of the exclusionary aspects of the system within the system mirrors my own elliptical and defensive explication. To do otherwise is to accept being polluted by the contagion of dishonor one describes in others.

The following account presents the other extreme: Lieutenant Salama's wedding was a model of disciplined image management that was well-financed, widely supported in the community, and actually somewhat amazing—even for someone who makes it his business to attend weddings. I heard about the wedding through his mother's family. They were excited to invite me to the wedding and made sure to emphasize his good family and rank. He was not just any old lieutenant—he was a lieutenant in the Air Force, which implies prestige, a high salary, and lots of opportunities to travel abroad for training. They even took me to his house, a two-story, white, stone-faced home. His relatives enthused about the fact that the kitchen was "on the American system" (*'ala an-nizam al-amriki*). Nevertheless, the wedding itself was studied in its down-home parochialism.

We arrived at the wedding to find about 200 people already present in plush chairs in a steel-framed tent with a colorful canvas tarp that could probably accommodate 500. After greeting the hosts, we took our seats and accepted our small cups of coffee from a man who had been hired to dress in traditional garb and fulfill the role of the *qahwahji*—a dependent quasi-slave who would serve coffee to guests of the premodern sheikh.[25] After shaking the porcelain cups to signify that we had drunk our fill, we stood up to get a better view of the proceedings. We positioned ourselves behind a sea of smartphones intent on recording the events unfolding. The older men were up front, dancing the *samir*. They stood in a line shoulder to shoulder and swayed slightly back and forth, bending their knees, clapping in time with the music, and chanting

Bedouin poetry in the old dialect. They sang about the hospitality and honor of their hosts with a minimum of the mockery and verbal repartee that often marks such poetry. As the line of men clapped and swayed, various individuals would break off from the group from an excess of enthusiasm and swirl their fine summer capes, walking sticks, or ceremonial swords.

In a pattern that would repeat itself for the rest of the night, the old men yielded to the young men, who were now rested from their previous bout of dancing at breakneck speeds in a spiraling, circular motion. As they retook the dance floor, one group was hard to miss: the lieutenant's men formed a distinctive bloc in their army fatigues. They danced the Iraqi *chobi*, holding hands and stomping in time with the music. Once again, men would break away from the group, swinging ceremonial swords and exhorting their comrades to greater levels of exertion. Meanwhile, other men strolled around with pistols, shotguns, and M16s, shooting in the air to express their joy at the happy occasion in a manner that nonetheless underlined their ability to live up to a very specific masculine ideal of aggression, martial prowess, and assertiveness in the face of any antagonism. So it went for the rest of the evening—we danced *dabka*, *samir*, and *chobi* while consuming cup after cup of tea and coffee. When I was shaking from the caffeine but could not bear to dance anymore, I found a ride back to my village. My hosts, however, would stay out for hours more, catching no more than a few hours of sleep before they began the massive task of preparing the next day's feast.

The next day, I arrived early and found the men hard at work over pot after pot of boiling meat, which they had set up in a half-finished house. The amount of work that goes into such events cannot be understated. I counted at least ten pots large enough for me to sit in atop massive gas stovetops. The heat was intense as the men described to me how they had butchered the animals at dawn, with very little sleep. From my own experience butchering for weddings, it would have taken at least twenty men half a day to do the job. They were exhausted and still had hours' worth of gracious hospitality to enact. Not wanting to be in the way and sweating profusely, I expressed my admiration for the hard work they were doing and joined the old men chanting poetry by the tent. As night came, the crowd swelled into the hundreds. The dance floor was soon covered with more than one hundred plastic tables. Next, a line of men came out bringing platter after platter of meat, each of which was at least one meter in diameter and about half a meter high. My video of the procession of platters went on for five minutes. When each table had been topped with meat, bottled water, and yogurt sauce, a round of gunfire went off as the hosts invited their guests to eat their fill. The crowd fanned out across the sea of platters. Four or five men gathered around each platter, urging their compatriots to eat from the huge piles of meat atop rice, parsley, nuts, and flatbread. When we were done, we went over to wash up and then sat down for tea as people began to drift away. The plates were then whisked away, and I thanked my hosts profusely for putting on such a wonderful display of hospitality.

The lieutenant and his family had succeeded in pulling hundreds of people into exchange relations of mutual hospitality, enacting a feast that most would struggle to match and thereby rendering their guests in their debt. The family had done so in a manner that mobilized both local kin networks (to provide both labor and attendees) and their highly visible involvement in transnational networks—in this case, most notably, those tied to the security services with its global flows of employment opportunities, military hardware, and training opportunities abroad. The promise of access to these different sources of wealth and power conspired to bolster the legitimacy of their position within the local system of patronage. These advantageous labor and property relations allowed them to continually exceed their neighbors in hospitality, producing a virtuous cycle (for the family in question) as the reverse image of the toxically synergistic forces ensuring that men like Mahmud would never rise above their station. Nevertheless, not all elite wedding spectacles cement relations with local kin groups so effortlessly or seamlessly. Access to money and foreign sources of power does not necessarily ensure a successful wedding.

"A Villa in Dubai"

Weddings can exacerbate tensions and alienate kin given their divergent attempts to inhabit the emerging cultural interzone. This blending necessitates a careful mix of deference to local norms and maintenance of an ironic distance from them. Too much ironic distance can lead weddings (and their hosts) to be evaluated negatively, as if polluted through their connections to external sources of power. Clumsily executed weddings can pollute the authenticity of traditional forms that elites seek to co-opt. In this final example, which is by no means unique, it is possible to discern some excesses associated with such weddings and why they might motivate a good deal of antipathy on the part of both individual Jordanians and more politically organized groups like the Chastity Society (the focus of chap. 6).

This focus on the mixture of attraction and antipathy that liberal and tribal values produce is a necessary corrective to the current Western fixation on why various facets of the broader Islamist project might or might not be appealing. As Roxanne Euben observes, "Few observers seem to have the same difficulties understanding 'democracy' as a value capable of inspiring an action as they do entertaining the possibility that Islamic fundamentalists may also seek an intrinsically compelling ideal" (1999, 14). To use Laura Pearl's language, they fall back on "structural functionalist" (2006, 34) explanations of Islamist appeal, as if there is no need for a symmetrical account of the appeal of liberal, democratic ideals. Whether labeled western or liberal or traditional or tribal, those aspects of weddings marked as specifically un-Islamic also strike Jordanians as alternately wholly appealing and wholly unappealing.

My neighbors told me with pride that the groom, Yasin, "works with a prince" in the Gulf. When I got there, they had already set up a traditional goat-hair tent and had padded chrome chairs stacked in the corner in preparation for the wedding. Yasin wore name brands from head to toe: a Burberry hat, a Porsche-branded T-shirt, and tight, distressed jeans rolled midway up his shins. His tight shirt revealed large, muscular biceps (perhaps the product of weight training and protein shakes rather than manual labor) and the bottom half of a tattoo. His uncles wore white robes and red headscarves. One of the main attractions of the village wedding (for Yasin, at least) was the prospect of shooting guns in the air—as he said repeatedly. He had a pistol tucked in his jeans against his back the whole time. Others, however, seemed to have different ideas on the matter. The prospect of shooting guns in the air appealed to the men from the city as a way of enacting a certain kind of transgressive masculinity; however, it clearly concerned the neighbors, who were experienced enough with guns to fear the possibility of property damage and the loss of life.

I arrived before sundown and greeted the family of the groom (most of whom worked in the entertainment industry in the Gulf). The feast was limited to the groom's family and the family of the bride—thus, they reasoned, no *nuqut* so as to keep it in the family. Like the family of the lieutenant, the hosts had hired men to dress up in traditional garb and serve tea and coffee to the guests out of traditional-looking coffee pots. Sporting white robes with leather straps filled with bullets, the hired help circulated with brass coffee urns that they heated on top of coals. At first, they worked with three porcelain cups, offering each guest a drink and then taking the cup back to serve the next person in line once the previous person had indicated they were satisfied by shaking the cup. As more guests arrived, they switched to plastic—both to handle the larger number of people and because of people's newfound concerns about the sharing of cups spreading disease.[26] Around sundown, the relatives of the bride arrived, and the family of the groom stood to greet them.

Soon after, the tables were brought out and bedecked with Pepsi, water, and giant plates of *mansaf*. The hosts let off a volley of gunfire (to announce the feast). But before the host had actually invited people to eat and before the yogurt sauce had been poured on the meal, people rushed toward the food. My hosts described this to me as an embarrassing breach of etiquette, as we participated in the minor stampede. After dinner, we washed our hands and took our seats as we let our food settle. Soon my neighbors were fulfilling their standard roles at weddings: dragging people up to dance and trying to get the party started. Over the course of the evening, they would perform songs allowing for the now-familiar genres of dance: *samir*, *dabka*, and *chobi*.

As the dancing got underway, Yasin pulled out his gun and shot a few rounds into the air. A couple of men did the same over the course of the next twenty minutes. Eventually, one of the family's patriarchs made his way up to the stage and said, "Welcome our honored guests. We respect you. Dance and enjoy yourselves. We say welcome, but if you're going to shoot, welcome and goodbye." With that, the dancing continued as it had before. We stood in a line shoulder to shoulder doing the *samir* or *dahiyya*. Those who were more enthusiastic would break out of the line and try to encourage the dancers to greater levels of exertion. Occasionally, people would grab at the crotch to tease. Meanwhile, the hired singers sang to congratulate the groom, and those who knew the words sang along—in the old days, the participants would have had to produce the verses themselves. There were occasional bursts of gunfire throughout from the dancers and from people more toward the fringes. The former tended to shoot pistols, whereas the latter favored shotguns and rifles.

The music stopped and I went to sit down, socializing a bit with some of the visiting city folk. The *dabka* began. Sporadic shooting continued. At some point, our hosts stopped the music, and the patriarch stood up on stage again, taking the microphone: "Because of God! Because of Muhammad! Don't shoot! Don't. Shoot. Don't shoot at our houses. Don't shoot at our market! Because of God, don't shoot! Because of Muhammad, don't shoot! By God, if you shoot . . . DON'T SHOOT!" The dancing went on for hours, and it was all good fun. Around midnight, someone tried to put a gun in my hand. My sense of horror at the prospect turned to relief as I saw an old man summoning me from the sidelines. I sat down to talk, and once again, we were exhorted to refrain from shooting. This time, it was the groom's father, Abu Yasin. He gave a more articulate if equally impassioned plea to avoid gunfire. This was followed by a volley of six shots.

At the time, my video camera was in my friend Abu Samir's hands. What it recorded was him asking repeatedly, "Was it in his face?" (*fi jakhimu?*; basically, "Is this a direct challenge to the man's authority and honor?"). The next thing I knew, Yasin (the groom), believing his father had been disrespected, began running toward the shooter, trying to throttle him while his relatives ran in to break up the ensuing fight between the groom and his new in-laws. The men were separated, and the band quickly began playing, although the party never really recovered. The man I had been talking to said, "I always like to leave occasions early while they're still happy. You don't want to stay too long." The music briefly paused, but the crowd demanded that the band play through the fight. At this point, I said goodbye to the older man, and I started walking toward the site of the altercation, sensing things had calmed down. The music stopped—this time for good—and the band said good night. I heard a man behind me exclaim, "Praise God, it ended with happiness. Now let's go home." I found Abu Samir, and he gave me my camera and asked if I was ready to leave. We picked up his wife and kids while I asked what happened: "Oh, the people from Amman were drunk. Their cars were full of liquor." The kids got in the car, and they pointed to a box on the ground: "That's 700 dinar whiskey! Chivas!" said one of the boys.[27] The wife also muttered about drunken troublemakers. As we drove out, Abu Samir waved to one of the few remaining guests "from Amman" and said, "This family only drinks Chivas!"

The hosts seemed relatively pleased with the event, but it is easy to see how such weddings could be exceedingly alienating to others. Drinking, fighting, and firearms at weddings can and do lead to injuries and even deaths—often involving innocent bystanders. Shooting at weddings in particular is nearly archetypal in Jordan, as the epitome of irrational "tradition." The exclusionary practices and sexual license of elite hotel weddings, in contrast, were seen as foreign imports to be treated with suspicion by large swaths of the public. The best illustration of this set of anxieties around elite hotel weddings is the fact that, in almost four years living in Jordan, no one has ever invited me to such a wedding. Perhaps the five-star hotel is the real zone of cultural intimacy for cosmopolitans, who are increasingly alienated from the rural social networks through which I primarily moved during fieldwork. Whether I was presumed too cosmopolitan or not cosmopolitan enough for five-star hotel weddings, this exclusion illustrates how elite celebrations are increasingly inaccessible (behind metal detectors and blast walls in five-star hotels).[28] It is arguably a testament to the increasing levels of inequality within Jordanian society that these class antagonisms have led to the emergence of distinct forms of weddings aimed and producing qualitatively different kinds of relationships. For their part, the poor increasingly wish their guests would stay home and spare them the cost and condescension. This emergence of competing models of wedding adds a new dimension to the social conflicts that have long played themselves out through weddings. At stake is the relative legitimacy of distinct pathways for enmeshing people in qualitatively different sorts of networks of affinity and alliance aimed at realizing qualitatively different futures.

The Islamic movement pushes these stakes to an extreme, railing against both liberal and tribal excesses in the realm of marriage and family. A close analysis of the movement's alternative framework for weddings will flesh out many of the marginalized critiques latent in this chapter's exploration of the wedding as part rite of passage, part exercise in self-aggrandizement, and part tool of ideological struggle. The Chastity Society no doubt hopes to provide beneficiaries with the same things, but it also brings the emphasis of weddings squarely back to broader questions of legitimacy at a time when people in many parts of the world increasingly see this issue as almost irrelevant to marriage. With its mass weddings and strident antitribal and anti-Western stances, the Chastity Society will never become hegemonic, but it represents a well-funded and articulate alternative that is not going to disappear anytime soon.

NOTES

1. In rural Jordan, *Pepsi* is often used as the generic term for carbonated beverages.

2. My preference for the phrase *semiotic struggle* in place of Vassos Argryou's "symbolic struggle" (1996) should be seen not as a critique of Argryou but rather an attempt to disassociate Argryou's contributions from the older "symbolic turn," which has tended to produce ethnographic studies that ignore exactly the forms of materiality that are crucial to both Argryou and my own ethnographic analyses of ritual.

3. It is easy to overestimate the lavishness of premodern Jordanian weddings. I collected many accounts like this one: "My wedding lasted a whole week! People came from all around. Everyone was there. They came from Jurayna, Hisban, Mushagar, and Ghurnata. We slaughtered goats and sang and danced. There were races. The women made bread. It was the sweetest thing!" It is easy to overlook a couple of key points here: The population density was very low in the 1950s. The poor quality of transportation infrastructure would have made it difficult to have a short wedding. Most notably, the guests of the wedding performed all of the labor themselves—almost always during a lull in the agricultural cycle after the goats had stopped producing milk and the grain had been harvested. More intensive questioning often revealed that people's weddings were modestly sized and heavily reliant on guests to bring meat, grain, coffee, and sweets, even if those guests might linger with their hosts for days on end.

4. Weddings tend to emphasize unity, but disunity, antagonism, and conflict generally linger just beneath the surface. As A. R Radcliffe-Brown and Daryll Forde noted, marriage is a "rearrangement of social structure" (1950, 43), and it is hard to imagine such a rearrangement ever being free of conflict, whether between generations

(cf. Boellstorff 1999; Cho 2009; Lash 2006) or between affines (cf. Bristol-Rhys 2007; Carsten 1997; Nguyen and Belk 2013). More generally, as Nadia Yaqub has argued in her review of the prominent place that weddings hold in Palestinian cinema, "The integrity of the wedding as a Palestinian event to be conducted in a Palestinian space is disrupted . . . filmmakers question the existence and the efficacy of various binaries (public/private, cultural/political, spiritual/material) and explore the ramifications of defying these divisions" (2007, 58). Although the context of Israeli occupation gives these films their rhetorical force and narrative arc, Yaqub points out that weddings often help to build up these kinds of binaries independent of specific political conditions— only to necessarily break them down so that the ritual may successfully affect a change in the social order. Consequently, although weddings may seem to embody the essence of propriety, there is (somewhat paradoxically) generally something at least a bit transgressive about them.

5. If one is going to go to the trouble of hosting such a public spectacle to emphasize one's deep connections to Bedouin identity, the American anthropologist is one such audience. Aside from the deep complicity of British and American colonial projects with the Hashemite monarchy's promulgation of Bedouinism (Massad 2001), there is a widespread recognition that cosmopolitans like myself often crave the kinds of authenticity that the properly packaged wedding seeks to enact.

6. Another possible wedding venue would be the halls that many tribes have built for hosting important events. Although I have been to plenty of funerals, delegations, and reconciliations in such spaces, they are not commonly used in rural areas for weddings—largely because of the availability of space and the heavy association between outdoor weddings and tribalism.

7. Many of these details signaled important information about one's background. For instance, some tribes (e.g., the Palestinian *bir Saba'* tribes) have the feast on Thursday night, as in Granqvist's (1935, 108–112) account. Most weddings I have attended include some combination of *dabka* and *samir*. Both are line dances, but whereas the former is associated with the peasants toward the west, the latter is associated with the Bedouins of the east. In *dabka*, participants hold hands and perform various sets of kicks and stomps to Arabic pop songs based on drum machines and synthesizers. According to local lore, the *dabka* was originally performed to tamp down the roof of the couple's new house. In *samir*, participants clap, sway from side to side, and stomp while chanting poetry. The goal is to display one's rhetorical virtuosity by composing verses mocking one's opponents. Because *samir* is an interactive, agonistic genre, it is at odds with a mass-mediated pop culture industry and has fallen into disfavor. However, the introduction of *samir* "teams" (who produce .mp3 files that people can chant along with) have led to a recent resurgence in the popularity of the genre. For a fuller analysis of poetry, verbal repartee, and mocking in Arab wedding celebrations, see Stephen Caton (1993, 2005).

8. The underlying mixture of antagonism and mutual dependency between the groups engaged in any marriage exchange has been central to anthropological understandings of marriage and kinship at least since Levi-Strauss's classic argument in *The Elementary Structures of Kinship*, that "mankind has always dreamed of seizing and fixing that fleeting moment when it was permissible to believe that the law of exchange could be evaded, that one could gain without losing, enjoy without sharing . . . of a world in which one might *keep to oneself*" (1949, 497; emphasis in original). A wide range

of anthropologists, many deeply critical of Levi-Strauss's larger project, took up the tension in competitive exchanges between "wife-givers" and "wife takers" as an object of study in the following decades (Dumont 1970, 109–129; Fox 1967, 175–209; Leach 1954, 136–140; Needham 1971). This literature is marked by a preoccupation with hierarchy, subordination, and the idea of the wife as a form of tribute. Few today would argue that concepts like the exchange of women, the wife-giver, and the wife-taker are universally applicable (Rubin 1975; Strathern 1984). As Peletz (1987) provocatively proposes, why not "The Exchange of Men?" Nevertheless, the aspect of conflict between the groups involved in marriage exchanges has proved to be an enduring theme in anthropological analyses of marriage (see also Carsten 1997).

9. Cars are a relatively recent addition to the ritual. As if to mock the idea of going back to the use of livestock like camels or horses to transport the bride, a number of Jordanians, playfully planning my own Jordanian wedding, have suggested I bring the bride to the wedding from the airport via camel.

10. I was not actually present for the literal washing of the groom. I have never participated in this aspect of the ritual, but videos are often shared after the fact, and I have watched a number of these.

11. The first of the rhymes is commonly featured on both state television and the radio—relatively novel modes of dissemination for wedding songs.

12. Pepsi is a relatively recent addition to wedding rites. However, even *kunafa* is novel. It is an urban specialty associated with the West Bank of the Jordan River, specifically Nablus. However, like Pepsi, it is a sweet and widely enjoyed foodstuff that can be given out as a way for the hosts to honor guests and demonstrate their generosity.

13. I say this because when I asked people about the bride's family refusing to attend the wedding or the bride's mother crying over the loss of her daughter, people always seemed eager to emphasize that men *used to be* angry about the "loss" of a sister or that they felt like they should be angry about the loss of a sister. I have never recorded an empirical example of someone actually expressing this sense of loss as a personal feeling. This is not to imply that people never miss their female relatives after they marry. Rather, that sense of loss is tempered by the joy that one's female relative has become a woman, wife, and mother with all of the increase in social status that the assumption of those roles entails.

14. In Karim's (2008) study, she shows how microcredit institutions in Bangladesh have figured out how to turn family honor into collateral (by offering poor women "collateral-free" loans and then threatening them with highly gendered forms of shaming ranging from gossip to prison and mob violence should they refuse to repay them). When Karim terms this a process of instrumentalization, she is highlighting the manner in which preexisting institutions (ranging from gossip to "house-breaking" or *ghar bangha*) become tools of transnational capital accumulation above and beyond their better established role in long-running conflicts between local notables and their dependents.

15. For more on Jordanian culinary nationalism and the emergence of *mansaf* as a peculiarly national dish, see Howell (2003) and Wojnarowski and Williams (2020).

16. In rural Jordan, it would be considered scandalous for women to serve food to large groups of strange men. Consequently, when it comes to weddings and other

displays of hospitality, it is incumbent upon men to take on much of this work of what autonomist feminists have called "affective labor" (cf. Hardt 1999).

17. Jordanians, like people in many parts of the world, can be highly distrustful of the public water supply. So-called "health water" (*ma'-sahi*) is incredibly popular, even among the relatively poor. This term sits uncomfortably with observations that the public water supply is ostensibly safe and that people often refill bottles of water with tap water.

18. As is usually the case in weddings, the men prepared the meat while the women prepared the rice.

19. There is a widely remarked-upon set of norms about the order in which people are supposed to eat at feasts. In most cases, women and children eat as they prepare the food. When it is ready, the male guests are served first, and then the food is taken to the women's section. Hosts are expected to eat last so that they can ensure the comfort of their guests (and in case there is not enough food to go around). However, I have been reassured at feasts that the women and children were already eating in an attempt to make guests relax and take their time.

20. The urban–rural contrast is not accidental; as I have argued, urban labor, property, and kin relations in Jordan are far less dependent on these complex norms of wedding hospitality than rural areas.

21. See similar complaints in Argryou (1996, 132–137).

22. Baylouny noted as early as 2006 in "Creating Kin: New Family Associations as Welfare Providers in Liberalizing Jordan" that the "near poor" were forgoing meat. This phenomenon has subsequently moved up the economic ladder.

23. Chicken, although served at the weddings of certain peasant groups for generations, is viewed as being beyond the pale by most who would consider hosting this kind of wedding. Those with this tradition are mocked by others who claim such people "are what they eat."

24. *Hawa'* (wind) is a common euphemism for *kharra* (shit).

25. Note the contrast between the use of wage laborers here and the poor and middle-class families who use family members to serve their guests.

26. Etiquette has traditionally dictated that until the guest shakes the cup, the server must continue to refill the cup. So long as the server is armed with two or three porcelain cups, this is all the more true because he cannot serve others without getting the cups back from his guests. At times, I have seen men use this fact to emphasize the subordination of the server by drinking cup after cup of coffee—holding up the line and daring the server to break protocol and chastise the guest for doing so. This is especially common when host and guest are roughly the same age but the server is younger and known for being impudent toward his elders. Plastic cups foreclose these kinds of negotiations over power relations; you get one plastic cup, and the server moves on.

27. At the time of research, Chivas was the only brand of alcohol (whiskey, to be precise) with which my largely teetotaling neighbors in the village seemed to be familiar. It was used alternatively as an index of urban decadence and decay as well as luxury and sensuousness. Chivas is a decent upper midrange blended scotch whiskey that does not cost anywhere near JD 700 per bottle—even in Jordan, where taxes on alcohol can approach twice the cost of the alcohol itself.

28. The deadliest terrorist attack in recent Jordanian history targeted five-star hotels. Most victims were attendees at a wedding celebration at the Radisson hotel in Amman (Fattah and Slackman 2005). By all accounts, the vast majority of Jordanians considered the attack an outrage and a particularly low blow. Fifty-seven members of the self-proclaimed mastermind Abu Musab Al-Zarqawi's tribe (the Khalayleh section of the Bani Hasan), including his brother and first cousin, responded by taking out half-page ads in Jordan's three major newspapers to publicly disown him (Howard 2005).

6

The Chastity Society

IN THE PREVIOUS CHAPTER, I EXPLORED HOW FAMILIES USE weddings to promote (and index their commitment to) competing visions of Jordan's future. This chapter poses a closely related question: Why weddings? Of all the rites of passage (birth, puberty, marriage, and death), why do weddings receive such a disproportionate amount of commentary, innovation, and resources in contemporary Jordan? The activities of the Chastity Society provide something of an answer. As an organization that has distributed millions of dollars to help thousands of Jordanians marry, their mass weddings and the accompanying training course for beneficiaries serve as yet another example of a clear articulation of a social vision centered on marriage. As its intellectuals make clear, the society views marriage as central to the foundation of an Islamic community. Consequently, it is unsurprising that they believe that much is at stake when it comes to weddings. Nevertheless, although tribesmen and rural patronage networks valorize weddings as helping emphasize the importance of reckoning widespread patterns of descent and alliance through lines of male filiation,[1] this need not be the primary focus of the rites of legitimation tied up with weddings. In fact, if the Chastity Society's concerns are any indication, one of the biggest threats to legitimate male filiation in contemporary Jordan (especially, at the level of the individual household) may be men themselves—as individuals lacking restraint and prone to tribalism and other vices that divert resources away from the household-level economic unit.[2] In short, men may suffer from *jahiliyya*: a state of being often likened to ignorance with connotations of immoderation.[3] As a result, Jordanians are increasingly exhorted to use weddings to enact one of a number of conflicting notions of legitimacy that emphasize either privileging the household (*usra*) or the extended kin group (*'a'ila*). The conflict itself further destabilizes the link between legitimate filiation and property relations, labor relations, and political affiliation more broadly, making weddings and a respect for their various ritual hazards seem even more important to the maintenance of the social order.

The Chastity Society's mass weddings, training courses, and literature had a decidedly male addressee. As the Sharia court judge Dr. Samir Qabah argues in a pamphlet published by the group, entitled *And Live with Them (f) in Kindness*, "The success of married life is a success for the whole community, because the successful individual is the one able to consolidate the success of his family, and the successful family is the one able to consolidate the foundation of an ascendant community" (2011, 9). This sentiment reflects an assumption that men pose the greatest threat to the family's ability to serve as a foundation for legitimate sociality. Challenging the forms of male sociality that were normatively valued in the previous chapter, the society endorsed the two-hour wedding format, transformed it into charity, and scaled it up to include thousands from families, ideally, drawn from across Jordan. All of this worked to systematically disrupt the use of weddings to promote tribal affinities, debt relations, and patronage networks, which the society portrayed as greedily preying on household finances and all but snatching needed resources from the mouths of women and children.

The speech at the mass wedding by Dr. Abdul-Latif Arabiyyat, the former head of Jordan's main opposition party (the Islamic Action Front), was particularly explicit in its denunciation of "tribal" and "familial" weddings (I will return to this speech in some detail at the end of the chapter). In contrast, he promoted the Chastity Society's celebration as "the wedding of the nation"—and not even the religiously inflected *umma* but rather the far more secular *watan*. As tribesmen and Islamic activists concerned themselves with realizing their positive social visions, they competed for the loyalties of the same people and (occasionally) came into conflict with each other. This competitive atmosphere made their organizational forms reminiscent of what the American sociologist Lewis Coser (1974) has called "greedy institutions," fighting for the "undivided commitment" of their constituents. Arabiyyat made even more explicit many of the antagonisms noted in chapter 5 (between different classes, generations, and affines) as well as antagonisms between town and country and conflicts between Palestinian refugees and "native" Jordanians. He also returned to the central theme of Judge Samir's lectures and writings—the role of Islam in constituting a legitimate order that binds together the individual, the family, and the community.

TRACING THE LIMITS OF LEGITIMACY

In tracing the limits of legitimacy, I am particularly indebted to the recent work of Morgan Clarke (2009). In *Islam and New Kinship*, he challenges the focus of many new kinship studies on the presence or absence of a "biogenetic" dimension to kinship and instead points to the importance (in the Middle East, at least) of the presence or absence of legitimacy. Mirroring Euben (1999) and Pearl's (2006) move (discussed in chap. 5) to use Islamic practice to problematize liberal democratic orthodoxy, he notes, "the Islamic focus on legitimacy, on being born in wedlock, throws into relief the extent to which this element of kinship has diminished in importance in 'the West', and thus perhaps helps explain the relative prominence of kinship's 'biogenetic' element in Western discourse" (Clarke 2009, 16). In this chapter, I extend his argument by showing that legitimacy here is not merely a family matter because filiation is still foundational to all other facets of legitimacy within society. Note, for instance, the powerful role that filiation plays in the governance of the Middle East at the highest echelons, both de jure (in monarchies like Jordan, Saudi Arabia, Morocco, the Emirates, and Bahrain) and de facto (the Assads in Syria, the Hariris in Lebanon).

Although the symbolic role of legitimate filiation in constituting the political order is important, the quotidian dimensions of the phenomenon deserve special attention.[4] As I argued in part 1, access to housing in Jordan is heavily dependent on accepted lines of male descent. A wealthy father can provide his son with land and, in many cases, the logistical support and a good portion of the money needed to build a house. Those who lack such a father figure must choose between renting or taking out a mortgage—both of which exhaust the monthly salaries of all but the most handsomely remunerated Jordanians. In the wedding, again, having a father or some other senior male relative who is invested in a particular young man is crucial for enacting a proper status-conferring marital rite. This is to say nothing of the labor that goes into such a wedding, which must be either purchased or finagled from a large pool of willing kinsmen. Moving beyond the marriage process, it is clear that many fathers play an important role in providing their children with business contacts, education, and even employment—and those young men who lack such a father figure (e.g., the brothers Muʿtasim and Mahmud in chap. 5) suffer for it. Filiation also plays a role in foundational aspects of the modern order that the more privileged members of the contemporary global order tend to overlook, like citizenship.[5] Clarke illustrates this most poignantly when he relates the stories told by his Lebanese interlocutors about how Palestinian refugees—denied citizenship, the right to own property, get an education, or join the professions—might abandon their children on the steps of an orphanage because it is better to be a Lebanese bastard than a stateless Palestinian (2009, 81).

If the ramifications of legitimate filiation extend far beyond the family, the legitimacy-conferring powers of the wedding do so as well. Commentators in the region are known to refer to upcoming elections as the *ʿurs watani* (national wedding). While they most likely mean to draw a simple parallel between what should be two different types of happy occasion, talk about a wedding celebration thrown by a local parliamentarian in one of my field sites provided some alternative readings. As it happened, I was sitting with two of the member of parliament's relatives watching the cars go by one day when one of them asked, "Have you heard about the lunch at the representative's?" I replied in the negative and asked about the occasion. ʿAwadh responded, "He wants to marry off his son Muhammad . . . *everyone* is invited! His son is going to marry a girl from . . . [the] in-laws of Prince [so-and-so]!" His uncle Ahmad Sweilem chimed in, asking, "Is it going to be a big occasion?" to which

'Awadh responded, "*Ya Salam!* [Oh, yeah!] He's going to make *mansaf* like no other!" However, if that was how his relatives explained the event, their neighbors had other ideas:

> ME: Are you invited to Abu Muhammad's lunch on Friday?
> ABU SAQR: Who's that?
> ME: He's the member of parliament
> ABU SAQR: No. Are you?
> ME: No.
> ABU SAQR: What's the occasion?
> ME: His son is marrying from the . . .
> ABU SAQR: Oh. They're from Amman. They're Prince [so-and-so's] in-laws.
> But it's not really an invitation for his son's wedding. It's an invitation for himself. The parliamentary elections are coming up at the end of the year. This way he can start the campaign early.

Whereas Abu Muhammad's relatives portrayed the event as an act of generosity, a distribution of largesse by a pillar of the community with a good heart, others took a more jaundiced view. Abu Muhammad's relatives were likely fully convinced of their account. Such acts of generosity have a purifying effect, banishing questions about where power or resources come from through generosity and helping to cow curious interlopers into silence. Nonetheless, attacking such gestures of shared commensality and wealth redistribution as cynical ploys (electoral or otherwise) was quite common in the catty world of village gossip about weddings. Indeed, Jad (2009, 244–246) notes in her study of Palestinian mass weddings that the phenomenon seemed to grow somewhat tainted amid the naked electoral machinations of the mid-2000s, when the foreign backers of the Fatah and Hamas factions used it as yet another arena in which they could compete for Palestinians' loyalties, with Fatah racing to copy the Islamic movement's successful innovation of the mass wedding.

Furthermore, lest one think that Abu Saqr's cynicism was merely a matter of petty village rivalries, he interpreted the Chastity Society through the same lens. When I discussed the Chastity Society with him, he wanted to know where the money came from, how much the beneficiaries paid, how people found out about it, and whether one had to be a part of the Islamic movement to benefit. I could tell him confidently that the beneficiaries of the Chastity Society paid little to nothing and that local businesses and the Jordanian Islamic Bank bore most of the cost.[6] I asked the charity's director, Dr. Mufid Sirhan, how beneficiaries found out about the society, and he replied curtly that it was advertised in advance and "everybody knows." Told this, Abu Saqr sniffed, "I've never seen an ad. I've never seen an invitation. How do people know when to sign up?"

My response, that beneficiaries were heavily concentrated in the refugee camps (where the Islamic movement's social services are stereotypically concentrated), only heightened his suspicion that this was a privilege reserved for supporters of the Muslim Brotherhood. The man was a veteran of the security services, a proud Bedouin tribesman from the East Bank of the Jordan River, an ardent nationalist, and a frequent critic of the Islamic movement—as well as the neighboring tribe and its political representative. Abu Saqr was no secularist, though. As he once told me, "If there was a *real* Jordanian Islamic movement, I would be the first to join. But there is no real Jordanian Islamic movement—just a Palestinian Islamic movement!" It was only when I described the educational levels and generally negative attitude among the beneficiaries that he became unsure about how it might fit in with the Muslim Brotherhood's electoral machinations. Reflecting my own uncertainty, though, I backtracked and offered, "I really wish I could talk to the women. They seemed more satisfied with the society. Maybe they're the ones who are with the Brotherhood." Abu Saqr replied, "Girls just want to get married. They don't care how." He continued, "Every man wants a wedding that is three days long with dinner every night and a dance team and a big tent. They want to be that kind of man. If they don't, it is a material [*maddi*; financial] problem."

People could be forgiven for seeing the stakes in the contemporary Jordanian marriage scene and throwing up their hands; there is no winning. Hosting a big wedding provokes envy. Not hosting a big wedding provokes pity. The Chastity Society offers a particular kind of escape hatch, albeit one that seems to be primarily appealing to certain segments of the urban poor. But if the Chastity Society is about opting out of certain circuits of exchange based around conspicuous consumption among related men, it preserves and augments the position of marriage in general and the wedding in particular through a concerted scaling-up of the crowd into the thousands and a rhetoric that places marriage at the center of social life. Through its training course and wedding, the Chastity Society unfolded a complex social vision for the largely poor young people who were attracted by the prospect of getting married for free. The society had identified a number of threats to its broader social vision and wanted to counteract them through training. Chief among those perceived threats were men themselves and, particularly, their perceived lack of self-restraint. The belief was that they would withhold resources and support from their family in the service of extravagant male sociality valorized by many of the celebrations in the previous chapter.

"Training for Every Institution"

I arrived at the offices of the Jordanian Engineer's Association at 9:30 a.m. for the Chastity Society's annual training course for couples.[7] I greeted the director, Dr. Mufid, who was standing with Dr. 'Adl Latfi, one of the "intellectuals" (muthaqqifun) whose work the society publishes. Dr. 'Adl was tall, white-haired, and kindly. Dr. Mufid soon left me with Dr. 'Adl, who began talking to me about the significance of the course: "There's training for every institution: the bank, teachers, of course the army. The army has lots of training. So there has to be training for marriage as well, since marriage is the most important institution. It should be as important as the medical test [required for marriage in Jordan]. One day, people will go to the courthouse, and they will bring a medical test and a certificate from a course like this." In total, there were four sessions, the first of which was given by Judge Samir, entitled, "The Rights and Duties of the Spouses." I will supplement a more careful narration of his lecture (largely drawn from "And Treat Her with Kindness") with additional material from lectures given by Muhammad Al-Aswad (a tall, slim man in his thirties with an immaculate beige suit with burgundy accents on the cuffs) and Mona Kalil (also in her thirties, a dentist and trainer who had studied psychology). Much like Dr. 'Adl's statement about the military and Judge Samir's interpellation of the male head of household ("and treat her with kindness," "his family") as central to the maintenance of the social order, the course largely addressed men. Men were seen as expecting too much, insufficiently capable of restraint, and prone to divert resources from their families towards various forms of male homosociality. These sentiments were reiterated throughout the day before a mixed audience, with women asked more or less explicitly at certain points to assert their presence. In the final portion of the course, participants were divided by gender for a frank discussion of what they could expect on their wedding nights. The male session was provided by Dr. Nidal Tariq. I highlight the first and the last sessions to emphasize the two major sources of authority, Islam and biomedicine, which were intermingled throughout the day.

I entered the room and surveyed the crowd. Most appeared to be in their early twenties. The women mostly wore colorful headscarves, although a few wore black and covered their faces. Some wore floor-length skirts, whereas others opted for the more demure robes running from the neck to the floor and down to the wrists. The young men wore the latest in working-class youth fashion: tight jeans, dress shoes, and the kind of buttoned shirts made to be worn untucked. I took my seat and waited. The men's side of the room was largely silent, whereas a number of women on the other side of the room chatted quietly, producing a good deal of subtle laughter. Dr. Mufid entered the room looking incredibly annoyed. "Brothers and sisters, no one is to remain except the brides and grooms. Could the chaperones please come to the other room we have for you?" He then walked out. A few mothers shuffled out. He came back (more annoyed), "I told you a week ago. Please. Look! They're all sitting here together!" Another mother left. Finally, he summoned a young man to come talk to him in the hallway, and he in turn summoned his bride. The bride came back in, went over to her mother, and coaxed her out of the room.

It is doubtful that the mothers were reluctant to leave because they feared for their daughters' honor. It seems far more likely that the mothers simply wanted to know what exactly it was that this organization was teaching. Perhaps they were right to worry and resist the organization's attempts to shut them out. If the Chastity Society took pains to position itself in relationship to the class antagonisms I described in the previous chapter, championing the poor, it also positioned itself in relationship to antagonisms between the sexes and generations. Broadly speaking, the training sought to take the *jahiliyya* (ignorance) of unreflexive tradition and replace it with scientific knowledge and the correct practice of Islam. Parents, far from being allies in this endeavor, were probably better off not knowing—at least from the perspective of the activists.

One of the central goals of the training and the larger social transformation being affected by the Chastity Society was the promotion of highly specific gender roles. I focus here on its vision of masculinity. To be sure, this vision was grounded in critiques of male behavior with deep histories not just in Jordan but also throughout the Muslim world. As Michael Peletz (1994) has argued, Islamic masculinities often portray men as quintessentially rational (possessors of *'aql*) at one (ideal) level while acknowledging their nearly universal shortcomings in that regard at another, more practical level.[8] According to Peletz, rationality here is not simply "about" gender. Rationality helps define all sorts of socially salient contrasts. It is what separates humans from animals. Children, non-Muslims, and the weak-minded all lack restraint and thus remain vulnerable to manipulation by the forces of evil: bad people, *jinn*, and, the devil himself. Religious practice, in a vital sense, is about developing one's reason to avoid such snares—regardless of gender. As we will see, however, "practical representations of gender portray men as less reasonable (i.e., having less 'reason'), and less responsible than women both with regard to managing money and other household resources, and in terms of honoring basic social obligations associated with marriage, parenting and kinship generally" (Peletz 1994, 152). What was potentially scandalous to the parental chaperones was the manner in which the contemporary Islamic movement in Jordan mobilized these practical representations to highlight the propensity of men to put their tribal loyalties, their masculine aggression, and their commitments to male sociality ahead of their own families, thereby undermining the basis for legitimate social relations both within and beyond the household.

Judge Samir's talk on "the rights and duties of the spouses" recapitulated many of the same critiques that religious scholars have been making for centuries (see chaps. 3 and 4). He readied the first substantial PowerPoint slide: a wall of yellow text on black background. Rather than read from it, he said, "In all things you have to prepare yourself. When you want to pray, you must do your ablutions (*wudu'*). A soldier going into battle must train, have a plan, have supplies. A teacher before going to the classroom needs a plan. Marriage is like that. In order that you do not oppress." Turning to the first slide, he said, "The first material right (*haqq maddi*) of the woman is the *mahr*. So sometimes, maybe the man gives the woman a thousand dinar in front of the people, and she returns it to him on Sunday?" People nodded along. "You know this is *haram* (forbidden). The *mahr* is her right [*haqq*; note that this word means both "right" and "price"]. If she returns it, this is what?" The women's side of the room replied in unison, "*Haram!*" "That's right," the sheikh continued, "it is what? Unrighteous (*athim*)." "The *mahr* is . . . for the woman. Her person remains autonomous (*yabqa shakhsiyyat-ha mustaqilla*). Many young men don't understand this." The sheikh moved on to the next slide, which was headed by *a hadith* about the dangers of men giving so much *sidqa* (*mahr*) that it instead creates '*adawa* (resentment).[9] The sheikh posed a question: "Does it do to request a high *mahr*?" The room was quiet. "Young men?" Again, silence. The sheikh tried another tack: "How many of you have *mahr*?" Dr. Mufid replied, "They all have *mahr*." The sheikh continued, "How many of you have *mahr* over five thousand?" No one raised their hand. "How many of you have *mahr* under two thousand?" No one raised their hand. Attempting a joke, he asked, "How many grooms think their *mahr* is too much?" I saw a number of people glowering. "How many women think their *mahr* is too little?" I looked over to see a bit of fidgeting. The sheikh went on to say that it was important that the woman be respected but that the *mahr* not be more than the man can afford so that he begins to hate his wife.

He moved onto the second material right: *nafaqa* (allowance). He asked, "How many of the men don't work?" One nearby man raised his hand a bit but thought better of it. No one else raised a hand. The sheikh continued, "Anything you eat, give some to your wife to satisfy her. As you dress, dress her. Not in pants and shirt!" The room laughed at this. Pleased with himself, the judge smiled and continued, "I mean from the same class. The husband is the one who brings the wealth and the wife is the one who preserves it." He switched the slide to the next one, "obedience" (*al-ta'a*), and continued: "If a man goes out every day and eats barbequed lamb while his wife buys her own bread, is this right?" The room replied, "NO!" The sheikh continued, "and if the wife eats barbequed lamb and the husband eats bread?" The room replied, less enthusiastically, "No." The sheikh said, "Actually, that's fine. As long as he's satisfied—it's his choice." Next, he asked, "If a woman's father gives her one hundred dinar, can the husband take it and hide it or spend it? No. It's her autonomous [*mustaqilla*] wealth." All of this was the stuff of village gossip in that everyone knew that excessive feasting and "borrowing" money from one's wife constituted forbidden forms of oppression that were, sadly, all too common.

He switched to his next slide: "The woman leaving the house." He asked, "Can the woman leave the house without permission?" The room replied, "No." The sheikh continued, "Will you young men give permission?" The room was quiet but one man said, "According to the request." The sheikh then went through the reasons why women could leave the house with or without permission—in direct contradiction of the general opinion among his audience: "To request their right, to request their allowance (*nafaqa*), to ask questions of scholars, because of emergencies in the spousal residence, to receive permission for divorce, for familial visits." The judge said that it was important to ask permission anyway and to do so nicely because "a son of people [a good person] would never say 'don't visit your family.'" He added that a woman has a right to visit her parents every week and her aunts, uncles, cousins, brothers, and sisters once a year. Summing up, he said, "There is mercy in the Sharia." The women let out a long and spirited note of assent: "aaaa."

He switched the slide forward and yet another block of yellow text on a black background appeared. At the top, it read, "The right of discipline." Once again, the sheikh emphasized the need for male restraint. He explained to the men, "First, talk with excellent words. Say that the house is dirty and that you would like it to be clean." He supplied a number of ways a man could register his displeasure while showing the proper degree of respect before continuing, "Second, distance your face from her [*iba'id wijhak minha*]. Let's say you return and the house is dirtier than ever. Keep away from her so that she knows the reason and knows that you want the house to be clean." He trailed off and paused before continuing, "Third, a justifiable blow [*darab mubarrar*], not with a stick or something hard." A man from the audience chimed in, "a hose!"

The sheikh demurred: "This is supposed to be light. Just so she knows that you are angry."

A good portion of the day was devoted to modeling and practicing appropriate forms of sociality for married life. As Mona said at the climax of her presentation, "Dialogue (*hiwar*)! Dialogue is the basis of everything! The salad, the rice, the fried tomatoes; if the food doesn't please you, tell her. Otherwise, it's all *waysting tiym*.[10] If the salad doesn't please you, tell her!" In his presentation, Muhammad counseled, "Talk with her like you talk with your friends," as he first mimicked the solicitous way men often talk with their friends ("my lover," "my age") before barking orders as he mimed a telephone with his hand. "Remember, she has left her father and brother!" He continued, "And the male is not like the female—in body, mentality, and self." He led the youths in an exercise in which they made lists of nice words they could say to their fiancées. A few men grumbled and claimed they did not know any, whereas others seemed downright enthusiastic. One man became frustrated and exclaimed, "This is something of the heart!" Muhammad replied, "You must change then!" When they were done, one group had eight, another twenty-four, and another eighteen. Muhammad told a man get up and read his group's list. He came to the front and read, "my honey, moon, my age, my lover." When he was done, Muhammad instructed us to clap. A second man stood up to read and looked directly (if bashfully) at his fiancée as he read his list, and the women giggled. The women were not asked to read their lists, but Muhammad counseled the entire group, "Accustom your tongue to them . . . this is not shameful."

In all three sessions, men's wrath was foregrounded and problematized, and trainers sought to develop strategies and rationales for helping men deescalate conflicts that could jeopardize the marriage. In a certain sense, this merely reflected a set of assumptions about power relations and antagonisms between the genders that should be familiar from chapters 3 and 4, especially the work of Sonbol (2008) and Tucker (1998, 2008) on premodern conflicts between Sharia courts and forms of male privilege otherwise enshrined in local custom. There, the diligent employees of the courts were convinced that there was an intrinsic potential for the *zulm* (oppression) of women in marriage and that it was up to pious Muslim men like themselves to prevent it. In the same way that the Sharia courts have designed procedures of guardianship, enumeration, stipulation, and consent, the Chastity Society seeks to promote its own interventions in the name of fighting women's oppression. In this particular case, the society chooses to work primarily on male notions of agency and self-worth, promoting the idea that men hold a good deal of the power to nurture or destroy their relationship with their future wives. In the case of the courts, it seemed that some women were able to manipulate these assumptions and the resultant procedures for their own benefit, whereas others were victimized and found that the discursive elaboration of their own powerlessness came to contribute to their actual powerlessness. Such observations apply, perforce, in the context of such discussions of domestic violence and masculine restraint.

After the sheikh's elucidation of the concept of a justifiable blow, silence settled over the room. The sheikh asked, "How many of you read the Quran daily?" No one raised their hand. "Yearly?" A few hands went up. "Who doesn't pray?" One person raised his hand. He repeated his questions for the women: some read the Quran every day. Most read it every year. They all prayed. He said, "It's important to read the Quran to know about your creation." The sheikh then said, "There are hormones (*hurmunat*). Do you know what hormones are? Sometimes she's angry without reason when she's pregnant, after she gives birth, before she gives birth. She says, 'I'm mad.' Just say you're sorry and walk with her."

The English loanword *hurmunat* was repeated throughout the day and, as we will see, constituted an important aspect of the repeated appeal to nature (*tabi'a*). It should serve to emphasize Peletz's caution that, gender ideology aside, rationality and its absence are often seen as qualities of both genders in practice (1994, 37–38). However, if female passions were dismissed as manifestations of *hurmunat*, they were not seen as in need of transformation in the same way that male passions were. As Muhammad counseled the men, "Mercy is not weakness, and it is not against romance." His PowerPoint slide clarified things further: "It's called the days of fertility." He claimed that "according to a scientific study in Europe, 90% of divorce happens in this period of the woman's monthly cycle. But our lord created woman like this.

Her body temperature rises by one degree. . . . You need to lighten up on her during these days. . . . If she's angry, let her talk until she's finished. . . . Memorize the monthly cycle of your wife. . . . This is the natural order." Mona, for her part, told the men at one point, "I'm going to talk to you about *adrenalin*. So you know what *adrenalin* is? If there is danger, it makes you *fiyt ur fliyt*. Understand? Decrease the distribution of adrenaline to the spouses. . . . Don't put gas on the fire! You need to be kind. You want to increase self-acceptance and *silf-istim*. This means *watsh yur wurds!*"

The sheikh concluded his presentation by saying, "Marriage is religious duty for us. Prayer is the first duty, but marriage is very important," and soliciting questions. Not receiving any, he began to quiz the audience. He asked, "What are the rights? I want to hear from the men." There was more silence. A few men shouted out "obedience, respect." Then a woman said "being able to leave the home." The sheikh asked, "When can the woman leave the home?" Unlike the men, who had not written anything on the paper they had been provided, a number of the women had taken careful notes—especially on key points like reasons for leaving the house and the protocol for the husband striking his wife. Reflecting the broader participation of women within the Chastity Society (as authors like Amal 'Abdeen, presenters like Mona, and especially as volunteers), the female beneficiaries gave verbatim accounts of what had been said on these topics. Dr. Mufid responded, "See young men? These women have been taking notes on the paper we gave them. I will give them prizes after this is over." A man said, "Thank you for your presentation. But you didn't talk about one important point. Sometimes women bring bad guests to the house. Their female friends cause problems. Is this not allowed?"

As he said, this I wondered how many men were starting to see the Chastity Society as a "bad guest" that they had unwittingly admitted into their relations with their future wives, upsetting the customary balance of power between the spouses. The sheikh replied, "Yes. The man can forbid any woman . . . or man!—from coming to the house if he isn't satisfied with them." With that, the sheikh said "congratulations, God willing," and the men responded in unison with a spirited, "God bless you too." The women left first to get their refreshments. Once they had finished and gone into the designated women's break room, the men burst forth to get their coffee and escape outside where they could smoke cigarettes. "Damn this course. It's not teaching anyone but my ass," rang out. I found about seven of the twenty-three men standing in a group talking. When I introduced myself, they all told me they were from the Jerash refugee camp. Then I listened as they complained about the session, making fun of the sheikh's language and mannerisms a bit before heading back down for the next session.

"You're All so Educated!"

At the end of the day, we were divided by gender for the sexual education portion of the course. The men were directed toward a room with a large conference table. When Dr. Nidal finally arrived, he brought with him a poster of the male and female reproductive systems and a plastic model of the female reproductive system. He was a jovial and rotund man with a white beard and a light gray suit. He set up his visual aids and began by saying, "There are the days of marriage and the days after. You're all so educated, young men," he said with a bit of knowing intonation. "What God Wills," he continued with a devious smile, "you have the internet. You have the Satellite. You have Facebook." The men began to laugh. "All of you are educated." He turned a bit more serious and said, "You should take information from respectful places." He explained to them that, of the religions, "our religion is the only religion that gives the woman her rights." He continued, "Marriage is a religious service/worship ['ibada] in our religion. Marriage is very important for Muslims. It's not like Europe. Now they have marriage between a man and a man—a man and an animal!" He continued, "A lot of youths think marriage is just for looking at her like a game. No. Marriage is worship."

If the day had started with appeals to religion bolstered by appeals to nature, it would end with the reverse: appeals to nature bolstered by appeals to religion. I found this appeal to nature to be particularly striking and emblematic of how self-consciously modernist the Chastity Society was in its outlook. It did not simply adopt modern technology (PowerPoint) or institutional forms (the nongovernmental organization). The society also exhibited a marked tendency to substitute nature (in the form of a particular construal of biomedicine) for God as what Strathern, writing in *After Nature*, has called a "grounding conceptualization for knowledge" (1992, 194). Such a shift, a "figure-ground reversal," should not be seen as modern in the sense of contemporary or coeval but rather as a latent potentiality in a myriad of longstanding symbols, tropes, and organizational forms (cf. Latour 1993; Wagner 1986). Just as Strathern has argued that nature has ceased to serve this "grounding function" for English kinship, the Chastity Society appears to have emerged as a creative attempt to stabilize *something* (e.g., "nature," "God"). The necessity is simply that there be something, "At once intrinsic characteristic and external environment, constitut[ing] the given facts of the world and the world as context for facts, thereby providing a ground to the life of persons and results of social enterprise" (Strathern 1992, 194–195). This seemed central to Judge Samir's search for "foundations" and carried throughout the course—relying alternately on appeals to God and appeals to nature. Dr. Nidal began his presentation by turning to his poster and listing off the various parts of the male anatomy using proper medical terms: prostate (*muwtha*), testicles (*khusitan*), and so forth. He explained how the testicles contained *hiywan manawi* (sperm), which were released from the penis. The penis, he explained is, "like a sponge" that collects blood, growing "from five or six centimeters to fifteen or sixteen centimeters." He attempted to explain the female anatomy as well—skipping rapidly upward toward the birth canal (*qannat al-wilada*) and womb (*raham*).

With this out of the way, we got to the heart of the matter: "Our women, what God wills, are shy. They're not like European women, you see.[11] Some of them are afraid. Slowly, slowly." This point was emphasized so extensively that at a certain point I stopped writing it down in my notes. It was a continuation of Dr. Samir's attempt to inculcate restraint as a masculine virtue, as well as a continuation of the nuptial advice given to Ali in the previous chapter. The use of the phrase epitomizes how the Chastity Society was drawing on a deep reservoir of "practical representations" of masculinity. Dr. Nidal continued, "There was a man down in the [Jordan] valley who tried and tried to enter the girl. And finally he tried violently (*bil-'unf*) and the girl died." He continued, "Think about the girl on the night of consummation. You haven't slept the night of the wedding or the night before. And a man can bare more. . . . Some people forget nice words, 'enough! Cut his head!'" Everyone laughed hysterically at this. A young man raised his hand and said, "Pray two *raka'at* (bows) and then enter slowly slowly—calmly." The doctor nodded. Returning to his cautionary tale he said, "It was all because he hurried. And it was worst in the old days. People would be looking from the windows, they came early in the morning. It was bad. But now they go to a hotel by themselves. This is a better way."

Talk of consummation quickly led to talk about the hymen (*al-bakara*) and its significance or, more accurately, its lack thereof to legitimate marital bonds—another long-term concern of Islamic reformers stretching back centuries. He said, "There are some women who don't have a hymen. Maybe 10 percent of women don't have one. Remember, it is a very small hole, but it can grow to 12 or 14 centimeters in childbirth because of the head of the baby. But there isn't always blood. My first daughter didn't have blood. This is very serious. This could affect the other daughters too." The men were hushed and concerned and nodded. The doctor continued, "And my daughter is an absolutely lawful girl. Luckily, we went to the doctor and brought a report and the other family accepted it."

At this point, he seemed to be running out of things to say. He reminded the men, "before you join, take a shower," and, he returned to his mantra: "slowly, slowly." He said, "Try one or two times only. If no blood comes out, don't try five times! If there's a lot of blood coming out, go to a doctor. It's getting better now . . . but people used to die. Are there any questions?" The director, Dr. Mufid, also asked, "Are there any questions?" The room was quiet. Dr. Mufid said, "If any of you have questions later," and one of the men blurted out, "Give me your phone number!" Immediately, every man had pulled out his phone and began to record his number in their phones. Dr. Nidal tried to return to important points: "Take [information] from cultured and religious sources." He also emphasized, "Give her her right. She is your partner (*sharak*) in all things—even sexual matters. One way or the other, it's important she's happy. She can go to the judge [and ask for divorce on these grounds]. . . . And if she doesn't have religion, she will go because of the tension to another by the unlawful (*haram*) path."

Dr. Nidal spoke to us of how he had participated in the founding of the organization in the 1990s when he saw young men putting off marriage and the government's unwillingness to address the problem. He said, "God willing, the situation will develop slowly. We could do one wedding every three months with thirty people. That's 120 in a year." The doctor talked about the financial barriers: "fifteen hundred for furniture, three thousand for *mahr*." He recommended "a marriage fund like social security: put one dinar in it every month and invest it.... Dinner alone can be three thousand dinar!" A young man said, "the Everest hotel [a notoriously upscale wedding venue] is twenty-five hundred!" The doctor replied, "I know, what God wills." Someone else said, "And her father isn't content until he brings one thousand gold and then the next day he returns it!"

Dr. Nidal agreed and said, "A lot of people damage their daughters. Now with the phones and internet and Facebook, the men and women can meet. Thank God! In every house, there's a spinster." Seeing me writing frantically, he said, "What are you writing?" "Notes," I replied. The men explained that I was a researcher, and I told him about my project. He asked me whether spinsterhood was a problem in the West. I replied, "Well, there are many women over twenty-five who aren't married, but people don't see it as a problem." He asked, "Do you have a word for spinsterhood?" and I assented but told him the word had fallen out of favor. There was a bit of silence and then Dr. Nidal said, "The woman thinks of sex last, young men.... Where does she want to go? We're not like Europe here. A woman who is twenty-five takes a man who is sixty-five." A young man asked, "If everyone took two [wives]? Isn't this the reason this is permitted in our religion?"

Dr. Nidal nodded and, betraying his own fondness for figure-ground reversals, explained my research to the young men like this: "What is interesting about Geoffrey's project is that he his doing it in the Western way. The Westerners start with the economic and move to the social and the ethical. We begin with religion and move to ethics." He then launched into his own family history. Studying medicine in Germany in the 1970s and living on the cheap, he met a "lawful girl," and her father "thank god" said, "It is enough that you are a good Muslim." He described their wedding: "We made *maqluba* (chicken and rice) for maybe ten or fifteen people and got an apartment." Later, he said he was inspired to start the charity by all of the unmarried men and women "when I saw the problems of the girls not marrying and the young men studying until they were twenty-four, twenty-five."[12] Arriving back at the macroeconomic level from which he saw my research project as springing, he repeated his advocacy for a national marriage fund, which he said has been successful in Malaysia: "When a young man turns eighteen, he gets a thousand or two to marry."

The Chastity Society is forthright in arguing that its project is, at least in part, a reaction to outside influences. In Dr. Nidal's formulation, this includes new technologies like the internet, TV, and Facebook, as well as new values—the diminution of marriage, secularism, and the expansion of the bounds for expression of legitimate sexual desire. However, these values and technologies confront preexisting antagonisms between the sexes, generations, classes, different ethnicities, and various categories of kin. Such outside influences do not confront people directly; rather, they are fed through preexisting antagonisms and affinities and affect people differentially. These kinds of internal family dynamics can push an Islamist intellectual like Dr. Nidal to advocate that young people take what would otherwise seem like drastic measures— in this case, using new media to circumvent their parents' attempts to enmesh them in marital strategies that are less about their development as pious Muslims and more about the maintenance and elaboration of extended kin groupings. In other words, the Islamic movement is no mere reaction to broad-based unsettling of the grounds of legitimacy—it is an active participant in that unsettling. The Chastity Society positions itself between nature and God, husband and wife, parents and children, rich and poor. It is looking for volunteers, for people who want to be extricated from kin-based forms of sociality that have proved either stultifying or neglectful.

THE WEDDING OF THE NATION

On the strength of the didacticism of the Chastity Society's training, it is easier to understand the society's symbolic rejection (through the mass wedding) of the forms of male homosociality valorized in the previous

chapter—especially when supplemented with Arabiyyat's metaprag-
matic commentary on the festivities to which I now return. Tribes and
the Islamic movement find themselves in competition at times for prospective loyalists. Coser's paradigm of "greedy institutions" likens this
form of competition to the "competition among users of scarce resources
in economic affairs" (1974, 1). He argues that "various groups having a
claim on individuals' energies and time compete with one another to
draw as much as they can, within normative limits" (1). Key to Coser's notion of the greedy institution is that, like Erving Goffman's notion of the
"total institution," it seeks to transcend modernity's partitioning of the
world, in which people "sleep, play and work in different places with different co-participants" (Goffman 1961, 4–5) or in which a man is "a father,
an employee, a trade unionist, and a church member" (Coser 1974, 4).
Where Coser seeks to differentiate his concept from that of Goffman is
the nature of the institution's action on individuals. Where the institution as a whole works through compulsion and isolation, the greedy
institution is liable to work through various blandishments, which are
used to exhort participants to go forth into the world and act upon it.

A recurrent theme is the control of human sexuality. Coser (1974)
proceeds from a discussion of eunichism to an analysis of "greedy families" and finally to an analysis of "greedy collectivities," concluding with
an essay comparing the celibacy imposed by the Catholic Church with
the promiscuity imposed by certain leftist revolutionary organizations
like the Communist Party, where he shows that monogamy was a more
common cause of censure than promiscuity. In both cases, the dyadic
relationship was seen to detract from the individual's loyalty to the
cause, possibly putting the greedy institution in question at risk. For this
reason, Coser claims that promiscuity and celibacy are "sociologically
equivalent" values in their mutual rejection of the dyadic marital bond.
However, one could take Coser's insight one step further: if the breaking of dyadic bonds can be instrumentalized by greedy institutions, why
would they not avail themselves of dyadic bonds as well?[13]

Rather than serving as a threatening competitor to a given institutional project, marriage can also be used to sunder preexisting loyalties
and reorient new adherents toward a novel institutional context. In fact,
one of Egypt's most scandalous and notorious Islamist splinter groups

became famous for attempting to do just that. The self-proclaimed "Society of Muslims" (known in the press as *takfir wa hijra* or "excommunication and retreat from the world") became infamous in the late 1970s not simply for kidnapping and murdering the former minister of religious endowments but also for enticing youths to run away from home and enter into "Muslim marriages" without parental consent. At its height, the group included no more than a few thousand members living communally in seedy furnished apartments on the margins of urban society, but it made terrific tabloid fodder, nonetheless (Hasso 2011; Kepel 2003, 86–89). While Kepel argues that the actual events of the case were completely distorted in the press, the surrounding moral panic is itself instructive. When Dr. Nidal celebrates marriages that blossom on social media without parental involvement and accuses his fellow countrymen of "damaging" their daughters by preventing them from marrying, he is courting similar censure—even if he possesses far more of the trappings of respectability.

It is hard to overemphasize the degree to which the Chastity Society had the distinctive feel of a Kawanis Club gala or some other wholly mainstream charitable event. Relations with families were cordial, if at times strained. It was clearly not a sex-negative organization like the Catholic Church, nor did it license the sexual hedonism of the revolutionary left in the West. In fact, it held up the dyadic relation of husband and wife as integral to its own organizational strategy. This strategy only makes sense against the backdrop of broader tribal affinities portrayed in the previous chapter, which its intellectuals denigrated, preferring to idealized the husband–wife bond. The Chastity Society painstakingly constructed its mass wedding to strengthen dyadic bonds between husband and wife at the expense of their bonds with extended kin networks.

"This Is Strange, Isn't It?"

When I arrived at the mass wedding the following week, I found a large number of boys dressed up as scouts in matching uniforms, standing for pictures. There were two groups: the Jerusalem Troop and the Badr Troop. They would be helping with the wedding in the way that all young boys do (as ushers and gofers), but the adult leader gave their mission a special urgency. He said, "The Chastity Society is a charitable society that helps people get married if they don't have the money. We are here to help them. We will bring people food and water and help clean up. We will also try to fix any problems. This one time, someone started shooting at one of these weddings. It wasn't anything with the wedding. It was a problem from before. But, God forbid." The boys fidgeted and roughhoused a bit as their leader was suggesting that they might be called upon to step in and put a stop to some sort of tribal violence. I smiled at the scene and turned to survey the rest of the grounds of the Islamic school that had donated its facilities to the mass wedding.

I inspected the various banners, all of which said "The Chastity Society welcomes our honorable guests"—a notable deviation from the ubiquitous wedding banners that read, "The sons of _____ welcome our honorable guests." I reflected on the social and political significance of such a shift in the locus of hospitality. Soon, Dr. Mufid came over and took me to the press area. There, journalists from local and international media (including South Korean and Kuwaiti TV) were set up to film the couples arriving. Knowing the event was being filmed, I focused on chatting with the male volunteers—four men in neatly pressed shirts who came from the Jerash refugee camp. The men told me they had come at the urging of Muhammad, the second presenter from the week before. Like the director, they seemed a bit defensive when I asked them specifically how people found out about the organization. They exclaimed, "Everyone knows about the society!" "They come to us." Pushing my luck, I asked what kind of role Muhammad played in the community. They told me he was a *mandub* (representative) for Jerash and, more generally, a driving force behind recruitment.

My elicitation here was quite clumsy, and the volunteers knew what I was after immediately. On one level, everyone (including the rather suspicious Abu Saqr, who was prone to denouncing the country's "Palestinian Islamic movement") knew that the camps were full of not just of Palestinians but also members of the lower classes from the East Bank who were desperate for housing. That does not mean, however, that there were not sensitivities around the relationship between place, identity, and political affiliation—and I had just tipped my hand. Asking the obvious sociological questions like, "Yes, I know you are theoretically open to anyone, but organizationally speaking, who do you serve? You seem to be drawing a lot from Jerash. Would you care to elaborate?" was rude, even if I tried to dress it up in a way that did not directly imply that I was dismissing their political vision as particularist rather than universalist. They saw me reducing them to another patronage network, for Palestinians, Muslim Brothers, camp dwellers, or perhaps Muhammad himself. I appreciated their graciousness in changing the subject to cars.

A more or less expensive car festooned with white fabric and flowers (the cars ranged from late-model BMWs to early 1990s Kias) would arrive in the *farida* (procession), trailed by cars honking behind them. Each car contained a male relative of the groom to drive, the bride's mother, and the couple in the back seat. The female volunteers would jump to help the women out of the car, with their long, billowing white dresses and veils, and the men would kiss the grooms on the cheeks and point the couples in the same direction. The couples were supposed to gather here and eat their "light dinner" first. Meanwhile, the press would frantically try to catch every moment. In the absence of arriving couples, I continued chatting with the volunteers about cars, the difficulties of getting married, and my research.

Once all the couples had arrived, it was time for the *zifaf*. In chapter 5, the most dramatic *zifaf* involved Ali being foisted aloft, carried, and shoved through the gate into the woman's section—the last we saw of him before he became a married man in the eyes of his community. In this case, the bride and groom walked side-by-side—often both tripping over the bride's huge dress, which covered her from head to toe in gauzy white. Under the glare of international media, they stepped into the women's tent together, where they stood on a large stage in front of a large crowd of women, surrounded by trilling and the standard wedding music. The journalists followed enthusiastically—so much for "lowering their gaze," as the Prophet's injunction goes.[14]

When the journalists were finally pushed out along with the grooms, we began the next phase of the procession toward the men's section. A group of boys led the march, singing many of the more family-friendly songs that people sing in the village on such occasions. We were accompanied by a man carrying a drum and, as we exited onto the street, a growing number of onlookers and family members of the grooms. We were soon taking up the entire street as we walked towards the men's tent. People began to hoist grooms on their shoulders. As we entered the school's courtyard, we were sprayed with foam from shaving cream cans and bursts of confetti. A musical team sang popular wedding songs, and there was general merriment between the stage and the seats. I ran into Dr. Nidal from the lecture the previous week, and he greeted me warmly. After the dancing ended, we took our seats.

Muhammad took the stage and welcomed us. He spoke at length about the Jordanian Islamic Bank, their services in providing loans for those hoping to marry, and their general contribution to the development of Jordan. He then introduced Arabiyyat, who spoke about the achievements of the Chastity Society. He spoke of the "over one thousand couples" married by the society in the past nineteen years and its soon-to-open permanent offices, which would include a library dedicated to the social sciences, a printing press, a scientific [research] center, and a hall for holding these mass weddings. He also emphasized that this was "a national wedding" ('urs watani)—that it included people from all over Jordan and transcended local and familial bonds to strengthen the nation as a whole. People's attention wandered a bit, but the atmosphere was largely respectful. I will return to his speech in greater depth in the following section.

As soon as he was done, they switched back to music and a *dabka* team came out to perform the iconic Levantine wedding dance. The men wore traditional robes with headscarves. They held hands and did the swirling line dance—left to right, stomp, kick, and so forth. Meanwhile, the boy scouts passed out water and off-brand candy bars. When the team had finished, Muhammad got up again and thanked all of the sponsors of the wedding. He then asked Walid Shabsuk (president of the society) and a representative of the Jordanian Islamic Bank to present a check to every groom as a "prize and support" (ja'iza wa da'im). With this concluded, another round of dancing began. This time, some of the grooms left the stage and were carried around by their relatives.

Circles for different sets of grooms began to form in the crowd. With this, the wedding singers sang the grooms out as they were carried away by well-wishers. Familial bonds reasserted themselves a bit even within the bounds of the Chastity Society's own ritual, although in highly attenuated form in the final moments. I lingered and spoke with the organizers as the chairs were quickly stacked. Dr. Nidal walked up to me and asked me what I thought: "It's strange, isn't it?" Not thinking about the fact that I was talking to a man who (as he had said the week before) was educated in Germany and was likely addressing me as a fellow cosmopolitan, I replied, "No, you have the *farida* and the *zifaf* and the musical team and *dabka*. It's actually a lot like a traditional wedding but with more people." We parted ways, and I began walking toward the main road as the couples sped away, honking and blasting music as they went.

Of course, Dr. Nidal was right. This wedding was strange. Rather than enticing families to expend precious household resources bolstering extended kin networks of debt and patronage through a celebration of male filiation, the mass wedding used economies of scale to save on costs while deemphasizing the extended kin group. Most dramatically, these bonds were dissolved by the large crowds of (supposedly unrelated) Jordanians. But it is also notable that the society, its representatives, and the Islamic Bank could stand in for senior men as financial backers. The cost and labor of the wedding were borne primarily by relative strangers to whom the bride and groom would theoretically owe nothing in return—even if men like Abu Saqr could be rightly forgiven for wondering if the society did not merely replace one kind of patronage network with another. Challenges to more traditional wedding practices continued with the training course, as sexual education and marital etiquette were made topics of open discussion outside of the family. By acting to check male passions and questioning certain forms of male homosociality and male privilege, the society was not simply challenging tribalism. These political forms are too inexorably bound up with deeper moral and aesthetic commitments to allow for such a simple line of causation to be drawn—despite the strong feelings on the matter of people like Arabiyyat. If the wedding itself had a positive vision of the future, it was largely tied to Islam, modernity, and efficiency. Nevertheless, in all of these ways, the mass wedding worked to destabilize the grounds of tribal legitimacy and relegate them to the past.

"By Themselves and for Themselves"

At the height of the wedding, after Arabiyyat had finished thanking the extensive list of groups that had helped make the wedding possible and sharing his vision for the future headquarters of the group, he began a didactic explanation of the aims of the ritual. He said, "I know that with the repetition of this work (*'aml*), we are building a higher value in this community." As he said repetition, he paused and made a cyclical motion with his hand. He had more effusive praise for the brides and grooms and then said, "When I saw them in this hall, I said to myself, 'this is a national celebration!' People celebrate familially; people celebrate tribally; people celebrate by different names, but this celebration is a national celebration—and the national celebration isn't like these other celebrations. We greet in the name of the *watan* (nation)!" The emphasis on nation (*watan*)—as opposed to the pointedly Islamic nation (*umma*)—seemed a direct challenge to people like Abu Saqr who would portray the Chastity Society and the Islamic movement more broadly as a foreign entity. Rather, he wanted emphasize to the crowd his desire to seize the mantle of essential Jordanian identity from the tribes.

More praise and good wishes for the brides and grooms followed, and then he said, "Welcome brothers and sisters, and welcome to the group, and I say to you that you have built and we are building a higher social good. And this is its meaning: leading all of the merit, your project succeeds, and your project succeeds in this country, leading change." Arabiyyat became more passionate as he stuttered, "And I, and I, and I ... there are places in Salt. There are tribal and familial marriages, which waste huge amounts. And all of the other resources go to the celebration, making food or for shooting fireworks and bullets for the occasion. And it's all an exorbitant cost. And it's all an ignorant (*jahil*) cost." He waved his hand dismissively as he listed off the excesses: fireworks, bullets, exorbitant cost, ignorant, unrestrained costs. The mention of Salt was striking because it was a suburb of Amman dominated by families that tend to maintain large patrilocal compounds and the accompanying nuptial rituals described in the previous chapter. Its representatives in parliament in recent years have been invariably tribal and tend to openly run on their last names (cf. Shryock 1997b). However, this was more than an urban–rural or urban–suburban conflict. What Arabiyyat was articulating was also quite familiar: for instance, a friend and devoted tribesman once rolled his eyes at the sight of men shooting off automatic rifles at a wedding and said, "Each one of those [bullets] costs a dinar, but if you asked them to give the money to the couple, they would refuse."

Arabiyyat, homing in on the theme of selfishness, concluded with a blistering denunciation of the "tribal" (*'asha'iri*) forces that he saw arrayed against the attempts of his movement to work for the betterment of all:

> Those doing this are doing it by themselves and for themselves. If you told them that door was good for the nation, they wouldn't know whether or not to advance. But we say, when we see this work, that we have worked with these previous celebrations for a very strong popular charter—that we are celebrating with it, that we are celebrating a higher value for the community and the prevention of wastefulness, and the image of brotherhood for the group. I'm very sorry, conversely, that I am creating opposition against others, but there is selfishness, there is self-interest, there is distance from the general meaning of national service, there is distance from its representatives and, for the youth, from the real sons of the nation, which deserve respect and deserve a celebration from the sons of the nation. To all of you brothers, welcome and respect with your celebration. And I say to you, with your help, you are leading in *khayr* [goodness, benevolence, welfare] in this country, and you, God willing, you will say this country, in other places [in the future], sates the hunger of this community, in order to win *khayr*, win its meaning of *khayr*, brotherhood, and love between the people, and in order to raise the purpose of the truth with the permission of the Most High, and bless you and peace be upon you and the mercy of God.

Arabiyyat concluded his remarks with a detailed dissection of the self-interested motives embedded within the tribal wedding, connecting his organization's efforts to a broad "popular charter" to provide a blistering denunciation of the political order. With that, he handed the microphone back to Muhammad and descended from the podium to applause as the latter repeated, "Yes, it is a celebration and a national celebration. Husband and wife, affection and mercy: its product is excellent progeny and a happy house." Muhammad, homing in on the dyadic relationship between husband and wife as key to the society's mission, continued, "We established in the Chastity [Society], bringing delight into the heart of every young man and young woman. And we draw for them a smile for tomorrow, a partner; [a partner] of their quality, of the chastity of themselves, to call them to their sides. The Prophet Muhammad, peace be upon him, said, 'I love the people for God most beneficent, and love the acts for God which bring pleasure to the heart of the Muslim.'"[15] He concluded, "Yes, it is the wedding of the nation, and the wedding for all Jordanians, and now for the second act, an artistic team and popular *dabka*."

CONCLUSION

In this chapter, I sought to explore the question of why weddings have taken on so much importance within contemporary Jordanian society. Having previously postulated that they could be used to produce (and index commitment to) competing visions of Jordan's future, I wanted to understand why weddings might be such an effective place to do so. The answer I put forth was that weddings were key to constituting a broad range of legitimate social relations within Jordanian society—more so than elsewhere. The Chastity Society and its intellectuals clearly said as much. However, even their detractors seemed to agree with the basic analysis; they too saw the wedding as key to legitimacy, broadly understood. When taken together, the weddings of rural tribesmen, the aspiring urban middle class, transnational elites, and the Islamic movement all evinced what William Roseberry has called a shared "language of contention," "a common material and meaningful framework for living through, talking about, and acting upon social orders characterized by domination" (1994, 361). This common framework was concerned with legitimacy, broadly understood, and involved a shared ritual template: the careful and highly stylized mediation of the relationship between affines through which husband and wife were brought together and, in the process, more or less alienated from their families. It also included a relatively uniform theory of exchange in which powerful networks were believed to distribute material rewards (up to and including various forms of sexual access) in return for loyalty. This was widely understood to be the grounds for domination. Whether or not it might be "legitimate" remained an open question.

It was the production of webs of loyalty through weddings, webs of loyalty that overflowed and extended beyond direct lines of filiation, which rendered Jordanian weddings and their concomitant modes of legitimacy thoroughly political. This political conflict expressed itself in a manner that, at first, I found very odd—as a conflict between religion and family.

This was surprising because, for all of their enthusiasm for "domaining" (Collier and Yanagisako 1987; Delaney 2004; Cannel and McKinnon 2013), contemporary Americans like myself tend to see religion and "family values" as isomorphic, something easy to believe for those in the ideological thrall of nuclear families.[16] However, where larger family units can pose a challenge to religious movements in the electoral arena and in the competition for adherents and the provision of social welfare, antagonisms are bound to surface between them. To emphasize this point, Coser (1974) borrows an extreme example from Luke (14:16) in which Jesus exclaims, "If any man come to Me and hate not his father and mother, and wife and children, and brethren and sisters, yea, and his own life also, he cannot be My disciple." As I argued in part 2, this antagonism between religion and family asserts itself in Islam as well. Leading lights of the Islamic revival like Sayyid Qutb have promoted quotations from the Prophet Muhammad's era that portray pre-Islamic Arabia as a society dominated by warring patrilines, each of which served its own false god. It was a society in which "the strong among us ate up the weak" (2000, 174), largely because men allowed themselves to be seduced by an excess of masculine passions, falling into the thrall of their patrilines in the process.

I would argue that the Abrahamic tradition has always struggled to work out the contradiction between religious and filial organizing principles for communities—at least from the perspective of Sunni Islam.[17] Take the three great prophets of the major heavenly religions (adiyan samawiya): Musa for Judaism, 'Issah for Christianity, and Muhammad for Islam. All three have fraught relationships to the patriline and produced no uncontested lineages of male descendants.[18] Musa was found in a basket, 'Issah had no human father at all, and Muhammad was an orphan who had many daughters but no adult sons. When I have shared this observation with Jordan's Sunni Muslims, a number have gone so far as to attribute this to divine will—that the men in question saw it as inconceivable that Islamic religious authority could be completely harmonized with patrilineal descent.[19] To be precise, they saw it as inconceivable that Muhammad could have ever produced a male heir.

This attempt to differentiate religious and familial authority places the Islamic movement in Jordan between tribalism and liberalism, criticizing both and, in many ways, contributing to the destabilization of the grounds of legitimacy for both. Ironically, the Islamic movement destabilizes received social orders at the same time that this destabilization drives at least some of its own activities—like the Chastity Society. As we saw, especially in Dr. Nidal's presentation, the encounter with "the West" has upset much of what was previously taken for granted, forcing people to think more seriously about the "grounding conceptualization for knowledge." But with the extension of the horizon of the possible, people seem not to linger on simplistic narratives of East versus West or religion versus science but rather set about remaking the grounds of legitimacy in their own community through everyday quotidian ritual work. In this regard, weddings are simply a ritual high point, with amounts of time, money, and thought invested in the ritual enactment of marriage and the concomitant production of families to make weddings a privileged site for such analysis.

NOTES

1. It would be interesting to study the relationship between the relative investment in different rites of passage and the degree to which the society in question can be considered to have a matrilineal or patrilineal kinship system.

2. Frances Hasso (2011) also writes about indigenous critiques of masculine excesses within the Arab world but shows that these may take on either a secular or a religious idiom, making the important point that many of these critiques are more a product of women's contestation of these masculine excesses than innate qualities of a given discourse. Here, the focus is more exclusively on how critiques of excessive masculinity are articulated through a particular, explicitly Islamist, organization.

3. William Shepherd writes in the *Princeton Encyclopedia of Islamic Thought* that *jahiliyya* (now commonly glossed as "ignorance" and used to describe pre-Islamic times) also means, "a tendency to go to extremes of behavior, whether in violence,

revenge, boasting, drinking, or even generosity, and was sometimes even considered a virtue" (2013, 269). Citing the Quran, Shepherd turns to verse 48:26, in which "we read the fierce arrogance of *jahiliyya* in contrast to the 'self-restraint *(taqwa)* imposed on the Muslims" (270).

4. I would even go so far as to argue that for many Americans, a focus on this symbolic importance of legitimate filiation at the highest levels of power is distracting because it reproduces these tensions and concerns as something people worry about in "other," "nonmeritocratic" societies. In fact, legitimate filiation remains crucial in Americans' (often unacknowledged) projects for multigenerational wealth accumulation that, as in Jordan, tend to involve substantial investments of time and money in amassing property and various kinds of social capital (especially educational credentials).

5. Because Jordan, like most countries in the region, confers citizenship only on the children of its male citizens, those born out of wedlock with no father willing to recognize them risk statelessness.

6. After the celebration, the society published quarter-page ads in all of the major newspapers to thank and list the donors. Many of the businesses had names involving phrases like *an-nur* or "light" that suggested an affinity with the Islamic movement.

7. The site was unsurprising, as the engineers association is one of the many professional associations in Jordan run by members of the Islamic movement and the Chastity Society is one of the numerous charities associated with the movement.

8. For more on what Peletz calls the "official" (1994, 137–138) account of gender that highlights the ideological connection of masculinity and *'aql*, see the work of Rosen (1984, 25–42), Mernissi (1975, 27–44), and Dwyer (1978). Wilson Jacob's (2011) *Working Out Egypt* offers an in-depth depiction of what he calls "effendi masculinity"—an elite Egyptian response to the colonial gaze at the turn of the twentieth century that sought to assert Egyptian men's fundamental rationality and masculinity at a time when those claims were under threat as never before.

9. The *hadith* (*Sunan Ibn Majah*, 1886), which is highly regarded, figures Muhammad as an exemplary individual who, in accordance with the nature of his exemplariness, obeyed community norms about *mahr* payments and limited the payments to his wives and daughters to twelve *uqiyyah* (measures of silver). His successor, the Caliph 'Umr bin Khattab, is recorded as having referenced this fact before warning that "a man may increase *mahr* until he feels resentment against her" (Ibn Majah 2007, 80–82).

10. Mona's frequent code-switching into English, while bolstering her authority as a well-educated member of the upper classes, was probably unintelligible to the mostly working-class audience.

11. The mention of "European women you see" is a reference to the ubiquity of Western pornography in contemporary Jordan.

12. As discussed at the end of chap. 4, the question of whether rates of singlehood are actually rising has proved more controversial than the question of whether divorce rates are rising. Evidence does point to a modest uptick, although not out of keeping with broader global trends.

13. This is highly reminiscent of Andrea Rugh's (1993) analysis of the Egyptian Islamic movement in the 1990s, in which she shows how the intensification of its women's movement led to tensions with its ideals of female domesticity and the

emergence of a reintegration of social order at a "suprafamilial" level. Although she reports that the most notable tendency was toward greater individuality, another tendency was to recognize and underscore "the continued importance of the specialized roles of husband, wife, mother, father, child and so forth" (Rugh 1993, 176).

14. Jad (2009, 47–49) also identifies the public display of the brides as a point of anxiety in Palestinian mass weddings, with a similar tendency to push them into separate, female-only spaces and to cover them from head to toe in mixed company.

15. In other words, because marriage is a form of 'ibada (religious service) that is supposed to bring pleasure to Muslims, the Prophet Muhammed loved it and would have approved of these efforts to facilitate it.

16. Nuclear families have never made up the majority of American households and have grown less and less relevant to the lives of most Americans over time. Conversely, extended families have been and remain an important safety net for many Americans.

17. The term "Abrahamic" itself reflects the tension between filial and confessional conceptions of community within much thought about religion in the contemporary world.

18. Because Muhammad's only son (Ibrahim) died in childhood, those who sought to graft a dynastic lineage onto the late prophet after his death were forced to champion his son-in-law and cousin Ali, leading to the schism that generally defines the broad Shiʻi–Sunni split within the Islamic tradition. Aspects of the Jewish tradition that attribute two sons to Moses (Gershom and Ezekiel) and even (in some cases) a short-lived priestly lineage to Moses's firstborn Gershom are largely absent in the Islamic tradition. There is no sense that Moses was celibate (like Jesus), but any progeny of his are largely irrelevant within Islamic cosmology.

19. These statements occurred against the background of the Sunni–Shiʻi conflict, which has become ever more vicious since the US-led Iraq invasion descended into sectarian conflict. This merely highlights that the tension between religious and familial foundations of authority are quite longstanding in Islam, even if they assert themselves more strongly in certain eras.

Conclusion

Affection and Mercy

AN EARLY FORMATIVE MOMENT OF ETHNOGRAPHIC INSIGHT
came to me while I was working as a Peace Corps volunteer teaching
English in a Jordanian public school in 2008. On this particular day,
I was riding home from school with the principal and some teachers,
including a new teacher who was submitting to the principal's stern questioning. Was he married? Engaged. When was the wedding? A long time
from now—money was tight, and the parents could only afford so much.
The wedding would have to wait. Did his fiancée work? Yes, she was a
teacher at another school. The questioning and the facts of our new colleague's biography were unremarkable; he was in the same position as
the rest of the teachers in the car. But instead of simply commiserating,
the principal urged the young man to take action. Pointing out what the
couple's combined income would be if they both continued to work, the
principal urged his new colleague to forget about his parents, marry his
fiancée now, host a "simple wedding," and lease an apartment instead
of waiting on the house.[1] As things stood, the principal observed that
the couple ran the risk of being led into temptation and spiritual ruin-
ation. The principal intoned that it was not natural for a young man to be
unmarried and pointed to the dire seriousness of the divine retribution
that awaits adulterers who have sex outside of wedlock.

In this conclusion, I would like to focus on the dynamics that led
some Jordanians to take such action to change their own family's marital practices and those of their broader community. I use the Quranic
phrase "affection and mercy" to emphasize the degree to which these
ideas had little to no need for Western inspiration because they were

already so firmly embedded within the Islamic discursive tradition—
often unconsciously so. However, I also suggest that these dynamics
run far deeper, actually predating Islam and arising out of much more
long-standing and widespread forms of kinship structures. I ask what
sorts of meanings this phrase conjures up and in what sorts of lifeworlds it might exist. Throughout the book I have argued that marriage in Jordan serves as a singularly privileged nexus among agnatic
kin ties, lines of legitimate male filiation, property relations, labor relations, and political authority. But I also want to focus on what Sylvia
Yanigasako and Carol Delaney (1995) have called marriage and procreation's "ontological dimension." As they point out, "Issues of gender
and procreation—marriage, family . . . are not just about the private,
domestic domain, but . . . the entire cosmological order" (9). As I argued
in the introduction, the relatively recent addition of a Quranic verse
to the marriage contracts of Jordan's Sharia courts indexes a subtle,
semiconscious shift that is afoot in the cosmological order for many
Jordanians.[2] The phrase "affection and mercy" stands in here for an
impetus championed by the Islamic movement (although not exclusively) to shift the focus away from the extended kin group and toward
the husband–wife dyad.

The phrase "affection and mercy" allows me to talk about contemporary notions of companionate marriage without ignoring their Islamic
precedents or falling back on the more loaded and value-laden concept
of romantic love. In fact, the word *affection* (*mawadda*) in "affection and
mercy" is sometimes translated as *love* (Abu-Lughod 1998, 253–254). But
the concept of romantic love generally implies forms of chivalry and
courtship that are much more carnal and immediate than what is at stake
here. Such forms of desire, which have long been widely disseminated in
Jordan and throughout the Arab world through poetry and song, contribute to the allure of companionate marriage. Indeed, the sense of
allure is only heightened by the manner in which these media provide
free range for fantasy and play by largely ignoring questions about the
marital household's division of labor, finances, and political representation. But these are precisely the matters of the greatest import when
families seek to reproduce a coherent cosmological order by harnessing
marriage's procreative powers.

Affection and mercy were part of both Islamic social engineering projects I studied but not their primary objectives. The phrase formed the background, the unremarkable wallpaper, for much of my research. Amira Sonbol (2008, 93) argues that the phrase has clear, pre-Islamic precedents. It was part of the formula used to conduct marriage contract signings at the courthouse. It was a favorite Quranic adornment to the frontispiece of all manner of books about marriage. It was directly invoked in the Chastity Society's rhetoric around mass weddings. But it was not merely *of* these social engineering projects. It predates them by well over a thousand years and, as I will argue, encompasses a set of concerns that extend far beyond the current purview of Jordan's contemporary Islamic movement. Chief among these is the idea that marriage, crucial for forming the lines of multigenerational filial bonds necessary to transmit wealth and power from one generation of male agnates to the next, could come to eclipse those broader agnatic kin ties in importance. To allow it to do so would have far-reaching effects—equal parts quotidian and cosmological.

Although the more narrowly defined kin formations that embrace this mantra of affection and mercy challenge the more extended kin groupings that they react against, they remain beholden to those extended kin groupings in important ways. The HUDC, the Sharia courts, and the Chastity Society had mixed results when it came to providing young people with pathways for disconnecting from their families—and thereby hijacking their own procreative potential away from the kin groupings from which they had emerged. Despite the best efforts of these three social engineering projects I studied to enlist individuals in their projects, the extended kin group retained a good deal of control over the marital prospects of most Jordanians I encountered. Families had a disproportionate impact on the choice of spouse, when the marriage happened, what the wedding looked like, and the nature of the couple's subsequent housing and employment situations. Housing and employment represented the most enduring and material set of linkages that kept couples tied to their families. Housing and communal defense repeatedly proved to be key concerns driving people to organize along lines of agnatic kinship. This was precisely where the Islamic movement remained the weakest—although this is beginning to change. One initiative in particular that is worth watching is the Jordan Islamic Bank—the major sponsor of the Chastity Society's mass wedding and one of the leading purveyors of Islamic home mortgages—which brings me back to the school principal's unorthodox ideas about marriage.

In retrospect, I should not have been surprised by the principal's unapologetic attempts to undermine parental authority (and the younger man's aspirations to someday being sole breadwinner) so much as his brazenness. All of his suggestions were possible—desirable even. But how could one blithely suggest a simple wedding without considering how the family would ever live down the shame? Who could propose renting and sending the wife to work without considering how this would alienate the couple, their resources, and their labor from the extended kin grouping anchored to its ancestral lands? How could the extended family survive if younger men started taking the initiative and putting their own sexual and spiritual needs first? In short, how could someone just casually upend what seemed like thousands of years of painstaking negotiations over the transfer of authority and wealth from one generation to the next?

To be fair, the principal himself had helped put precisely these questions in my head. Over the course of a number of prior conversations, he struggled to understand how I could be so blasé about the idea of extramarital sex and I struggled to understand the problem. He would urgently ask me, "How else would we know [na'rif; or recognize, ni'tarif] our fathers [without marriage]?" It was only because I had come to take the authority of these patrilineally reckoned kin groups over their members so much for granted that I could be shocked by the impertinence of an authority figure telling a young man to simply go his own way. But what if kinsmen had become fundamentally unable to reinforce the kin group's authority by following its actual dictates and found that they had to disobey those dictates in particular ways to preserve the broader kin group's authority—perhaps even its very existence?

I would argue that these projects tended to gain traction precisely because of this double bind (cf. Bateson 1972/2000; Fortun 2001). For all their modernizing rhetoric and enthusiasm for planning, the HUDC, the Sharia courts, and the Chastity Society flourished only where they could legitimate preexisting relationships that were relevant to the sexual, property, and labor concerns of larger kin-based collectivities. Especially in the case of the latter two projects, their sometimes fraught relations with the extended kin group belied the degree to which their whole raison d'être was to further cement the bonds of male filiation on which the extended kin group was based. In the face of such seeming paradoxes, I want to emphasize that the resulting practices that I hope to highlight lacked the ideological purity or coherence needed to reduce them to a simple outgrowth of the Islamic revival movement, tribalism or, emphatically, Western/colonial liberalization initiatives. Nor were these practices reducible to any simple interaction between such rival ideologies. Rather, they emerged from the interaction of belief systems with the material constraints that Jordanians encountered and the systems of meaning and affinity that they created to overcome those constraints.

In part 1, I approached marriage as a fundamentally housed relationship, emphasizing the forms of embodiment, spatial practice, labor, property, and gender associated with contemporary Jordanian houses. I focused on the diverse and changing nature of the Jordanian marital abode and divergent possibilities for its future. In recent decades, forms of dwelling based on the collective male defense of land have promised to give way to increasingly independent household units that rely on the government to protect their claims. Where kin bonds primarily intended to support the communal defense of land do atrophy, those resources and energies can be devoted to following consumer fashions—for instance, by embellishing the home. For those who embrace this lifestyle, women's involvement in the workforce becomes an attractive option for increasing the household's purchasing power to better project the image of success and respectability that consumerism promises. However, repudiation of consumerism, private property, and obedience to the state has never quite ceased to be an alternative possibility. Older men in particular see the increasing replacement of kin bonds with market relations as a threat to their authority. Rural and working-class people continue to valorize the strength, endurance, and self-reliance associated with securing one's own housing free from state interference or assistance. Most important, when Jordanians lack the money to secure land through the market, they have shown a willingness to unite with their agnates and unrelated neighbors to seize it.

Islamic or even mainstream finance could potentially upend this state of affairs—if young people, their kin networks, and capital markets were amenable. Already with the "Decent Housing" initiative, two Islamic banks were available for customers in search of Sharia-compliant mortgages. Whether or not Islamic finance will ultimately be successful in extending market relations into the very heart of the attempts of families to reproduce themselves is another matter. Nevertheless, a number of factors make this an obvious and appealing move. As I have argued, marriages—especially where they involve housing—are incredibly economically significant events for the finances of the larger extended kin group. Older men may not sign over the deed to the land to their children for decades after their marriages.[3] However, dwelling in a house on one's ancestral lands makes a powerful claim to ownership while suggesting a host of obligations to one's senior kinsmen, encompassing demands for political allegiance, care, communal defense, and other forms of labor.

These dynamics around the intergenerational transfer of wealth help to constitute strong social norms, enhanced through their association with Islam, that directly militate against the elaboration of a thriving market in home mortgages in Jordan. All manner of debts proliferate over the course of a couple's marriage. These remain largely unregulated from the standpoint of Islamic finance because such debts are largely limited to kinsmen and, at least ideologically, are gifts given unconditionally; therefore, they cannot be considered forbidden forms of interest-like *riba*.[4] Were these forms of indebtedness formalized, marketized, and institutionalized through the medium of money, a powerful set of forces would arise, struggling against the sundering of "individual and local limitations" on the way to direct, promiscuous, and increasingly abstracted "money for money" transactions that define unbridled contemporary capitalism (cf. Marx 1976, 207).

Market relations are subjected to a rigorous spatiotemporal discipline in Islamic law that regulates all associated exchanges. In the case of money, the standards are the most exacting: "like for like, equal for equal, hand to hand." These are not pedantic points, either. They are common knowledge, and people do not need extensive schooling to take them seriously. In some cases, Quranic injunctions such as "when you contract a debt for a specified term, write it down" (2:282) seemingly have no need whatsoever for metaphysical speculation as justification. A farmer friend who decided against secondary school rehearsed these points without prompting when I asked him about his dealings with Islamic banks by saying, "The important thing in Islamic finance is that there has to be a particular [concrete] commodity [*sil'a mu'ayyna*]. . . . One time, I took a loan from the Jordan Islamic Bank for a bedroom [furniture set]. They didn't give me the money." So far so good: according to the dominant strain of analogical reasoning within Islamic law, the lender should only give him some sort of commodity in exchange for the money or "gold" (in this case, Jordanian dinars) that he would have to repay later on an installment plan. Exchanging money now for more money later would be *riba*. However, he then proceeded to tear into the Islamic Bank on exactly this point. He complained, "The employee came with me to the store and stood outside while I bought the goods. We came out, and he signed the receipt. You see? It's all lies. He didn't see the furniture, its cost, its quality. He didn't see if I took it. See? It's all lies." My friend's outrage was borne of his understanding that when one introduces strangers, money, and institutional responsibilities into the work of financing social reproduction, the complexity of those transactions and their ritual hazards (Keane 1997) are greatly exacerbated.

Conversely, with a bit of attention to these strictures that mandate this rigid spatiotemporal discipline around the exchange of money, the mavens of Islamic finance could use housing, land, and building materials to structure loans that could be assimilated into the categories of mainstream finance. This struggle is at the heart of Sarah Tobin's (2016) ethnography of Jordan's second largest Islamic bank. As I pointed out in part 1, this is already happening on a small scale in building supply stores across Jordan. Those with access to capital leverage their knowledge of local kin networks, extending credit to relatives and neighbors in return for selling their wares at higher asking prices than urban merchants. For such operations, building materials make a good counterpoint to money. Like money, they have a standardized value and form, generally tied to the transformation of cement, aggregate, water, and rebar into square meters of dwelling space. What's more, from the perspective of finance, housing is great collateral: it is durable, immovable, hard to hide, and, unlike so many other commodities, its depreciation takes decades rather than years. For instance, it has been unsurprising to watch the Saudi Al-Rajhi group (the largest Islamic investment group in the world) move aggressively into both home finance and the production of building materials. Al-Rajhi was one of the first companies to open a cement factory in Jordan after liberalization, and the company has been an enthusiastic advocate for the enactment of the first mortgage law in its native Saudi Arabia (Khan 2013).

More remains to be done from the perspective of Islamic finance. The cost of Sharia-compliant capital can be quite high, and people remain reticent about borrowing from banks. When I spoke to Sharia court judges, many of whom sit on the advisory boards of these banks, they blamed the high cost of borrowing on a lack of "political will." However, there is also a question of making sure the loans are eventually repaid—or that the underlying asset can be extricated from delinquent borrowers. In the case of the HUDC's "Decent Housing" initiative, when it was time to collect on the loans, employees complained of supplicants who came to them looking for help because "the bank has no heart." Jordan's own leading Islamic bank has moved aggressively into the mortgage market and proudly publicizes its involvement in providing access to housing in its annual social justice report. The bank's JD 236 million in loans for housing in 2012 represented only about 10 percent of its JD 2.3 billion in investment activities (Jordan Islamic Bank 2012, 38). Nonetheless, with more than 17,600 beneficiaries of these loans, the bank has learned how to entice twice as many people into taking out loans as the "Decent Housing" initiative—every year.

These ventures into home finance may push the Islamic movement and the larger, predominantly Palestinian banking sector into real estate (one of the last bastions of economic dominance for East Bank kin networks; see Reiter 2004). Similarly, the Jordan Islamic Bank's role in hosting mass weddings seems like a play for the kind of political dominance that East Bank tribes have worked to reify through their own wedding rites. As I noted in chapter 6, the mass wedding was heavily branded as being connected to the Jordan Islamic Bank, which also earned plaudits from the organizers as they distributed cash gifts to the young couples from the stage. The Chastity Society represents one of the largest charitable initiatives of the Jordan Islamic Bank, to the tune of JD 4.6 million (Jordan Islamic Bank 2012, 6).

By offering to house young people, host their weddings, and even teach them about marital etiquette and sex, the contemporary Islamic movement is poised to replace many of the most important roles that kin play in the lives of young people. It remains to be seen how many young people will take them up on the offer. The activities of the Islamic movement are predicated on the notion that there is something onerous about having to rely on one's kin. As we have seen, where money is tight or young people's desires are ignored, this is likely the case. But having kin remains an intrinsic good for many, who cannot even imagine the point of a wedding if not to embed oneself within complex webs of indebtedness.

In contemporary Jordan, an objectified past of tents, communal lands, female seclusion, and powerful associations of male agnates persists in the present day in talk, ritual, storytelling, and aspects of the built environment. It persists despite its logics appearing increasingly inscrutable to many young people who dream of disconnecting from their family obligations and becoming more independent consumers. For its part, though, we have seen that the HUDC's focus on engineering a housing market instead of providing housing to individual citizens has tended to encourage people to rely on agnates—*despite* their intense concern with registering land to individuals.

Those working for a more Islamic society—both inside and outside of government—have also had fraught relationships with extended kin groups. Islamic facets of the Jordanian state like the Sharia courts have been forced to compromise with extended kin groups and local tradition, altering their procedures to take the prerogatives of extended kin groups into account. The Chastity Society is nongovernmental and independent and thus free of many pressures that have been brought to bear on the Sharia courts. Nevertheless, the society remains a significant but politically marginal alternative to more powerful regime loyalists who emphasize their tribal pedigrees. Historically, it is only in moments of liberalization that the Islamic movement can pose a threat to regime-affiliated notables who mobilize agnatic kin as their base of support (Baylouny 2008, 2010; Brynen 1992; Peters and Moore 2009). In contrast, the expansion of military aid and the uncertainty around housing has the potential to bolster networks of agnatic kin. If rival state-building projects in neighboring areas continue to send new waves of refugees toward Jordan and provoke a more aggressive response from the Jordanian state, the most likely beneficiaries will be precisely those extended kin groups that contemporary states are generally concerned with monitoring and managing (through careful attention to property relations, the registration of populations, and the organization of patronage networks). Regardless, Jordanians will likely continue to develop and adopt various institutional initiatives designed to free themselves from those kinship and gender obligations that have grown too onerous—as they have throughout Jordan's short history.

NOTES

1. The word *ista'jar* can mean "to rent" or "to lease." The issue of Islamic finance was not broached, but such a devout community leader would have meant either renting or taking on a Sharia-compliant lease. In many cases, these leases can be structured to end with the lessee owning the asset, which makes these leases quite mortgage-like. The crucial distinction is that, whatever the asking price of the underlying asset tied to the Sharia-compliant lease and no matter how exorbitantly greater it may be than the normal market price, it cannot be figured as "interest" in the sense of being calculated on the basis of time to repayment, and it cannot compound (see Obaidullah 2005, 79–93).

2. The Jordanian Sharia courts made a statement about their growing commitment to emphasizing the ontological stakes of marriage in 1995, when they added the Quranic verse from which this phrase is taken to the top of their form marriage contracts.

3. Often, property is officially transferred from one generation the next via the Sharia Courts as inheritance only once the original owner is deceased.

4. As I discussed in chap. 1, transactions that involve the exchange of a smaller amount of money at one point in time for a larger amount of money later are considered *riba*. A good deal of social stigma is attached to such transactions, even though they continue discretely. These sentiments against *riba* find expression in sayings of the Prophet like the one that declares that God damns not only the person who takes or "eats" *riba* but also the person who pays it, the two witnesses to the contract, and the scribe (Muslim 2007, 319). While those who study Islamic finance are correct to argue for nuance in understanding words like *riba*, there are somewhat specific and well-defined explanations of the concept. For instance, there is the rather concrete definition of the Prophet in the *hadith* literature, "gold for gold, silver for silver, wheat for wheat, barley for barley, dates for dates and salt for salt be exchanged, like for like, equal for equal and hand to hand; one who demanded extra or paid extra, indulged in

riba (interest)" (Muslim, cited in Islahi 2004, 51). Here, we have an enumeration of the six most important commodities in the markets of pre-Islamic Arabia, including the two commodities that most closely approximate the abstract money form and four essential foodstuffs for the early Muslim community. Crucially, however, an exchange of other commodities for these commodities can be endlessly exploitative and unequal without, however, being *riba*.

BIBLIOGRAPHY

'Abdeen, Amal. 2010. *Divorce before Marriage and in the First Year of Marriage: Social and Psychological Causes and Effects* (*At-Talaq Qabl Ad-Dukhul wa fi As-Sinna Al-Uwla min Al-Zawaj: Al-Asbab wa Al-Ithar An-Nafsiyya wa Al-Ijtima'iyya*). Amman, Jordan: Al-'afaf.

Abu-Lughod, Lila. 1986. *Veiled Sentiments: Honor and Poetry in a Bedouin Society.* Berkeley: University of California Press.

———. 1989. "Zones of Theory in the Anthropology of the Arab World." *Annual Review of Anthropology* 18:267–306.

———. 1998. *Remaking Women: Feminism and Modernity in the Middle East.* Princeton, NJ: Princeton University Press.

Abu Rish, Ziad. 2012. "Jordan's Current Political Opposition Movements and the Need for Further Research: An Interview with Tariq Tell (Part 2)." *Jadaliyya.* http://www .jadaliyya.com/pages/index/7007/jordans-current-political-opposition-movements -and. Accessed April 15, 2020.

Adely, Fida. 2004. "The Mixed Effects of Schooling for High School Girls in Jordan: The Case of Tel Yahya." *Comparative Education Review* 48 (4): 353–373.

———. 2012. *Gendered Paradoxes: Educating Jordanian Women in Nation, Faith and Progress.* Chicago: University of Chicago Press.

———. 2016. "A Different Kind of Love: Compatibility (*Insijam*) and Marriage in Jordan." *Arab Studies Journal* 24 (2): 102–127.

Agmon, Iris. 2003. "Text, Court, and Family in Late-Nineteenth-Century Palestine." In *Family History in the Middle East: Household, Property and Gender*, edited by Beshara Doumani, 201–228. Albany, NY: SUNY Press.

Agnes, Flavia. 2009. "Patriarchy, Sexuality, and Property: The Impact of Colonial State Policies on Gender in India." In *Family, Gender, and Law in a Globalizing Middle East and Southeast Asia*, edited by Kenneth Cuno and Manisha Desai, 19–42. Syracuse, NY: Syracuse University Press.

Agrama, Hussein. 2010. "Ethics, Authority, Tradition: Towards an Anthropology of the Fatwa." *American Ethnologist* 37 (1): 2–18.

———. 2012. *Questioning Secularism: Islam, Sovereignty and the Rule of Law in Egypt.* Chicago: University of Chicago Press.

Ahmed, Leila. 1992. *Women and Gender in Islam: Historical Roots of a Modern Debate.* New Haven, CT: Yale University Press.

Al-Abbadi, Ahmad Oweidi. 2006. *Bedouin Justice: The Customary Legal System of the Tribes and Its Integration into the Framework of State Polity from 1921–1982*. Amman, Jordan: Dar Jareer.

Al-Albani, Muhammad. 2000. *Sahih Al-Taghrib wa Al-Tahrib*. Riyadh: Maktaba Al-Ma'arif Lil-Nashr wa Al-Tawzi'.

Al-Hindi, Rania. 2012. "Business Man Releases Road Map to Solve the Problem of Communal Lands" (Rajul 'Amal Yatluq Kharita Tariq li-hal Mushkila Al-Aradhy Al-Musha'). *Al-Rai*. http://alrai.com/article/26498.html. Accessed August 24, 2014.

Al-Nimry, Jameel. 2009. "A Story of Building and Trade in the National Company and Decent Living!" (*Qissa Al-Imareh wa Al-Tijareh fi Al-Sharikah Al-Watuniyyah wa Al-'Aish Al-Kareem!*) *Al-Ghad*. Accessed April 2, 2013. http://www.alghad .com/?article=12717.

Al-Sana'ani, Muhammad. 2011. *Tanwir Sharh Al-Jami' As-saghir*. Vol. 2. Riyadh: Maktaba Dar As-Salam.

Alon, Yoav. 2007. *The Making of Jordan: Tribes, Colonialism and the Modern State*. New York: I. B. Taurus.

Amman Embassy. 2007. "US Embassy Cable—07AMMAN3162: Jordanian Municipal Elections: The Islamist Government Showdowns in Irbid, Karak, and Madaba." Wikileaks. https://wikileaks.org/cable/2007/07/07AMMAN3162.html. Accessed August 24, 2014.

Antoun, Richard. 1967. "Social Organization and the Life Cycle in an Arab Village." *Ethnology* 6 (3): 294–308.

———. 1968. "On the Modesty of Women in Arab Muslim Villages: A Study in the Accommodation of Traditions." *American Anthropologist* 70 (4): 671–697.

———. 1980. "The Islamic Court, the Islamic Judge, and the Accommodation of Traditions: A Jordanian Case Study." *International Journal of Middle East Studies* 12 (4): 455–467.

———. 2006. "Fundamentalism, Bureaucratization, and the State's Cooptation of Religion: A Jordanian Case Study." *International Journal of Middle East Studies* 38 (3): 369–393.

Appadurai, Arjun. 1986. *The Social Life of Things: Commodities in Cultural Perspective*. Cambridge: Cambridge University Press.

Argryou, Vassos. 1996. *Tradition and Modernity in the Mediterranean: The Wedding as Symbolic Struggle*. Cambridge: Cambridge University Press.

Asad, Talal. 2003. *Formations of the Secular: Christianity, Islam Modernity*. Palo Alto, CA: Stanford University Press.

———. 2004. "Where Are the Margins of the State?" In *Anthropology in the Margins of the State*, edited by Veena Das and Deborah Poole, 179–188. Santa Fe, NM: SAR Press.

Austin, J. L. 1975. *How to Do Things with Words*. Edited by J. O. Urmson and Marina Sbisà. Cambridge, MA: Harvard University Press.

Badraneh, 'Adal. 2009. *The Guide: Indicators of Marriage and Divorce in Jordan* (*Ad-Dalil: Mu'ashshirat Az-Zawaj wa At-talaq fi Al-Urdan*). Amman, Jordan: Al-'Afaf.

Badran, Faruq and Mufid Sarhan. 1999. *Spinsterhood: The Reality, the Causes, and the Solutions* (*Al-'anusiyya: -Al-Waqa' -Al-Asbab -Al-Halul*). Amman, Jordan: Al-'Afaf.

Baer, Marc. 2008. *Honored by the Glory of Islam: Conversion and Conquest in Ottoman Europe*. Oxford: Oxford University Press.

Bahloul, Joëlle. 1999. "The Memory House: Time and Place in Jewish Immigrant Culture in France." In *House Life: Space, Place and Family in Europe*, edited by Donna Birdwell-Pheasant and Denise Lawrence-Zúñiga, 239–49. Oxford: Berg.

Bakhtin, M. M. 1981. "Forms of Time and the Chronotope in the Novel." In *The Dialogic Imagination*, translated by Caryl Emerson and Michael Holquist, 84–259. Austin: University of Texas Press.

Baram, Amatzia. 1997. "Neo-Tribalism in Iraq: Saddam Hussein's Tribal Policies 1991–96." In *International Journal of Middle East Studies* 29 (1): 1–31.

Barr, James. 2011. *A Line in the Sand: Britain, France and the Struggle for the Mastery of the Middle East*. New York: Simon & Schuster.

Bateson, Gregory. (1972) 2000. "Double Bind, 1969." In *Steps to an Ecology of Mind: Collected Essays in Anthropology, Psychiatry, Evolution, and Epistemology*, 271–279. Chicago: University of Chicago Press.

Baylouny, Anne Marie. 2008. "Militarizing Welfare: Neo-liberalism and Jordanian Policy." *Middle East Journal* 62 (2): 277–303.

———. 2010. *Privatizing Welfare in the Middle East: Kin Mutual Aid Associations in Jordan and Lebanon*. Bloomington: University of Indiana Press.

Bechdel, Alison. 1985. *Dykes to Watch out For*. Ithaca, NY: Firebrand.

Berkes, Fikret. 1999. *Sacred Ecology: Traditional Ecological Knowledge and Resource*. Philadelphia: Taylor & Francis.

Boellstorff, Tom. 1999. "The Perfect Path: Gay Men, Marriage, Indonesia." *GLQ* 5 (4): 475–510.

Bourdieu, Pierre. 1977. *Outline of Theory and Practice*. Cambridge: Cambridge University Press.

———. 1984. *Distinction: A Social Critique of the Judgment of Taste*. Cambridge, MA: Harvard University Press.

Bonte, Pierre, Édouard Conte, and Paul Dresch. 2001. *Émirs et Presidents: Figures de la Parenté et du Politique dans la Monde Arabe*. Paris: CNRS Editions.

Bowen, John. 2016. *On British Islam: Religion, Law, and Everyday Practice in Shari'a Councils*. Princeton, NJ: Princeton University Press.

Brand, Laurie. 1995. "Palestinians and Jordanians: A Crisis of Identity." In *Journal of Palestine Studies* 24 (4): 46–61.

Bristol-Rhys, Jane. 2007. "Weddings, Marriage, and Money in the United Arab Emirates." *Anthropology of the Middle East* 2 (1): 20–36.

Brynen, Rex. 1992. "Economic Crisis and Post-Rentier Democratization in the Arab World: The Case of Jordan." *Canadian Journal of Political Science* 25 (1): 69–97.

Bukhari, Muhammad. 1996. *The English Translation of Sahih Al Bukhari with the Arabic Text*, translated by M. Khan. Riyadh: Darussalam.

Callon, Michel. 1998. *The Laws of the Markets*. Oxford: Blackwell.

———. 2005. "Why Virtualism Paves the Way to Political Impotence: A Reply to Daniel Miller's Critique of *The Laws of the Markets*," *Economic Sociology* 6/2 (February): 3–20.

Cannell, Fenella, and Susan McKinnon. 2013. *Vital Relations: Modernity and the Persistent Life of Kinship*. Santa Fe, NM: SAR Press.

Carsten, Janet. 1997. *The Heat of the Hearth: Process of Kinship in a Malay Fishing Village*. Oxford: Clarendon Press.

———. 2004. *After Kinship*. New York: Cambridge University Press.

Carsten, Janet, and Stephen Hugh-Jones. 1995. *About the House: Lévi-Strauss and Beyond*. Cambridge: Cambridge University Press.

Carver, Terrell. 1996. "'Public Man' and the Critique of Masculinities." *Political Theory* 24 (4): 673–686.

Caton, Steven Charles. 1993. *Peaks of Yemen I Summon: Poetry as Cultural Practice*. Berkeley: University of California Press.

———. 2005. *Yemen Chronicle: An Anthropology of War and Mediation*. New York: Hill & Wang.

Charrad, Mounira. 2001. *States and Women's Rights: The Making of Postcolonial Tunisia, Algeria, and Morocco*. Berkeley: University of California Press.

Chatterjee, Partha. 1993. *The Nation and its Fragments: Colonial and Postcolonial Histories*. Princeton, NJ: Princeton University Press.

Cho, John (Song Pae). 2009. "The Wedding Banquet Revisited: 'Contract Marriages' between Korean Gays and Lesbians." *Anthropological Quarterly* 82 (2): 401–422.

Clarke, Morgan. 2009. *Islam and New Kinship: Reproductive Technology and the Sharia in Lebanon*. New York: Berghahn.

Cohen, Amnon. 1973. *Palestine in the 18th Century: Patterns of Administration*. Jerusalem: Hebrew University.

Cohen, David. 1989. "Separation and the Status of Women in Classical Athens." *Greece and Rome* 36 (1): 3–15.

Collier, Jane F., and Sylvia J. Yanigasako. 1987. *Gender and Kinship: Toward a Unified Analysis*. Palo Alto, CA: Stanford University Press.

Conklin, Lindsay, and Sandra Nasser El-Dine. 2015. "Negotiating Courtship Practices and Redefining Tradition: Discourses of Urban, Syrian Youth." In *Gender and Sexuality in Muslim Cultures*, edited by Gul Ozyegin, 197–216. London: Routledge.

Coser, Lewis. 1974. *Greedy Institutions: Patterns of Undivided Commitment*. New York: Free Press.

Cronon, William. 1996. "The Trouble with Wilderness; or, Getting Back to the Wrong Nature." In *Uncommon Ground: Rethinking the Human Place in Nature*, edited by William Cronon, 69–90. New York: Norton.

Cuno, Kenneth. 2003. "Ambiguous Modernization: The Transition to Monogamy in the Khedival House of Egypt." In *Family History in the Middle East: Household, Property, and Gender*, edited by Beshara Doumani. Albany, NY: SUNY Press.

———. 2009. "Disobedient Wives and Neglectful Husbands: Marital Relations and the First Phase of Family Law Reform in Egypt." In *Family, Gender, and Law in a Globalizing Middle East and Southeast Asia*, edited by Kenneth Cuno and Manisha Desai, 3–18. Syracuse, NY: Syracuse University Press.

———. 2015. *Modernizing Marriage: Family, Ideology, and Law in Late Nineteenth and Early Twentieth Century Egypt*. Syracuse, NY: Syracuse University Press.

Dalakoglou, Dimitris. 2010. "Migrating-Remitting-'Building'-Dwelling: House-Making as 'Proxy' Presence in Postsocialist Albania." *Journal of the Royal Anthropological Institute* 16 (4): 761–777.

Deeb, Lara, and Jessica Winegar. 2012. "Anthropologies of Arab-Majority Societies." *Annual Review of Anthropology* 41:537–558.

Delaney, Carol. 1986. "The Meaning of Paternity and the Virgin Birth Debate." *Journal of the Royal Anthropological Institute* 21 (3): 494–513.

————. 2001. "Cutting the Ties that Bind: The Sacrifice of Abraham and Patriarchal Kinship." In *Relative Values: Reconfiguring Kinship Studies*, edited by Sarah Franklin and Susan McKinnon, 445–467. Durham, NC: Duke University Press.

————. 2004 "Relatives and Relations." In *Investigating Culture: An Experiential Introduction to Anthropology*, 177–220. New York: Blackwell.

Donzelot, Jacques. (1977) 1997. *The Policing of Families*, translated by Robert Hurley. Baltimore: Johns Hopkins University Press.

Doumani, Beshara. 2003. *Family History in the Middle East: Household, Property, and Gender*. Albany, NY: SUNY Press.

Dresch, Paul. 1994. *Tribes, Government, and History in Yemen*. Oxford: Oxford University Press.

Dumont, Louis. 1970. *Homo Hierarchicus*. Chicago: University of Chicago Press.

Dwyer, Daisey. 1978. *Images and Self-Images: Male and Female in Morocco*. New York: Columbia University Press.

Edwards, Jeanette, Sarah Franklin, Eric Hirsch, Francis Price, and Marilyn Strathern. 1999. *Technologies of Procreation: Kinship in the Age of Assisted Conception*. New York: Routledge.

Euben, Roxanne. 1999. *Enemy in the Mirror*. Princeton, NJ: Princeton University Press.

Evans-Pritchard, E.E. (1966) 1990. *Kinship and Marriage among the Nuer*. Oxford: Oxford University Press.

Fabian, Johannes. 1983. *Time and the Other: How Anthropology Makes its Object*. New York: Columbia University Press.

Fattah, Hassan, and Michael Slackman. 2005. "3 Hotels Bombed in Jordan; At Least 57 Die." *New York Times*, November 10, 2005. Accessed October 1, 2013. http://www .nytimes.com/2005/11/10/international/middleeast/10jordan.html?_r=0.

Federici, Sylvia. 2012. *Revolution at Point Zero: Housework, Reproduction, and Feminist Struggle*. New York: PM Press.

Feeley-Harnik, Gillian. 1984. "The Political Economy of Death: Communication and Change in Malagasy Colonial History." *American Ethnologist* 11 (1): 1–19.

Ferguson, Heather. 2003. "Property, Language, and Law: Conventions of Social Discourse in Seventeenth-Century Tarablus al-Sham." In *Family History in the Middle East: Household, Property, and Gender*, edited by Beshara Doumani, 229–244. Albany, NY: SUNY Press.

Ferguson, James. 1994. *The Anti-Politics Machine*. Minneapolis: University of Minnesota Press.

Fernea, Elizabeth. 1965. *Guests of the Sheik: An Ethnography of an Iraqi Village*. New York: Anchor.

Fischbach, Michael R. 2000. *State, Society, and Land in Jordan*. Leiden: Brill.

Fortun, Kim. 2001. *Advocacy after Bhopal: Environmentalism, Disaster, New Global Orders*. Chicago: University of Chicago Press.

Foucault, Michel. 1991. "Governmentality." In *The Foucault Effect: Studies in Governmentality*, translated by Rosi Braidotti, edited by Graham Burchell, Colin Gordon, and Peter Miller, 87–104. Chicago: University of Chicago Press.

Fox, Robin. 1967. *Kinship and Marriage: An Anthropological Perspective*. Harmondsworth, UK: Penguin.

Franklin, Sarah, and Susan McKinnon. 2001. *Relative Values: Reconfiguring Kinship Studies*. Durham, NC: Duke University Press.

Gal, Susan. 2002. "Language Ideologies Compared: Metaphors of Public/Private." *Journal of Linguistic Anthropology* 15 (1): 23–37.

Gerasa News. 2012. "What's the Story of the Lands That the Kuwaiti Ambassador and the Brother of Kilani Bought!!" (*Ma Qissa Al-Aradhy Ilati Yishtariha Al-Safir Al-Kuwaiti wa shafiq Al-Kilani!!*). Accessed April 15, 2020. http://www.gerasanews .com/index.php?page=article&id=82563.

Gerber, Haim. 1980. "Social and Economic Position of Women in an Ottoman City, Bursa 1600–1700." *International Journal of Middle East Studies* 16 (1): 3–41.

Gerholm, Tomas. 1985. "Aspects of Inheritance and Marriage Payment in North Yemen." In *Property, Social Structure, and Law in the Modern Middle East*, edited by Ann Elizabeth Mayer, 129–151. Albany, NY: SUNY Press.

Ghannam, Farha. 2002. *Remaking the Modern: Space, Relocation, and the Politics of Identity in a Global Cairo*. Berkeley: University of California Press.

Ghazal, Muhammed. 2008. "60,000 Applications Distributed in 2 Days." *Jordan Times*. Accessed April 2. http://www.jordantimes.com/?news=6673.

Gilsenan, Michael. 1986. "Domination as Social Practice: 'Patrimonialism in North Lebanon: Arbitrary Power, Desecration, and the Aesthetics of Violence.'" *Critique of Anthropology* 6 (1): 17–37

———. 1996. *Lords of the Lebanese Marches: Violence and Narrative in an Arab Society*. London: Tauris.

Gocek, Fatma. 2003. "Ottoman Empire: 15th to Mid-18th Century." In *Encyclopedia of Women and Islamic Cultures*. Vol. 1, *Methodologies, Paradigms, and Sources*, edited by Suad Joseph, 72–81. Boston: Brill.

Goffman, Erving. 1961. *Asylums: Essays on the Social Situation of Mental Patients and Other Inmates*. New York: Doubleday.

Goldman, Michael. 2005. *Imperial Nature: The World Bank and Struggles for Social Justice in the Age of Globalization*. New Haven, CT: Yale University Press.

Goody, Jack. 1986. "The State, the Bureau and the File." In *The Logic of Writing and the Organization of Society*, 87–126. London: Cambridge University Press.

Gough, Kathleen. 1971. "The origin of the family." *Journal of Marriage and family* 33 (4): 760-771.

Granovetter, Mark. 1973. "The Strength of Weak Ties." *American Journal of Sociology* 78 (6): 1360–1380.

Granqvist, Hilma. 1931. *Marriage Conditions in a Palestinian Village*. Vol. 1. Helsingfors: Akedemische Buchhandlung.

———. 1935. *Marriage Conditions in a Palestinian Village*. Vol. 2. Helsingfors: Akedemische Buchhandlung.

Hacking, Ian. 1982. "Biopower and the Avalanche of Printed Numbers." *Humanities in Society* 5 (3–4): 279–295.

Haraway, Donna. 1984. "A Cyborg Manifesto: Science, Technology, and Socialist-Feminism in the Late Twentieth Century." In *Simians, Cyborgs, and Women: The Reinvention of Nature*, 149–181. New York: Routledge.

Hardt, Michael. 1999. "Affective Labor." *Boundary* 2 26 (2): 89–100.

Hart, Kimberly. 2007. "Love by Arrangement: The Ambiguity of 'Spousal Choice' in a Turkish Village." *Journal of the Royal Anthropological Institute* 13 (2): 345–362.

Hasso, Frances. 2009. "Shifting Practices and Identities: Nontraditional Relationships among Sunni Muslim Egyptians and Emiratis." In *Family, Gender, and Law in a Globalizing Middle East and Southeast Asia*, edited by Kenneth Cuno and Manisha Desai, 211–222. Syracuse, NY: Syracuse University Press.

———. 2011. *Consuming Desires: Family Crisis and the State in the Middle East*. Palo Alto, CA: Stanford University Press.

Hattar, Musa. 2012. "'Rape Law' Triggers Fury in Jordan." *The Daily Star*. Accessed September 10, 2020. https://www.dailystar.com.lb/ArticlePrint.aspx?id=178574 &mode=print.

Herzfeld, Michael. 1985. *The Poetics of Manhood: Contest and Identity in a Cretan Mountain Village*. Princeton, NJ: Princeton University Press.

———. 1997. *Cultural Intimacy: Social Poetics in the Nation-State*. New York: Routledge.

Holy, Ladislav. 1996. *Anthropological Perspectives on Kinship*. London: Pluto.

Hoodfar, Homa. 1997. *Between Marriage and the Market: Intimate Politics and Survival in Cairo*. Berkeley: University of California Press.

Hourani. Albert. 1991. *A History of the Arab peoples*. Cambridge, MA: Harvard University Press.

Howard, Michael. 2005. "Zarqawi's Family Disowns Him after Bombing." *The Guardian*, November 20, 2005. Accessed October 1, 2013. http://www.theguardian.com/world /2005/nov/21/iraq.michaelhoward.

Howell, Sally. 2003. "Modernizing Mansaf: The Consuming Contexts of Jordan's National Dish." *Food and Foodways* 11 (4): 215–243.

Howell, Signe. 2006. *The Kinning of Foreigners: Transnational Adoption in a Global Perspective*. New York: Berghahn.

Hughes, Geoffrey. 2018. "Cutting the Face: Kinship, State and Social Media Conflict in Networked Jordan." *Journal of Legal Anthropology* 2 (1): 49–71.

Hull, Matthew. 2003. "The File: Agency, Authority, and Autography in an Islamabad Bureaucracy." *Language Communication* 23 (3–4): 287–314.

———. 2010. "Democratic Technologies of Speech: From WWII America to Postcolonial Delhi." *Linguistic Anthropology* 20 (2): 257–282.

Husseini, Rana. 2017. "In Historic Vote, House Abolishes Controversial Article 308." *Jordan Times*, August 1, 2017. Accessed July 20, 2018. http://www.jordantimes.com /news/local/historic-vote-house-abolishes-controversial-article-308.

Hutchins, Ed. 1995. "How a Cockpit Remembers Its Speeds," *Cognitive Science* 19:265–288.

Ibn Al-Kalbi, Hisham. 1952. *The Book of Idols*, edited by Nabih Amin Faris. Princeton, NJ: Princeton University Press.

Ibn Majah, Muhammad. 2007. *Sunan Ibn Majah*, translated by Nasiruddin al-Khattab. Vol. 3. Riyadh: Darussalam.

Inhorn, Marcia. 2012. *The New Arab Man: Emergent Masculinities Technologies, and Islam in the Middle East*. Princeton, NJ: Princeton University Press.

Islahi, Abdul Azim. 2004. *Contributions of Muslim Scholars to Economic Thought and Analysis (11-905 A.H./632-1500 A.D.)*. Jeddah, Saudi Arabia: IRTI.

Jabiri, Afaf. 2016. *Gendered Politics and Law in Jordan: Guardianship over Women*. New York: Palgrave Macmillan.

Jacob, Wilson. 2011. *Working Out Egypt: Effendi Masculinity and Subject Formation in Colonial Modernity, 1870–1940*. Durham, NC: Duke University Press.

Jad, Islah. 2009. "The Politics of Group Weddings in Palestine: Political and Gender Tensions." *Journal of Middle East Women's Studies* 5 (3): 36–53.

Jordan Islamic Bank. 2012. *2012 Social Responsibility Report*. Amman, Jordan: Jordan Islamic Bank.

Joseph, Suad. 1999. *Intimate Selving in Arab Families: Gender, Self, and Identity*. Syracuse, NY: Syracuse University Press.

Kandiyoti, Deniz. 1988. "Bargaining with Patriarchy." *Gender and Society* 2 (3): 274–290.

Karim, Lamia. 2008. "Demystifying Micro-Credit: The Grameen Bank, NGOs, and Neoliberalism in Bangladesh." *Cultural Dynamics* 20 (5): 5–29.

Karmi, Ghada. 1996. "Women, Islam, and Patriarchalism." In *Feminism and Islam: Legal and Literary Perspectives*, edited by Mai Yamani and Andrew Allen, 69–85. Reading, UK: Ithaca Press.

Keane, Webb. 1997. *Signs of Recognition: Powers and Hazards of Representation in an Indonesian Society*. Berkeley: University of California Press.

———. 2003. *Christian Moderns: Freedom and Fetish in the Mission Encounter*. Berkeley: University of California Press.

Kepel, Gilles. 2003. "The Society of Muslims." In *Muslim Extremism in Egypt*, 70–102. Berkeley: University of California Press.

Khan, Mazhar. 2013. *Saudi Mortgage Law: Planning for the Long Term*. Riyadh: Al-Rajhi Capital.

Khan, Ruqayya. 2000. "On the Significance of Secrecy in the Medieval Arabic Romances." *Journal of Arabic Literature* 31 (3): 238–253.

Khater, Akram. 2001. *Inventing Home: Emigration, Gender, and the Middle Class in Lebanon, 1870–1920*. Berkeley: University of California Press.

Kholoussy, Hanan. 2010. *For Better, for Worse: The Marriage Crisis That Made Modern Egypt*. Palo Alto, CA: Stanford University Press.

Khoury, Philip and Joseph Kostiner. 1990. *Tribes and State Formation in the Middle East*. Berkeley: University of California Press.

Kisiara, Richard. 1998. "Some Sociopolitical Aspects of Luo Funerals." *Anthropos* 93 (1): 127–136.

Lash, Shari. 2006. "Struggling with Tradition: Making Room for Same-Sex Weddings in a Liberal Jewish Context." *Ethnologies* 28 (2): 133–156.

Latour, Bruno. 1993. *We Have Never Been Modern*, translated by Catherine Porter. Cambridge, MA: Harvard University Press.

Latte-Abdallah, Stéphanie. 2009. "Fragile Intimacies: Marriage and Love in the Palestinian Camps of Jordan (1948–2001)." *Journal of Palestine Studies* 38 (4): 47–62.

Layish, Aharon. 1991. *Divorce in the Libyan Family: A Study Based on the Sijills of the Sharia Courts of Ajdābiyya and Kufra*. New York: New York University Press.

Layne, Linda. 1994. *Home and Homeland: The Dialogics of Tribal and National Identities in Jordan*. Princeton, NJ: Princeton University Press.

Leach, Edmund. 1954. *Political Systems of Highland Burma: A Study of Kachin Social Structure*. London: Athalone.

———. 1967. "Virgin Birth." *Proceedings of the Royal Anthropological Institute* 1967:39–49.

Levi-Strauss, Claude. (1949) 1969. *The Elementary Structures of Kinship*, translated by James Bell and John von Sturmer. Boston: Beacon.

———. 1963. *Totemism*. Boston, MA: Beacon Press.

———. 1987. *Anthropology and Myth: Lectures, 1951–1982*. Oxford: Oxford University Press.

MacKenzie, Donald. 2006. *An Engine, Not a Camera: How Financial Models Shape Markets*. Cambridge, MA: MIT Press.

———. 2009. *Material Markets: How Economic Agents Are Constructed*. Oxford: Oxford University Press.

Mahmood, Saba. 2005. *Politics of Piety: The Islamic Revival and the Feminist Subject*. Princeton, NJ: Princeton University Press.

Malinowski, Bronislaw. (1922) 2014. *Argonauts of the Western Pacific: An Account of Native Enterprise and Adventure in the Archipelagoes of Melanesian New Guinea*. New York: Routledge.

———. 1929. *The Sexual Life of Savages in North-Western Melanesia*. London: Routledge.

Marx, Karl. 1976. *Capital: A Critique of Political Economy*. Vol. 1, translated by Ben Fowkes. New York: Penguin.

Massad, Joseph. 2001. *Colonial Effects: The Making of National Identity in Jordan*. New York: Columbia University Press.

Maurer, Bill. 2002. "Repressed Futures: Financial Derivative's Theological Unconscious." *Economy and Society* 31:15–36.

———. 2005. *Mutual Life, Limited: Islamic Banking, Alternative Currencies, Lateral Reason*. Princeton, NJ: Princeton University Press.

McKinley, Robert. 2001. "The Philosophy of Kinship: A Reply to Schneider's *Critique of the Study of Kinship*." In *The Cultural Analysis of Kinship: The Legacy of David M. Schneider*, edited by Richard Feinberg and Martin Ottenheimer, 131–167. Urbana: University of Illinois Press.

Melly, Carol. 2010. "Inside-Out Houses: Urban Belonging and Imagined Furtures in Dakar, Senegal." *Comparative Studies in Society and History* 52 (1): 37–65.

Mernissi, Fatima. 1975. *Beyond the Veil: Male-Female Dynamics in a Modern Muslim Society*. Bloomington: Indiana University Press.

Messick, Brinkley. 1986. "Subordinate Discourse: Women, Weaving, and Gender Relations in North Africa." *American Ethnologist* 14 (2): 210–225.

———. 1993. *The Calligraphic State: Textual Domination and History in a Muslim Society*. Berkeley: University of California Press.

Mills, C. Wright. 1959. *The Sociological Imagination*. Oxford: Oxford University Press.

Mir-Hosseini, Ziba. 1993. *Marriage on Trial: A Study of Islamic Family Law in Iran and Morocco*. New York: Tauris.

———. 1999. *Islam and Gender: The Religious Debate in Contemporary Iran*. Princeton, NJ: Princeton University Press.

Mitchell, Timothy. 2002. *Rule of Experts: Egypt, Techno-Politics, Modernity*. Berkeley: University of California Press.

Moore, Pete. 2004. "Political Economy of Acronyms." *Middle East Report* 234:18–25.

Moors, Annelies. 1995. *Women, Property, and Islam: Palestinian Experiences, 1920–1990*. Cambridge: Cambridge University Press.

———. 1999. "Debating Islamic Family Law: Legal Texts and Social Practices." In *A Social History of Women and Gender in the Modern Middle East*, edited by Margaret Meriwether and Judith Tucker, 141–175. Boulder, CO: Westview.

————. 2003. "Women's Gold: Shifting Styles of Embodying Family Relations." In
Family History in the Middle East: Household, Property, and Gender, edited by Beshara
Doumani, 101–118. Albany, NY: SUNY Press.

————. 2008. "Registering a Token Dower: The Multiple Meanings of a Legal Practice."
In *Narratives of Truth in Islamic Law,* edited by B. Dupret, B. Drieskens, and A. Moors,
85–104. London: Tauris.

————. 2011. "Mahr Meanings—Dower Dealings: Reflections from Palestine." In
Embedding "Mahr" (Islamic Dower) in the European Legal System, edited by R. Mehdi,
& J. S. Nielsen, 21–34. Copenhagen: Djøf.

Morgan, Lewis Henry. 1871. *Systems of Consanguinity and Affinity of the Human Family,*
Smithsonian "Contributions to Knowledge," XVII. Washington, DC: Smithsonian
Institution Press.

Mundy, Martha. 1979. "Women's Inheritance of Land in Highland Yemen." *Arabian
Studies* 5:161–188.

Mundy, Martha, and Richard Saumarez Smith. 2003. "'Al-Mahr Zaituna': Property and
Family in the Hills Facing Palestine, 1880–1940." *Family History in the Middle East:
Household, Property, and Gender,* edited by Beshara Doumani, 119–150. Albany, NY:
SUNY Press.

Muslim, Abdul-Hussein. 2007. *Sahih Muslim,* Vol. 4, translated by Nasiruddin
Al-Khattab. Riyadh: Darussalam.

Na'amneh, Mahmoud. 2009. "Cultural Heritage and Collective Identity: The Status of
Intangible Heritage in Jordan from an Anthropological Perspective." *Al-Manarah*
15 (3): 29–45.

Needham, Rodney. 1971. *Rethinking Kinship and Marriage.* New York: Tavistock.

Nguyen, Thuc-Doan, and Russel Belk. 2013 "Harmonization Processes and Relational
Meanings in Constructing Asian Weddings." *Journal of Consumer Research* 40 (3):
518–538.

Obaidullah, Mohammed. 2005. *Islamic Financial Services.* Jeddah: King Abdulaziz
University Press.

Ong, Walter. 1982. *Orality and Literacy.* London: Methuen.

Ortner, Sherry. 1995. "Resistance and the Problem of Ethnographic Refusal."
Comparative Studies in Society and History 37 (1): 173–193.

Ozyegin, Gul. 2009. "Virginal Facades: Sexual Freedom and Guilt among Young
Turkish Women." *European Journal of Women's Studies* 16 (2): 103–123.

Parker, Christopher. 2009. "Tunnel-Bypasses and Minarets of Capitalism: Amman as
Neoliberal Assemblage." *Political Geography* 28:110–120.

Pateman, Carole. 1988. *The Sexual Contract.* Palo Alto, CA: Stanford University
Press.

Peacock, Sandra L., and Nancy J. Turner. 2000. "Just Like a Garden." In *Biodiversity
and Native America,* edited by Paul E. Minnis and Wayne J. Elisens, 133–179. Norman:
University of Oklahoma.

Pearl, Laura. 2006. *The Girls from the Prayer Room: The Women's Islamist Movement at
Yarmouk University, Jordan.* PhD diss., University of Michigan, Ann Arbor.

Peletz, Michael. 1987. "The Exchange of Men in 19th-Century Negeri Sembilan
(Malaya)." *American Ethnologist* 14 (3): 449–469.

————. 1994. "Neither Reasonable nor Responsible: Contrasting Representations of
Masculinity in a Malay Society." *American Ethnologist* 9 (2): 135–178.

Peters, Anne, and Pete Moore. 2009. "Beyond Boom and Bust: External Rents, Durable Authoritarianism, and Institutional Adaptation in the Hashemite Kingdom." *Studies in Comparative International Development* 44:256–285.

Petra. 2008. "Al-Malik Yatlaq Al-Mubadira 'Sukan Kareem Li'aish Kareem' Bikalifeh 5 Milyarat Dinar." *Al-Ghad.* Accessed April 2, 2013. http://www.alghad.com/?news =310182.

Pitt-Rivers, Julian. 2017. "The Role of Pain in Rites of Passage." In *From Hospitality to Grace: A Julian Pitt-Rivers Omnibus,* edited by Giovanni da Col and Andrew Shryock, 267–273. Chicago: University of Chicago Press.

Porter, Theodore M. 1996. *Trust in Numbers: The Pursuit of Objectivity in Science and Public Life.* Reprint ed. Princeton, NJ: Princeton University Press.

Proctor, Robert, and Londa Schiebinger. 2008. *Agnotology: The Making and Unmaking of Ignorance.* Palo Alto, CA: Stanford University Press.

Qabah, Samir. 2011. *Wa 'ashiruhun bi-al-ma'ruf: dirasa shira'iyya wa-filsafiyya fi al-haquq al-zawjiyya* ("And Live with Them (f) in Kindness": A Legal and Philosophical Study in Marital Rights). Amman, Jordan: Al Afaf.

Qutb, Sayyid. (1953) 2000. *Social Justice in Islam,* translated by John B. Hardie, translation revised by Hamid Algar. New York: Islamic.

Radcliffe-Brown, A.R., and Daryll Forde. 1950. *African Systems of Kinship and Marriage.* London: Oxford University Press.

Rafeq, Abdul-Karim. 1966. *The Province of Damascus, 1723–1783.* Beirut: Khayats.

Razzaz, Omar. 1991. *Law, Urban Tenure, and Property Disputes in Contested Settlements: The Case of Jordan.* PhD diss., Harvard University, Cambridge, MA.

———. 1994. "Contestation and Mutual Adjustment: The Process of Controlling Land in Yajouz, Jordan." *Law and Society Review* 28 (1): 7–39.

Reiter, Yitzhak. 2004. "The Palestinian-Transjordanian Rift: Economic Might and Political Power in Jordan." *Middle East Journal* 58 (1): 72–92.

Rogan, Eugene. 1999. *Frontiers of the State in the Late Ottoman Empire: Transjordan, 1850–1921.* Cambridge: Cambridge University Press.

Roseberry, William. 1994. "Hegemony and the Language of Contention." In *Everyday Forms of State Formation: Revolution and the Negotiation of Rule in Modern Mexico,* edited by Gilbert Joseph and Daniel Nugent, 355–366. Durham, NC: Duke University Press.

Rosen, Lawrence. 1984. *Bargaining For Reality: The Construction of Social Relations in a Muslim Community.* Chicago: University of Chicago Press.

Rubin, Gayle. 1975. "The Traffic in Women: Notes on the 'Political Economy' of Sex." In *Toward An Anthropology of Women,* edited by Rayna R. Reiter, 157–210. New York: Monthly Review Press.

Rugh, Andrea. 1993. "Reshaping Personal Relationships in Egypt." In *Fundamentalisms and Society,* edited by M.E. Marty and R.S. Appleby, 151–180. Chicago: University of Chicago Press.

Salem, Rania. 2014. "Trends and Differentials in Jordanian Marriage Behavior: Marriage Timing, Spousal Characteristics, Household Structure, and Matrimonial Expenditures." In *The Jordanian Labour Market in the New Millenium,* edited by Assaad Ragui, 1–28. Oxford: Oxford University Press.

———. 2016. "Imagined Crises: Assessing Evidence of Delayed Marriage and Never-Marriage in Contemporary Egypt." In *Domestic Tensions, National Anxieties: Global*

Perspectives on Marriage, Crisis, and Nation, 231–266. Oxford: Oxford University Press.

Sartre, Jean-Paul. 1965. "Bad Faith." In *Essays in Existentialism*, 147–186. Syracuse, New Jersey: The Citadel Press.

Schneider, David M. 1972. "What Is Kinship All About?" In *Kinship Studies in the Morgan Centennial Year*, edited by Priscilla Reining, 32–63. Washington, DC: Anthropological Society of Washington.

Schwedler, Jillian. 2010. "Amman Cosmopolitan: Spaces and Practices of Aspiration and Consumption." *Comparative Studies of South Asia, Africa, and the Middle East* 30 (3): 547–562.

Seyed-Gohrab, A. A. 2009. "Leyli O Majnun." *Encyclopedia Iranica*. http://www.iranicaonline.org/articles/leyli-o-majnun-narrative-poem. Accessed August 10, 2013.

Shelter Unit. 1987. *National Housing Strategy*. 24 vols. Amman, Jordan: Ministry of Planning.

Shepherd, William. 2013. "Jāhiliyya." In *The Princeton Encyclopedia of Islamic Political Thought*, edited by Gerhard Bowering, Patricia Crone, Wadad Kadi, Devin J. Stewart, Muhammad Qasim Zaman, and Mahan Mirza, 269–270. Princeton, NJ: Princeton University Press.

Shryock, Andrew. 1995. "Popular Genealogical Nationalism: History Writing and Identity among the Balqa Tribes of Jordan." *Comparative Studies in Society and History* 37 (2): 325–357.

———. 1996. "Tribes and the Print Trade: Notes from the Margins of Literate Culture in Jordan." *American Anthropologist* 98 (1): 26–40.

———. 1997a. "Bedouin in Suburbia: Redrawing the Boundaries of Tribalism and Urbanity in Amman, Jordan." *Arab Studies Journal* 5 (1): 40–56.

———. 1997b. *Nationalism and the Genealogical Imagination: Oral History and Textual Authority in Tribal Jordan*. Berkeley: University of California Press.

———. 2000. "Dynastic Modernism and its Contradictions: Testing the Limits of Pluralism, Tribalism, and King Hussein's Example in Hashemite Jordan." *Arab Studies Quarterly*, 22 (3): 57–79.

———. 2004a. *Off Stage/On Display: Intimacy and Ethnography in the Age of Public Culture*. Palo Alto, CA: Stanford University Press.

———. 2004b. "The New Jordanian Hospitality: House, Host and Guest in the Culture of Public Display." *Society for Comparative Study of Society and History* 46 (1): 35–62.

Shryock, Andrew, and Sally Howell. 2001. "'Ever a Guest in our House': The Emir Abdullah, Shaykh Majid Al-'Adwan, and the Practice of Jordanian House Politics as Remembered by Umm Sultan, Widow of Majid." *International Journal of Middle East Studies* 33 (2): 247–269.

Silverstein, Michael. 1979. "Language Structure and Linguistic Ideology." In *The Elements: A Parasession on Linguistic Units and Levels*, edited by R. Cline, W. Hanks, and C. Hofbauer, 193–247. Chicago: Chicago Linguistic Society.

Singerman, Diane. 1995. *Avenues of Participation: Family, Politics, and Networks in Urban Quarters of Cairo*. Princeton, NJ: Princeton University Press.

Sonbol, Amira. 2008. "A History of Marriage Contracts in Egypt." In *The Islamic Marriage Contract: Case Studies in Islamic Family Law*, edited by Frank Vogel and Asifa Quraishi, 87–122. Cambridge, MA: Harvard University.

Spivak, Giyatri. 1988. "Can the Subaltern Speak? Speculations on Widow Sacrifice." In *Marxism and the Interpretation of Culture*, edited by C. Nelson and L. Grossberg, 271–313. Urbana: University of Illinois Press.

Star, Susan. 1999. "The ethnography of infrastructure." *American Behavioral Scientist* 43 (3): 377–391.

Strathern, Marilyn. 1984. "Marriage Exchanges: A Melanesian Comment." *Annual Review of Anthropology* 13:41–73.

———. 1985. "Kinship and Economy: Constitutive Orders of a Limited Kind." *American Ethnologist* 12 (2): 191–209.

———. 1988. *The Gender of the Gift: Problems with Women and Problems with Society in Melanesia*. Berkeley: University of California Press.

———. 1992. *After Nature: English Kinship in the Late Twentieth Century*. Cambridge: Cambridge University Press.

Tapper, Nancy. 1991. *Bartered Brides: Politics, Gender, and Marriage in an Afghan Tribal Society*. Cambridge: Cambridge University Press.

Tobin, Sarah. 2016. *Everyday Piety: Islam and Economy in Jordan*. Ithaca, NY: Cornell University Press.

Tucker, Judith. 1998. *In the House of the Law: Gender and Islamic Law in Ottoman Syria and Palestine*. Berkeley: University of California Press.

———. 2008. *Women, Family, and Gender in Islamic Law*. Cambridge: Cambridge University Press.

Turner, Victor. 1967. *The Forest of Symbols: Aspects of Ndembu Ritual*. Ithaca, NY: Cornell University Press.

van der Geest, Sjaak. 1998. "Yebisa Wo Fie: Growing Old and Building a House in the Akan Culture of Ghana." *Journal of Cross-Cultural Gerontology* 13:333–359.

van Gennep, Arnold. (1909) 2004. *The Rites of Passage*. New York: Routledge.

Vom Bruck, Gabriele. 1997. "The House Turned Inside Out: Inhabiting Space in a Yemeni City." *Journal of Material Culture* 2 (2): 139–172.

Wagner, Roy. 1986. "The Western Core Symbol." In *Symbols that Stand for Themselves*, 96–125. Chicago: University of Chicago Press.

———. 1991. "The Fractal Person." In *Big Men and Great Men: Personifications of Power in Melanesia*, edited by Maurice Godelier and Marilyn Strathern, 159–173. Cambridge: Cambridge University Press.

Wahlin, Lars. 1988. "The Occurrence of Musha' in Transjordan." *Geografiska Annaler. Series B, Human Geography* 70 (3): 375–379.

———. 1994. "How Long Has Land Been Privately Held in Northern Balqa', Jordan?" *Geografiska Annaler. Series B, Human Geography* 76 (1): 33–49.

Walker, Sarah. 2013. *Fragile Bonds: An Ethnographic Investigation of Marriage-Making amongst Muslims in Cairo*. PhD diss., University of Edinburgh.

Warner, Michael. 2002. "Publics and Counterpublics." *Public Culture* 14 (1): 49–90.

Warrick, Catherine. 2009. *Law in the Service of Legitimacy: Gender and Politics in Jordan*. London: Ashgate.

Watkins, Jessica. 2014. "Seeking Justice: Tribal Dispute Resolution and Societal Transformation in Jordan." *International Journal of Middle East Studies* 46 (1): 31–49.

Weiner, Annette. 1992. *Inalienable Possessions: The Paradox of Keeping-While Giving*. Berkeley: University of California Press.

Welchman, Lynn. 1988. "The Development of Islamic Family Law in the Legal System of Jordan." *International and Comparative Law Quarterly* 37 (4): 868–896.

———. 2009. "Family, Gender, and Law in Jordan and Palestine." In *Family, Gender, and Law in a Globalizing Middle East and Southeast Asia*, edited by Kenneth Cuno and Manisha Desai, 126–144. Syracuse, NY: Syracuse University Press.

Werner, Cynthia. 2004. "Women, Marriage, and the Nation-State: The Rise of Nonconsensual Bride Kidnapping in Post-Soviet Kazakhstan." In *The Transformation of Central Asia: States and Societies from Soviet Rule to Independence*, edited by Pauline Jones Luong, 59–89. Ithaca, NY: Cornell University Press.

———. 2009. "Bride Abduction in Post-Soviet Central Asia: Marking a Shift towards Patriarchy through Local Discourses of Shame and Tradition." *Journal of the Royal Anthropological Institute* 15 (2): 314–331.

Weston, Kath. 1991. *Families We Choose: Lesbians, Gays, Kinship*. New York: Columbia University Press.

Wilson, Mary. 1987. *King Abdullah, Britain, and the Making of Jordan*. London: Cambridge University Press.

Wojnarowski, Frederick, and Jennifer Williams. 2020. "Making Mansaf: The Interplay of Identity and Political Economy in Jordan's 'National Dish'." *Contemporary Levant*, DOI: 10.1080/20581831.2020.1767325

Yanigasako, Sylvia, and Carol Delaney. 1995. *Naturalizing Power: Essays in Feminist Cultural Analysis*. New York: Routledge.

Yaqub, Nadia. 2007. "The Palestinian Cinematic Wedding." *Journal of Middle East Women's Studies* 3 (2): 56–85.

Zaloom, Caitlin. 2006. *Out of the Pits: Traders and Technology from Chicago to London*. Chicago: University of Chicago Press.

Ze'evi, Dror. 1998. "The Use of Ottoman Sharīʿa Court Records as a Source for Middle Eastern Social History: A Reappraisal." *Islamic Law and Society* 5 (1): 35–56.

Index

Note: Page numbers in *italics* refer to images.

GEOFFREY F. HUGHES is Lecturer in Anthropology at the
University of Exeter.

CPSIA information can be obtained
at www.ICGtesting.com
Printed in the USA
JSHW030434151122
33201JS00001B/14